I Slept Through The American Dream

Written and lived by D. Waters

First Printing, 2015

ISBN-13: 978-1511594462

ISBN-10: 1511594462

CreateSpace.com

Thank you to all the people that kept me writing, even on sunny days. You know who you are.

Edited by Steven Dillon, MA

Whisper House Publishing

www.whisperhousepublishing.com

Whisper House
Publishing

For *Angie*
My dearest friend

FORWARD

Anyone who has ever claimed membership in the human race is entitled to an autobiography. Self-told life stories can be interesting and worthwhile and D. Waters' methodically-narrated review of his existence is certainly that.

Although it might be judged in part as pedestrian in pace and not building to a roaring climax, that too is Waters' substance and style. But he is a superb storyteller nevertheless and in his natural and unpolished hand, he spins a chronical web of a life that a reader may sum up as wasted – of crime, working the system, defying authority – but he is never rueful nor apologetic.

Anecdotes are recalled in precise, often raw, detail, along with the working of a criminal mind, tracing the genesis of a criminal-to-be from the juvenile pranks of an Oxnard beach boy, to heavy drug trade activity and eventually to robbing banks and then surviving a decade of daily tension and scheming to survive that decade in a notorious federal penitentiary.

Whether all this defines a "hardened" criminal, may be subject to debate. Evident in Waters' saga is a definite sense of arrogance and occasionally the reader may discern signals of a generous soul, vis-à-vis other prisoners, and human frailty and vulnerability. Some mixed emotions, for sure, but the over-riding theme is that of an individual with an inborn mindset of ignoring the norms of society and marching only to his own cadence.

Any sense of morality is left to the reader. Redemptions, likewise. Although one turning the final page can ponder his own thoughts on the man, his story and the fact that, after riding on the edge for so long, Waters is now at peace with himself and the world.

Larry Press, Ventura, CA, March, 2015

The reviewer, an occasional acquaintance of D. Waters, was a long-time sports editor and columnist for newspapers in Casper, WY and Bakersfield, CA.

Einstein said, "Imagination is more important than knowledge."

That would make me an A student, top of my class, valedictorian of the school of the imagination.

Growing up in southern California, everyone watered their grass, and I believe everyone had a son for the sole reason of mowing that grass. But with the sprinklers going day and night, the gutters were always flowing. My imagination would take me to sharpening a Popsicle stick to a point on the sidewalk, placing it in the gutter, and walking along side it as it traveled down the street. My mind would create a speedboat, a pirate ship, or a working barge, which would occupy my mind for who knows how long. As a kid, you don't have any concept of time, and as I look back, that is a beautiful thing. Not having a schedule, not having to look forward to weekends. Every day was a new page growing up. I wasn't the only one with this imagination. There was a kid down the street who would hit .22 caliber bullets with a hammer on the sidewalk. I had no idea what his mind was imagining. But he was the only one surprised when he blew off his thumb. But my little Popsicle boat would just sail and sail through the ripples and whirlpools. I would often narrate the sticks travels. I could picture myself on it, or sometimes put a rollie-pollie bug on it to create this very vivid picture of a boat with a captain racing in the ocean.

My imagination has never left me, and I am glad for that. As a kid I was very energetic, never able to channel my energy. One minute sailing my Popsicle stick boat, the next minute watching trails of ants bumping into each other and never figuring out where they were going or coming from. I, along with the neighborhood kids, often would end up in a vacant lot, sitting on boxes, rocks, or the ground and just telling made up stories for hours. We would create a corporation one day and talk about traveling the world the next, never leaving the vacant lot. But somehow at five o'clock, everybody would have to be home for dinner. Without having a watch, or any idea of the time, I would be washed up and at the dinner table by five o'clock sharp. Being there was mandatory and not being there on time seemed to be against the law. Sitting with my family and eating, I had to become a non-imaginary person. Practice my manners and compliment my mom on the food, always saying yes to my dad about finishing my chores. The worst thing of all was waiting for everyone to finish eating before I could leave the table. The big build up and perfect wording of the most important question ever was next; "Can I go back out and play?"

Remember my motor was running, I mean running. I always felt like I couldn't miss anything, and something cool was gonna happen next and I needed to be there, wherever *there* was. And that imagination that I had to put in a box when being around my family was let loose again.

We all went to school. Most of us had to go to church. That wasn't important in our lives and was pretty much never talked about. I always said my homework was done because nobody ever checked, and my room was always clean. For some reason, I was a very neat kid.

The older kids in the neighborhood were our reality. They were bigger than life. The trickling down of a story of what an older kid did would sometimes grow so much, that when it was your turn to tell the story, you would say you were there when it happened. I am sure the stories were more stories than fact, but these older kids would walk around the neighborhood and to us they owned it. If they ever gave me the nod of existing, it would just make my whole world complete. Make no mistake; these older kids would whoop your ass, and tell you it was for staring at them, or heard you said something about them, but the truth is they whooped your ass cuz they could.

And those gutters which were always full from everyone watering their grass. Many times there would be older kids cruising down the street, packed six to a car. As I would be walking alone, or with my best friend of the week, the older kids would put the two passenger side tires in the gutter as they drove past. This caused the car to spray nasty gutter water on you and your clothes, usually a clean white T-shirt and pegged Levi 501's. That is, if you could find a mother that would sew them into that style. Forty-six years later, they call them skinny jeans. Things really do change, yet stay the same. Nobody had thought of making colored T-shirts, and part of the pecking order was the whiteness of your shirt. So, when the car filled with older kids splashing dirty gutter water passed, this would cause our conversation to turn to young tough-guy threats among each other.

"They better not stop. I swear next time they're gonna have trouble with us."

3

More times than not the car would pull over, some or all the guys would get out and yell back at us.

"YOU GOT A PROBLEM?"

"No, no problem," was always our answer as we looked down. But in my active mind, that connected me more to the kids in my neighborhood that I idolized.

That became a pattern in life, learning to negotiate the best outcome of situations without thought, without hesitation. I paid more attention than most and my clothes stayed clean and I received less ass-kickin's, which was fine by me. You don't know when it happens, but this rite of passage gave me the most euphoric feeling I have ever had. Some tribes in Africa jump from platforms with a vine wrapped around their leg. If the vine holds and they live, they become men. They make that transition that quick. In my neighborhood in southern California, the transition wasn't as abrupt, but being noticed by the older kids reinforced my rite of passage. We would branch out from the vacant lot and end up further and further away from home. I was on my way to being a young man, but at five o'clock I was always at the dinner table, saying I did my chores and my homework, even if I hadn't.

There are a few unwritten facts in life. One of them being, you are usually doing the same exact thing as the people you hang around with. I was mischievous and my little crew was mischievous. Through my young life, my father would catch me doing things that I shouldn't. I never knew how he knew, but he would always say, "I can tell what you are doing by who you are hanging around with."

No truer words were ever spoken and yes we were mischievous. One of my favorites was putting rocks in people's hubcaps. Waiting for them to drive

4

off and listening to a sound that seemed to have every nut and bolt falling out of their engine. When the car was moving, the rocks would tumble against the metal hubcap, the driver would pull over and open the hood and the engine would sound fine. They would drive off again and the clanging would start, they'd stop open the hood and scratch their head. I don't know how long they did that, if they found the rocks or if their mechanic would find them, but we would get a laugh and move on. Hubcaps were a big deal back then. If we found one, we would argue who would get to bring it home and somehow we were gonna get the other three, the tires, the wheels, and build a car around that one hubcap. They were shiny. They were big. They were heavy, and usually had a crest on them from the manufacturer. They looked so cool hanging in the parents' garage to show your friends, and create that story of being able to turn that hubcap into an entire car. There was always that one kid that wanted to go for a ride when the one magic hubcap became a car. We would just look at him crazy and laugh. Our conversations never materialized and we would move on to the next idea or thought. None of us knew what an alternator was or could even spell alternator, but I had one, and it was a connection to things that made you older. We'd end up in my garage passing it around, oohing and ahhing, with me controlling the time you could hold it before I would announce "It's mine and from my father's Cadillac."

Reputation was everything.

I mentioned that I grew up in southern California; the name of that town is Oxnard. Produce farms, beaches, Navy Base, and tract homes. It was a mixture of Hawaiians, Samoans, Chicanos, and whites. We weren't separated by ethnic groups, but more by reputation. When I was nine years old, I was in the back seat of one of my dad's many oversized cars. I distinctly remember driving by a group of people. The guys had pompadours, ducktails, and each one looked like he was posing for a Hollywood movie set. They moved gracefully, spoke with their hands, and the cars that they were leaning on seemed better than my father's car. In actuality they weren't, with primer for paint and chrome rims, but to a nine-year-old boy trying to find his spot in life, they just seemed nicer.

My mother turned to my father and said, "Look at those hoodlums; they all have reputations around town." She then turned around to look at me in the back seat saying, "You will never be like that."

In my mind at that moment, all I wanted was to be exactly like that. And get me one of those reputations, even though I had no idea what a reputation was.

We walked everywhere, or ran to get there faster so as not to miss out on anything. I ran to school, to other kid's houses as well as meeting up at those vacant lots. I discovered that I was faster than all the other kids, and could out run everybody. I would challenge other kids at school to races, walking up to some random schoolmate and challenging him to run to the next unofficial finish line. I usually staged it so that other people were watching, and hopefully there would be girls in the vicinity of the finish line. I can remember the pride I had from winning these little races, and I felt, true or not, that people were starting to take notice of how fast I was. In between classes there might be a small group, and I would walk up and someone would comment what a fast little kid I was. It felt like my insides were coming out because I felt so big. At the time, I felt unbeatable in life; I was somebody different than the others. That was the start of my reputation.

Oxnard was a pretty tough town. Watching some of the Hawaiians fight amazed me. Their bodies seemed to not have ankles or wrists; their thickness just ran to their hands and feet. The Samoans were very similar. As a rule in my neighborhood Hawaiians and Samoans didn't like each other, and when they fought each other the fight seemed to never end. The Chicanos were like little buzz saws with their repeated, well-placed hits, winning with speed and big hearts. To fight any one of these groups and win, meant you had to fight more of their family members, older, bigger, male, female, and they all had big families. I didn't have a brother, so part of my arsenal was my humor and charm. There was a park right next to the junior high school, and when there was a problem that is where it got solved. All day in school everyone's conversation was about the big fight after school. Everybody was asked if they were going to the park to see the fight? This happened quite often and for the same major reasons: he looked at my girl, he talked to my girl, or he bumped my shoulder in the hallway. I don't remember any other reasons for the after school fights. It taught some proper manners at an early age. You have to realize, one kid hitting another kid doesn't hurt that much. But having the crowd watching, living in town and going to that school every day, winning or losing contributed to your reputation.

One of my personal stories is when I got shoulder bumped. It was at the local shopping plaza with Grants, Thrifty's (both department stores), and a Chess Kings clothing store along with a couple other independent shops. Everybody hung out for hours at this tiny little Mayfair Plaza and being seen there was everything. I got shoulder bumped by this big kid. He was a drop out, had a five o'clock shadow and already looked to me like he'd been to prison, even though he was probably only twelve. Anyway, he shoulder bumped me and he was wearing a white fur vest, which would have looked like women's clothing on me, but on this guy it looked like a warrior vest worn by Vikings.

After being bumped he said, "What? You wanna fight me?"

"Of course I will," came out of my mouth without a thought.

Most fights back then were by appointment, and looking back I realize that young kids really didn't want to fight for the simple reason that it could change the status of their reputation. That day I was with a couple other guys and they asked, "You're not gonna show up are you?"

"Of course I am." But deep inside, I was frozen and my life was over as far as I was concerned.

That night I *did* show up, peering around the back corner of Grants department store. I waited, still frozen without any clue of why I was there or what was I going to do. But I was there. Long story short, the other guy never showed up and I doubt it was because he was in fear of me; he was probably busy fighting a dozen other guys across town. I can't describe the relief of living another day. When I tell you I was frozen, I was frozen. Going to school on Monday, the friend that was with me at the plaza when I got bumped had already told the story. He was telling everyone how I beat this guy down and how I looked like the ghost of Rocky Marciano. Funny, but my friend didn't show up that night at Grants to help me (or take me to the hospital), but he was sure telling everybody how he saw it all. Gradually his story grew and he was telling anyone who would listen how he saw the whole thing and how they should have been there.

Now I was fast and tough, making a name for myself in South Oxnard. Reputation was everything.

Southern California is warm most of the time, but in December there is a wind that blows down from the mountains. We don't suffer from the Nor'easters of Boston or the snow storms of Buffalo, but that chilly wind does blow. And like everywhere else, Christmas comes. From my earliest memories, to today, I love Christmas. Money was tight in my house, but it wasn't the gifts I loved. It was the lights, the tree, and all the Christmas stuff around the house. It was the same every year: a little snow scene at the bottom of the tree made of cotton, a mirror for a lake with two skaters, surrounded by a snap-together white fence. Next to the tree was a manger scene where the wise men were too tall to fit into the inn.

There were two rules growing up: don't touch anything and act right.

But I was a kid and it was Christmas. So when no one was around, I would have to touch the mirror to see if it was wet or touch the cotton to see if it was cold like snow. In doing so, I would always knock the little fence over and because of my lack of patience and hurriedness of righting a wrong, I could never get the entire fence to stand up and go back together. Every time when asked if I knew what had happened, I would simply reply, "I don't know."

I would have to help my dad decorate the outside with a string of lights around the house and a cut out of Santa and his sleigh that went on the roof. Dad, always saving money, took a big picture of Santa and glued it to a piece of plywood and used a jigsaw to cut it out. My other job was always to check the bulbs to see if they worked, because back then if one bulb was out the entire strand wouldn't work. There I would sit, surrounded by a strand of non-working lights trying to figure out which bulb was bad. It made me crazy inside. We'd get the lights up around the house, and then it was time to put the big waving Santa up on the roof. Awkward, big, and near impossible to carry up the ladder, we'd finally get it up to the roof. My father had a cable system that didn't really work. He used the same cables used to hold up the old-fashioned television antenna. My job was to hold the waving Santa straight while dad secured the proper length of cable, front and back, side to side. Well, it never worked. For years it never worked, but that was part of our Christmas tradition. The wind would knock it down and we would get up on the roof and go through the process of righting Santa.

Throughout my young life, we moved around a lot, but Christmas always had the same feel. The ice skaters on the mirror lake were less than an inch tall, the wise men were too tall to fit into the inn, creating this eclectic Christmas village of odd proportions, all surrounded by a white fence that must have come from a cowboy toy collection. But it was Christmas, and Santa was coming. I would become so excited, counting the days and every year promising myself to stay awake so I could see Santa face-to-face. I never did meet him, but I was always the first one to wake up and be at the tree on Christmas morning.

There would be a few boxes with our names on it and always one gift that was unwrapped, that would always be the coolest gift. Because of the no-touching rule, I would stare at everything under the tree while waiting for everyone else to wake up. I would cough, close cupboard doors, anything to make noise to wake up the rest of my family. Doesn't anybody understand that Santa came and I want my stuff? Finally the house was awake. My dad poured the slowest cup of coffee ever poured and then we could all open gifts one at a time. Since we didn't have much money, my mom would cut out pictures from a magazine of a shirt, a pair of pants or some shoes, put it in a box and wrap it with a name on it. If you got a picture of a shirt that meant you would get a shirt sometime that year. A picture of pants the same, and so forth. Both my grandmothers lived far from us, so we received their gifts in the mail and they were the same every year. Queen Elizabeth (her real name) would send me a two-dollar bill every year. The family would get a pecan pie made by her from her pecan tree in Georgia. When she got older she would just send me a two-dollar bill and the family a bag of pecans so mom could make our own pecan pie. We called her Queen Bee and nobody ever questioned her way of doing things. My other grandmother, Mama Stan, short for Stanfield, would also send the same gift every year. A pack of white BVD underwear and every year she would send the same size. She never saw me growing so she didn't realize that I was a lot bigger at twelve years old than I was at four. I would put them in my drawer and never wear them, but my mom always made me write a thank-you note. I never understood why no one ever told grandma that I was three times as big as I used to be. Grandparents seem to have this special power where nobody ever corrects them.

Santa had come again and like most kids, I pretended to believe in Santa longer than I really did. One year when I still believed, at the age of eight, there was a Christmas event where if you showed up Santa gave you a gift. Santa was going to arrive in a helicopter from the local Navy Base, big stuff back then. There I am, waiting with the other kids, and when we saw the helicopter the excitement multiplied. Finally the helicopter landed and Santa stepped out with a big bag. He waved to the crowd and in doing so the blades chopped off the tops of his fingers. That fast, everything changed. I'd never seen anything like that, and chaos ensued. Santa was bleeding badly and all I remember is thinking... Am I still gonna get my gift?

Kids are selfish and I was no exception. We still got our gifts. So I was ok. But my believing in Santa stopped; to me a real Santa wouldn't be so stupid as to lose his fingers that way. I pretended to believe a few more years, mostly for my parents wanting to be Santa.

But the unwrapped gift, that always made Christmas worth waiting for. One year it was a used bike that my dad cleaned up and spray-painted. Another year it was a Hula Hoop. But the best unwrapped gift I ever got was a used AM radio. Big, maroon with gold lightning bolt lettering that said Zenith. That radio changed my life, bringing music right into my room. I would listen to KACY 1520 on the AM dial. Listening to Ricky Nelson, Neil Sedaka or hearing The Righteous Brothers doing *Unchained Melody* for the first time captured my spirit. Motown was born and I would sit in my room for hours listening. To this day when I hear the first bass note of *My Girl* by The Temptations it takes me back to a good and simpler time. I was thirteen and had connected to something different than anything I had ever experienced.

My friends were growing and changing along with me, which gave me others in my life that truly understood what my family didn't.

My father was a character. He grew up on a dirt
road and came from a big family. The same dirt road
my grandmother Queen Bee died on at a hundred and
one-years-old. I have many stories about my father
and looking back, that's when I realize what a
character he really was. He picked cotton as a young
boy to help support his many brothers and sisters,
joined the military before he was of legal age, met my
mother and made a plan for creating a life for our
family. My father was a young boy during the Great
Depression and served in World War II, as well as
Korea. He never spoke of any of these times in his life.
Only after his death did I learn of his life changing
triumphs. He was good to people, always willing to
help someone else. My manners, humor and
cleanliness are a direct result of my father's impact on
me, although when I was young my imagination and
adventure for life would cause me to separate from
what he was really trying to teach me. The
neighborhood kids all liked him and he was good to
them. His one love outside his family was his cars.
And he always had the nicest cars. Back then cars had
personality, with oversized chrome accents, mirrored
paint jobs and big engines. As a young boy I could get
lost in the back seats of my father's cars along with my
dad's rule for riding; don't touch anything, ever. Which
to me meant something good would happen if I touched
the interior. Somehow my father would always know
anytime I touched anything. He had the ability to
drive, look forward and bring his long arm to the
backseat and thump me in the head, all without ever
taking his eyes off the road.

My father's father believed in heavy discipline,
which made my father believe in heavy discipline. I
would get the belt and then be told not to cry. This
confused me, but I learned to take a beating and not
show any pain or any signs of being hurt. Don't
misunderstand me, my father was a very good man

and when all is said and done I turned out okay. And when I say I turned out okay, I'm referring to the quality that comes from having good manners, considering others and realizing that everybody has problems and I am not unique with mine. But to avoid the belt, I became slicker and would lie my way out of situations. Deny till I die, that was my creed. But once in a while, I would get caught and have to pay the price. I figured everybody had to pay the price sometimes, but the less you get caught the less you pay. My father trusted me so when I lied he would believe me most of the time; after all I was his son.

I never really liked childlike things and the adult world interested me from a very young age. I was exploratory and interested in the world around me. As I said, we didn't have much money, only later I realized my mother and father were saving money for the future. But eventually we got a little black and white television set, back then there were only three channels: ABC, NBC and CBS. They wouldn't come on until four in the afternoon and end at one or two a.m., with the playing of the national anthem and a picture of an Indian Chief centered on a gray test pattern. I thought this was very strange. But late at night the old movies would be shown. While my family was asleep I would quietly get up and turn on the television, volume way down low and watch an old movie. It was usually a gangster flick with Edward G Robinson, Humphrey Bogart or some unknown actor playing a tough guy. I loved the way they dressed, the way they talked and their not give a fuck attitude about life. They always got the girl, had the nicest cars and their dialogue was unmatched by any. As a young kid, I wouldn't get tired, so sneaking and watching the late movies became part of my young routine. My values and mindset of rules in life were forged by the movies I would watch at night. These gangsters wouldn't talk to the police, never tell on their friends, get shot, die or get sent to prison, but to me it always seemed like they won. Their coolness under pressure impressed me so much that I became aware of how I would talk, stand and look. I don't know if everyone in my house was a heavy sleeper or I was just so good at being sneaky, but at age ten, I never got caught watching these midnight movies.

My personality was forming to the point that if I didn't get caught doing something wrong I kept doing it over and over, and over. But no matter how many nights I would sneak up and watch Jimmy Cagney movies, I was still my father's son and needed to act accordingly. I would have to do my chores. Empty the house trash, mowing the lawn on Thursday, rake and have the lawn clippings in the trash can for Friday pickup, and never fail to be at the dinner table at five o'clock. We had a push mower that to me never seemed to cut right, although my dad would sharpen it by hand, which never seemed to help. I believe the day I moved out of my parents' house, my father bought his first gas-powered mower.

Dad would take me places, tell me stories and point out different types of cars. Eventually, I knew every year and every make of automobile, including the different state license plates and their slogans; New Jersey—Garden State, Missouri—Show me State and New Mexico—Land of Enchantment. I knew them all. But the only thing that was ever really interesting to me was the adventure of the unknown. Staring out my dad's car window I would picture myself in different parts of the world doing anything but what I was doing right then. My imagination was still working twenty-four seven. But hanging out with my dad was cool and I was very entertained by adults. I didn't know then what I know now; my dad was a true character. This was evidenced on more than one situation.

One time, my sister and I wanted to get a cat. Dad said, sure. There was a stray black cat in the neighborhood and my father told us that was now our cat. We named it Blackie and would see it every few days. My dad would come home from work and I would often ask if he had seen Blackie? Dad's reply was always, "Seen him yesterday. Blackie is doing just fine." I would be okay for that moment, knowing my cat was good. But Blackie never set one paw in our house.

Another time my dad was having a clambake with his friends and I wanted to hang around to hear what the adults talked about and my father agreed to my presence. With a big washtub boiling on an open fire and the clams waiting to be cooked he gave me a small hammer and told me, "When you see the clams open, tap them lightly so they close back shut."

So there I was watching clams starting to open and with a light tap they would close again, my dad would occasionally glance at me and say, "Good job." This kept me occupied and also insured that I didn't bother the adults. But there were other times when my father would get so upset with me that he would just look at me saying, "What were you thinking?" One particular Sunday ended with that phrase.

Sunday was church and family day. I would have to go to church in the morning in my oversized little suit, scratching and itching from the tweed material. Mom would always buy clothes that were too big for me, saying I would grow into them. My clothes were usually used, but my shoes were always brand new and I would wear my clothes out before outgrowing them. After church we'd do some sort of family thing. I didn't mind it, but I always worried that I would miss something in the neighborhood, like maybe someone falling out of a tree and dislocating their shoulder or finding something cool we could all pass around and put a story to.

Our family was going to picnic at the beach this one Sunday. I bounced around waiting for everybody to get in the car, because I was ready to go. Finally, we were all in the car, my dad's 1950 black Cadillac. Twenty-one coats of black lacquer hand rubbed paint, gangster white wall tires that were white from the center of the tire to the entire outside face of the tire, and big chrome hubcaps like giant mirrors that I would often stare at myself in. This 1950 Cadillac was truly beautiful and my dad loved this car. With the riding rules of no touching, no eating and keep your little fingers off the glass in effect, finally the whole family was on the way to the beach.

My mom prepared the picnic area as I wandered like I always did looking at stuff. I walked on the beach for a little ways and saw these two men were pulling this big fish out of the ocean. I was seven-years old, so the fish looked even bigger to me. I watched for a while as they pulled this enormous fish onto the sand, then I realized it was a shark. Because my father would take me to the movies, I always noticed that the wealthy people in these films had fish on the walls of their plush homes. So my little brain starts working overtime on how to contribute a look of wealth to our own house. I devise a plan that will make me not only the hero of the day, but a son that my dad will be truly proud of.

I asked one of the men, "What are you going to do with that fish, Mister?"

"Nothing, do you want it?" he said.

Do I want it? I couldn't believe it, they were gonna give me this five-foot shark! My plan was coming together better than I could ever have imagined. I start dragging my fish by its tail along the

18

beach towards my dad's Cadillac, having to stop and take little breathing breaks because this fish is much larger than my seven-year-old body. I'm so excited, my heart's pounding in my chest thinking about how happy everyone will be when their little hero gives the family this fish to put on the wall of our house. They might have a little mini parade for me and I'm hoping my dad won't crush my ribs when he hugs me from sheer uncontrollable pride brought on by his only son. So there I am dragging the fish, creating a little line in the sand from the shark's nose as I tug the shark towards my dad's car.

Opening the Cadillac's back door I climb up pulling the shark by the tail into the back seat, struggling until the entire fish is on the floorboard of my dad's Cadillac. The tail touched one door and the nose the other. Now the hard part of keeping this surprise to myself as I roll up the windows to make completely sure that nobody steals my fish. I go back to the picnic area looking like the cat that ate the canary, but somehow I manage to keep it a complete secret. Time starts to go slow. I just want the picnic to be over, see my dad open the door of his car and the smile on his face. But it did not happen quite like this. There was no parade; no bone crushing hugs, just that look that always went with the words, "What were you thinking?"

My father was past upset.

My dad has passed for quite a while now and I miss him still to this day. He would take me to the movies, where I would see Paul Newman, Steve McQueen, or Marlon Brando for my first time.

Or think about the time we bought a dog. He said he didn't have enough money for the dog, that he was two dollars short. So my sister and I put in one dollar each and dad told us, "You don't get an entire dog for only a buck."

My dad said my sister got the head for her dollar, my dad got the body and legs for eight dollars and I only owned the tail for my buck. Then he told my sister since she owned the head she had to feed him, and since I only could afford to own the tail I had to pick up the poop. My dad was a funny guy.

He also would make rubber band guns for the kids in the neighborhood. Pieces of wood that look like a pistol with a clothes-pin for a release, crosscutting an inner tube from a car tire to make the rubber band ammunition. As I got older he would always bring a screwdriver out of the garage and make sure my friends cars were idling just right by adjusting the carburetor. He didn't talk much and never complained about coworkers or having to work at all. His weight stayed the same his entire life by wearing the same size pants, never sweatpants or any type of elastic waistband. When his pants would get tight he would just eat less. When he quit smoking, he never mentioned smoking again. I never heard him talk about the two wars that he had fought in, even after coming back from Korea and being on the front lines of that war. Getting shot at caused the dark brown color of his eyes to vanish, making them light for the rest of his life. Fear of dying can make your body react strangely. But he never talked about that either.

Walking into the house and smelling the macaroni and cheese casserole was one of my favorite things. Mom was a good cook, always creating a variety of dishes. But mac and cheese was on the top of my list, and we are talking oven baked, not on top of the stove. She also kept a very clean house, along with keeping herself dolled up at all times and she was quite a looker. My sister and I didn't have that many toys, but playing outside most of the time I would always find something to do. But if the weather kept me inside that day, Mom would give me a Quaker oats container; the old-school round cylinder type along with a couple of pencils and I'd have me a drum set. Mom was creative in ways of keeping me busy. And I was always finding ways to create my own little world.

Under the house I had an old Prince Albert tobacco can that would hold my prize possessions. Nobody knew about this can and I might have a penny in it, a couple of marbles and an old tuna key. Cans in those days included a key on the bottom that you would break off guide a little piece of metal through the slot of the key and twist clockwise. This would open the can.

My mother would always worry about me, but I was only doing boy stuff. The neighborhood kids and I would play football or baseball in the street and anytime a car was approaching simultaneously we would yell, "CAR."

This drove my mother crazy for some reason.

My mother and I were never close and if my dad was the executioner on punishment, this would make my mother the judge. And what she said went with my father, never a negotiation. Her words of, "When your father gets home, he will take care of this," would always send me into a tailspin. That was my cue to incorporate humor in hopes of a lesser sentence. This never did work; nonetheless I would make my mother laugh. Then I would have to sit in my room waiting for my father to get home to give me the strap. I hated this, truly hated this. Hearing my father's car pull up and then the car door shut, the sound of the back door of our house open then close with conversation in the kitchen, and me never being able to make out what was being said. My bedroom door would open and periodically my father would tell me, "Anytime you think you're too big for this whipping let me know."

Many times I would sit in my bedroom saying this is the day that I tell him, "You are not gonna hit me no more."

But when my bedroom door would swing open I wouldn't say a word. But I can tell you that the day finally came. My dad came in my room and I found enough courage, "No more, you are not gonna do this to me anymore!" and I stood up.

He looked at me for a split second, hit me in the chest knocking me back on the bed and said, "I won't punish you with whippings ever again."

But with my Mother, there was never any gray area, she felt like I knew better and should act better. But she sure could cook some good macaroni.

4

It was 1962, Bobby Vinton was singing *Blue on Blue* on the radio, and this new good-looking singer named Elvis had everybody talking. Going from Parkview Elementary School to E.O. Green Junior High School, I was changing and my friends were changing. I didn't know it then, but the world was changing also, never to be the same.

I loved summer with no school, but eventually school would start again. With kids growing and changing during that three-month school break, 1962 seemed to have more changes than usual. Some of the girls returned to school with *bumps*, it was amazing. During my late-night TV watching, I would watch The Tonight Show with Jack Parr having Sophia Loren or Brigitte Bardot as guests. I'd never seen anything like those women, but in person to see girls with bumps truly amazed me.

Our choice of clothes wasn't that big a deal. Going to school meant wearing jeans, a collared shirt and some tennis shoes, but you still would lay out that special shirt the night before the first day. It was all about your entrance on the first day of school. It would wear off quick though when you realized that eight other kids in the school were wearing the same shirt as you. Moms pretty much shopped at the same place.

We had lockers where we kept our books and papers when we were back in school and that's where they stayed during school times, we may have been trouble but we weren't the only ones. Some of my teachers would slap kids in the back of the head for not paying attention and even the principal had a big paddle with holes drilled for wind resistance hanging in his office, and he would whack kids with it. One homeroom teacher I had was angry all the time; sometimes putting kids in the closet and closing the door for the entire class. Or, he would shake a kid until they cried. And often he would make kids stand during the whole class with a textbook in each hand and arms ninety degrees out, yelling if the student's arms started to drop. He was unanimously hated.

But I was a smart kid and avoided all this; I had figured out limits and lines not to cross, mostly from trying to outwit my father. I never did my own homework, always cheated on tests, and never carried a textbook. I became too cool for school, and with some cutie always offering to do my homework, I would graciously accept.

Other activities would distract me also, like some junior high kids sneaking cigarettes. I didn't smoke since my father would kill me, but on a foggy day while walking to school, I would pretend to. Blowing my fog breath into the sky like it was cigarette smoke to the point of stopping, throwing this imaginary cigarette on the ground and grinding it with my foot pretending to put it out. I thought everybody was watching from their windows of the houses I passed on the way to school. Yes, I was that fucked up.

My reputation shadowed me everywhere, I was well known in the neighborhood, liked and respected. Funny thing about reputation, it's hard to get and harder to get rid of. But I loved the adventures of life I was involved with and after school we would always find some kind of mischief or ride our bikes around town. I had a nice used Royce Union bicycle; ten speeds with racing tires, because when traveling on flat ground for a few blocks you need a European style bike with ten gears. Our bikes were more status than functional and I kept my bike shining. I would sometimes ride to school, parking in the cool kids parking area where we never locked our bikes. We figured everybody should know who we thought we were. But after school one day, I walked to the *cool* section and my bike was not there. Probably just an oversight I thought, I might've parked it somewhere else that day, although I know I hadn't. I wasn't ready to come to grips with somebody stealing my bike, but they had. I walked around the parking lot thinking it has to be here somewhere, but it wasn't. Devastation set in as I walked home that afternoon, still not fully accepting somebody had stolen from me. This was a first and I didn't like the way it felt. At home after telling my dad he only said, "You should have locked it."

"But dad..."

"You should have locked it. Bikes don't grow on trees."

After that day, I would look at every bike thinking it might be mine. I was starting to steal little things from the stores, but never thought how it would feel on the other end. *It ain't no fun—when the rabbits got the gun...* another life lesson that I didn't pay attention to. About a year later, somebody applied to where my dad worked, riding my stolen bike. Recognizing my Royce Union my dad put it in his trunk and brought it home to me. The thief hadn't taken care of it; the rims were dirty and bent, and the handlebar tape was torn. I didn't want it anymore and it sat in my garage and I never rode it again. But everything else in life was so good. My little crew along with myself would wander further and further away from home, cutting it closer to getting back home for the five o'clock dinner hour.

This Elvis character started to create quite a stir, from his clothes to his hair, and that became who we all wanted to be. With some talking, I convinced my father into letting me wear my hair in a pompadour and a ducktail. A four-fingered pompadour at that! Combing your hair straight back and with four fingers put in the front, you pull just a little and this would get it just right, the duck tail was both sides in the back brushed toward the center with some Pomade hair product on it and there I was, a little Elvis. Our way of dress also started to change, wearing slacks on the weekends and sometimes a suit. You could pick up a sharkskin suit with a velvet collar at Chess King for about eighteen dollars, which took some hustling. Get a pair of Flag Brother Boots with a Cuban heel for about six dollars and matching socks and a white shirt for a couple more bucks, and you could see thirteen year old Elvis Presley's everywhere. We still walked to school, but now we walked slower and with purpose, sat in the back of the classroom and just soaked in coolness, never ever engaging in actual school. Teachers wouldn't flunk us or hold us back a grade, because they didn't want us for another year in their class. Also, the school mailed our report cards home, which we would always intercept, find a kid whose parents had a typewriter, and erase the bad grade and type in a good grade. Trying to line up the typewriter just right was not that easy and the paper would become frayed from the erasing. But it worked and in my parent's eyes, I was a good student with a high B average. Giving yourself all A's was too suspicious.

School started cracking down on the dress code, probably because we were all looking like little hoodlums. A belt became mandatory, so we chose thin belts or cut the belt loops off our pants altogether; can't wear a belt without belt loops. Shirts had to be tucked in, so we started wearing Jack shirts (squared at the bottom with little buttons on the side). Taps on your shoes were also forbidden, but some of the kids would get what was called a full house on their entire shoe. That was a horseshoe tap on the heel, one on the point and one on each side. Walking into the classroom with taps would demand all the attention from the tapping sound on the tile floor. My father would never allow this, so I would put thumbtacks on the bottom of my soles. In class if the teacher got on to me, I would pull the tacks out. But when the guys with the real taps got caught, they would be sent home, which was the coolest thing that could happen to you in school. My mother got wind of the school's dress code and would give me the once over every morning before leaving the house, but I had an extra set of clothing in the garage which I would change into and off to school I would go.

We were seen all over town, at the bowling alleys or the hamburger stands, always combing our hair and posing as if a picture was being taken paying extra attention to every detail when girls passed by. And there was always a couple of girls doing the same as us, hanging together and looking good. We would position ourselves to be able to look and see if they were looking back at us. The guys would talk to each other but our whole focus was glancing at the girls. I liked the girls a lot; they were like these creatures that were so different from us, and the eye-to-eye contact with them would boost me to a level I've never known. There would be school dances and dances at the recreation center. We would get ready early to arrive late, sneaking some of my dad's Old Spice after shave and buying a pack of Sen-Sens (a small box of tiny licorice squares), life couldn't get no betta'. With Mary Wells singing *My Guy*, "Nothing you could do—could make me untrue—to my guy..."

In our young minds every song was about us.

The dances we would do were The Shimmy and The Slawson and chaperones watched to ensure we weren't gravitating and gyrating inappropriately. Walking the Dog was forbidden, so naturally that's the dance we couldn't wait to do. Walking the Dog consisted of putting your left hand in front of you, your right hand on your jewels with both feet shuffling forward; it looked like you were riding a bull without the bull. And at the end of the night a slow song always played. Girls on one side of the room and boys on the other created the opportunity to slow walk across the room and pick that one, that special one, for the last dance and maybe for your girlfriend that week. A girlfriend consisted of someone you would usually walk home from school carrying her books and talk with on the phone.

Phones only had five digit phone numbers with a word for a prefix. Mine was Hunter 66650. Mom would make me memorize our number and carry a dime for that emergency that never happened. Five numbers, that's all you needed to dial. The first two letters of the prefix were for long distance, and long distance calls were only made on Sunday after six p.m., because it was cheaper. The only time I was involved in a long distance call was talking to my grandmothers and being asked the same questions.

"How is school? Are you growing?"

My reply was always the same, "Doing well in school and I'm getting big."

Waiting for these calls would make me crazy because I wanted to be outside. By the time it was my turn on the phone and asked these repetitive questions by my grandmothers, I wanted to blurt out, "I'm cheating in school and getting smaller from some mutant life form I contracted." Of course I never said this, only thought it.

We also had a party line, which meant that somebody else shared the same phone line. Not the same number, but the same line. They could live close or across town. You'd pick up the phone to call out and there would be two other people talking on the line. We devised methods to get our way and use the phone when we wanted, hanging it up loud or make a sighing sound when trying to dial out and hearing two strangers talking. Some people would stay on the phone all day, but if I needed to call my girl I needed to call her now. Our methods worked sometimes; sometimes it wouldn't affect the other two parties at all.

My cronies and I didn't use the phone that often to call each other because we knew each other's routine and schedules. I did have one friend Billy Forert though who would often call me telling me to hold on a minute, then he'd get on his bike and speed to my house knocking on my front door while I was on hold. Having to put down the phone because phones weren't cordless to answer the door, there stood Billy, we thought that was so funny.

The phone was added to the arsenal in our bag of mischief. We'd call random people telling them they won a vacation or a set of golf clubs, anything we could think of on short notice. If they could answer one question they would be declared the winner of the nonexistent prize, "Who's buried in Grant's tomb?"

Surprisingly most people didn't know, and some of the people stayed on the line with us thinking we were fooling them. But most people hung up. We weren't good at sounding adult with our conversations.

Fast food places didn't exist because everyone ate at home. But there was this one innovative company called Chicken Delight that drove around in Volkswagen Beetles, with a big chicken on top, delivering chicken. Their slogan was "Don't Cook Tonight – Call Chicken Delight". Often we would call in a big order of chicken and have it delivered across the street, peering through the curtains we would watch and giggle while the resident would be explaining they didn't order any chicken. We thought that shit was so funny.

There was no 911, but there was 411, which was called information. Dialing 411, a lady would answer and look up the number for you, having the same phone book as everyone else did at home. You could hear her flipping through the pages, as she looked up the number you requested. There was a lady in town named Francis Fuchs, we would call information and ask, "Could you please give me the phone number of Francis FUCKS?"

The operator's would reply, "WHAT did you say?"

Then we would spell it, F-U-C-H-S and then the operator would say, "Hold on a minute I have the number right here." Again that was so funny. Calling a butcher shop, we would ask the butcher, "Do you have pig's feet?"

"Yes."

"Wear shoes, nobody will notice," we'd say, laughing and hanging up. The phone was a good addition to our mischief.

I was a teenager and disconnecting from my family more and more. Still having to go to school as well as church, my family seemed boring and slow and when at home, I would be in my room with the music. Motown was coming on the scene and I was lost in my own little world and stealing a lot more by now. I had an official California State flag from the post office, which I had stolen right off the flagpole. It covered one wall in my room along with construction lights that would blink at night. My room was my world. Anytime my father would ask where I got this stuff, I would lie so naturally saying some guy down the street was throwing it out and said I could have it.

Often my mother would come in my room with me sitting with the lights off, my sunglasses on and listening to Motown. I was on a road of self-destruction, unaware of where it was leading me while feeling misunderstood. My friends were doing the same. My friends became my only refuge. We didn't go to school to learn. It was all about a good time, with a little hot-female schoolmate doing your homework and always cheating on your tests. I'd tape the answers upside down on my shirt tail, and if the teacher walked by I would just put my shirt tail down. Sitting next to a smart kid was another one of my tricks. I would just give him a tough look and he would scoot the paper closer, so I could read his test answers.

I was also made to go to church, but never engaged in the message being delivered. As a child I would have to go with my grandmothers when they would visit, both Southern Baptists. The older women would be wearing fox stoles; seventy-something degrees out and they would have on a fox stole with the head still on it. The eyes were made out of glass balls and sitting in church next to my grandmothers, I couldn't help staring at those fox heads. They looked alive and seemingly staring back at me. My mind would tell me they were gonna jump off the old lady's shoulder any minute and grab me by the neck. That was my mindset during the longest hour of my week, church.

School and Church wasn't for me, I didn't know a lot but I knew this.

There was a Foster Freeze hamburger stand and Mayfair shopping center, places we could be seen at on a regular basis. Hanging out and doing our best James Dean impression, because being seen was everything. The weekends we would go to the movies at the Vogue or the Melody; ten cents got you in for the matinee. There we would be, kicking back in the oversized chairs and putting our feet up, as ushers would come around with flashlights telling us to put our feet down. We'd slowly comply, mostly for the sole reason the usher was an older kid who would kick your ass. We would flatten popcorn boxes, throwing them in the air during the movies, creating a silhouette on the screen, disrupting the movie and making people groan.

From my earlier practice of late-night television, I could understand the adult dialogue and get lost in the movie, but if there was a girl inside the movie house, that's where I would set my sights. It took a lot of courage to go sit next to her, even more courage and about three quarters of the movie to maybe put your arm around her. It was awkward for everyone involved, as if my actions with girls took on a life of its own. Most kids then feared rejection. For me, not taking a shot was far worse than a failed attempt. I was a highly confident little guy and wanted the whole world to know.

Always working an angle, we would crack the back door open to the movies to let our friends in, as well as reaching over the glass snack counter and grabbing candy bars. If ever confronted on anything, we would just start running. No time to deny it, no time for any conversation, we would just run. Almost getting caught created a better story than actually getting away clean. Although people seldom chased us, the story by the time you told it a couple times would become a huge crowd chasing behind you, but you were faster and smarter. And any time we bought something it was a big *to do*. You would become the big shot with the money; it seemed everybody didn't have money on the same day. One of us would usually come up with money, thus making that person in charge of where we went and what we bought. The whole crew would wait for your decision, "I'll take one of those." Then you'd turn and look, asking, "You guys want one?"

"Sure!" was the unanimous reply.

"Give me three more for my friends."

These are some of the things that bonded us as a crew. We would *have* together and we would *have not* together. You weren't able to be with us if you were selfish, hanging around when you had *nothing* and not to be seen when you had something. Unacceptable.

But once in a while mom would give you money and you had to go to the store for something specific. Mom would give me five dollars and send me to Grant's department store to buy a new pair of Levi originals; they had little metal rivets on the front pockets and were against the dress code at school. Something I never understood, not being able to wear the Levi originals to school—a dress code violation— but that's what mom would buy me, and telling me she wanted the change back because Levi originals were less than five dollars back then. I felt like John Gotti as I walked to the store with five dollars in my pocket. And the fact that there was an older girl working at Grant's, who was probably twenty years old who would help you in the pant department made the anticipation even greater. Pretending not to know my own pant size, I would ask her for help. She would proceed to tell me when she buys new Levi's she washes them and wears them wet for a better fit. She would also spin around to show me how her Levi's fit. Mesmerizing is the word that comes to mind.

We really didn't like new Levi's though, thick, stiff and had to be washed by themselves several times so the blue dye wouldn't get into your other clothes. Just when you were getting a pair just right, mom would tell you that you needed a new pair, making your old pair non-school pants and the new pants school pants. Levi rotation was a big process even though both pairs violated the dress code.

5

We were considered characters and we were, but we weren't the only ones. I can remember so many. One girl in particular who had pasty white skin and stringy blonde hair whose name was Vikki Wite. What made her unique is she wore a black raincoat and carried a black umbrella every day to school. We live in Southern California, rain is not our strong suit, but every day you could see Vikki on her way to school looking like a witch on Halloween. Someone would always sneak up behind her and yell, "SPOOK!" She would chase them swinging her umbrella, a lot of the kids did it, "SPOOK!" and the chase would begin.

Another kid named Walter Bartholomule wore a sweater vest and carried a briefcase to junior high school. He had a real big head and his eyes were always wide open. Really, a briefcase Walter? We're in seventh grade, not splitting atoms. The thing to do when you saw him was you would get real close to his face and go, "HEY WALTER BARTHOLOMULE!" Somehow that was funny too.

But the character of that era was Joe Pace. We would be hanging at the Foster Freeze hamburger stand. Joe would show up on his Schwinn Stingray bicycle. This bike had to be seen, with reflectors everywhere, multicolored streamers coming out the ends of the butterfly handlebars, and playing cards held on by clothespins on the spokes to make it sound like it had a motor. Joe also had strange facial features. His face was real long and his nose and mouth seemed like they were on the side more than in the middle of his face. Nobody knew where he lived; he never went to school and would just show up at the Foster Freeze riding in circles in the parking lot. We figured he was mental because he never got off his bike, just riding in circles as he talked to us. If the Los Angeles Rams were playing that weekend he would say he was on the team, and of course we would engage, "You play quarterback don't ya Joe?"

"That's right," would be his reply.

"Don't you date one of the Ram cheerleaders also Joe?"

"Sure do and she really likes me a lot, oh yeah she loves me."

Suddenly somebody would scream, "YOU'RE LYING! You don't play for the Rams. You don't date a cheerleader."

Then he would get all crazy and start riding around the parking lot real fast, faster and faster and yelling back at us, "I DO, YES I DO!"

Every time we would see Joe he would tell another story. He was Grand Marshal at the Harbor Day Parade or knew the President of the United States personally, and with us eventually yelling at Joe, "YOUR LYING!" he would pedal fast and scream back at us, "NO I'M NOT!" and ride off to nobody knew where.

We were just kids being kids, no harm intended and if anybody ever took it past those lines of just playing we would step in and defend Vikki, Walter and Joe; very odd relationships indeed.

As a group, we soon realized life with money is better. Putting our heads together, we concocted ways to have some sort of cash flow at age twelve. I was mowing the neighbor's yard on Saturday, which consisted of cutting the grass front and back using a push mower, hand edging, and raking and putting everything in the trash can. I would then knock on the neighbor's door and hear, "Good job," and receive one dollar for my labor.

I saw no future in this and it was only for one day a week anyway. We needed to learn how to make money fast, easy, and as a group. One of our better schemes was painting house numbers on the curb of the sidewalk. In California, addresses are located on the curb as well as on your house, so the fire department can locate the street address in an emergency. We set off to make pocket money by spray painting house numbers on the curb. We searched our parents' garages to find stencils and spray paint. Spray paint was big back then, people spray painted everything: bikes, tables, and even house furniture. My dad was the spray paint king. He would spray paint everything and say how it would look brand new. I always thought it looked the same just spray painted. So there we were, with a can of white spray paint, a can of black spray paint, stencils and a piece of cardboard cut in a rectangle for the background.

Knocking on a random door, for a dollar you could have your house numbers in front of your house. One group of us was in charge of the white spray painted rectangle, the next group in charge of doing the black numbers. Having no patience as kids, often the numbers would run from too much paint, or the two colors would mix together from not allowing ample time to dry. When the black paint ran out usually first we would still knock on doors offering the same services, telling the customer that a couple of kids are painting numbers around the corner and will be here next to do yours. With only the white background rectangle painted, we would get our dollar. With both cans of spray paint now empty, we continued knocking. Now, the entire paint department was around the corner, but we represented marketing and accounts receivable and paying us a dollar *now* would ensure your house numbers would be painted next. With the quick buck in our hot little hands, we would be gone with nobody showing up to paint. All of us would meet up at the park, splitting the loot and planning our trip to the store. We stayed away from the houses that never saw the paint crew, only the finance department.

Other kids I knew had paper routes, collecting money monthly. Northside Stevie, who could porch the newspaper with one throw, would go two or three times to the same customer during the month collecting money, having multiple receipt books to satisfy both customer and paper. Although unorthodox, we always had pocket money.

Plastic was a relatively new product, so everything was glass: jars, milk containers and pop bottles (soda). Recycling wasn't the trend yet, but you could get three cents for a bottle. At vacant lots and parks you could always find a couple of discarded bottles and go from broke to having nine cents in your pocket in a matter of minutes. Nine cents doesn't sound like much now, but it meant you could buy nine items at the penny candy store: wax lips, candy cigarettes, bubble gum with a baseball card and a large variety of other penny treats. But as I said, we wanted fast and easy group money.

Markets would give you three cents for a bottle and stored the returned bottles in wood crates, stacking them in the back outside of the store, usually with a chain link fence around the storage area. Our plan would be to bring in a couple of bottles, get our six cents, while telling the clerk we are meeting friends here and they would be bringing bottles also. This diversion allowed the others to go around back, lift the fence and grab some more bottles. The clerk would pay for the same bottles over and over. That was *our* recycling in the early sixties.

School had become easy, but I was still always looking for that angle. If I overheard my mother saying she had errands to do that day, I would become an Oscar award-winning actor, pretending to be sick. Anytime you mentioned not feeling good, mom would put a thermometer in your mouth. You could twist your ankle and mom would take your temperature. One morning, I didn't want to go to school and allegedly I didn't feel good, so into my room comes my mother with the thermometer. Putting it in my mouth she left the room leaving her coffee by my bed. I put the thermometer inside of her coffee to ensure a day off from school. A minute later she returned, looked at my temperature and said smiling, "You have a fever of 126°. You're going to school, you're not that sick."

Most of the time, I thought I was slicker than I really was. Being in eighth grade now, I was considered a senior in the junior high school. I had the place wired. It seemed we always had pocket money and mom would give you a quarter for a hot lunch at school, which consisted of walking through the food line and having the cafeteria ladies fill your tray with food, complete with a miniature carton of milk. With a bowl of quarters in a kitchen drawer at home for my lunches, I would grab more than one many times, and spread the quarters around the bowl to make it look like I wasn't stealing. Having the sound of change in my pocket became a security for me, knowing I could buy anything at any time.

There were Helms bakery trucks around the neighborhood, blue and yellow trucks that would honk this odd noise to let you know they were in the area.

Swing open the back doors and big trays of doughnuts would appear. For six cents you could get an apple fritter or a bear claw. After school the Good Humor ice cream trucks would play their ice cream song and we would get a nutty-buddy or 50/50 bar (they call them dream-sickles now). We were eating all the time.

Even in the morning on the way to school, I sometimes stopped at Hugh's Market because they sold candy by the pound. Ordering fifteen cents worth, the clerk would then put the candy in a white paper bag, and off to school you would go. Offering everybody some, as people stuck their hands in the bag you became the Godfather for that moment. One morning I had the white bag filled with Chocolate Stars. On the school grounds, the principal grabbed my bag questioning me about the candy. I told him that I bought it for him and was on the way to his office to give it to him. He lit up with a smile and said, "Thank you very much." Not getting caught at anything had become my main objective in life at age thirteen.

Eventually the school cracked down, calling the Helms Company and banning their trucks from the school area and anyone seen with a white bag would fall under heavy suspicion. But for me that became a game of cat and mouse and I enjoyed playing.

As usual the boredom set in, and I found myself in school staring out the window, wishing I was anywhere but right here, right now. Most of the teachers didn't hold my attention, but this one in particular, Mr. Rusnak my eighth grade math teacher was completely different than all the others. He would start his tests with a cap gun and time us, teaching us to multiply ten digit numbers by ten digit numbers, not using scratch paper. This was called the Trachtenberg method of multiplication. Some guy named Trachtenberg, a P.O.W. in wartime, would keep himself sane by doing numbers in his head and came up with this method. In other classes, I would have to read a book and give my opinion of that book and sometimes the teacher would say "No, that's not quite right." I would think to myself: My opinion is always right, as my opinion. But with math there was only one right answer and I liked that concept, plus doing numbers came easy for me. Mr. Rusnak was missing half of his middle finger on his left hand and often laid his left hand on the overhead projector silhouetting his missing finger to scare the girls. We thought that was so cool.

When President Kennedy got shot, there was this one kid named Sullivan who came into the class listening to his transistor radio and told Mr. Rusnak the president just got shot. Mr. Rusnak started slapping him in the face telling Sullivan, "Don't you ever say that about the President." Sullivan, this white-haired skinny kid, kept telling him it was true. Mr. Rusnak slapped the dog shit out of him that day.

In other classes we would watch these outdated movies about farming and growing wheat, or how the Boll Weevil bug would destroy an entire cotton crop. I'd think to myself, when am I going to use this knowledge in life?

In October they would bring black-and-white televisions in the classroom for everybody to watch the World Series. But, I really didn't want to be there ever, no matter what was happening.

High school was next with the rumors already swirling what could or might happen to you at the hands of the seniors. Threat of the *Royal Flush* was having your head put in the toilet by the older kids as it is being flushed. Or another rumor was about the one high school kid that would pee on you in the community showers after gym class. That rumor turned out to be true. His name was Art and he would walk over to guys while showering, start talking and peeing on them to start a fight. From the rumors everything seemed to advance to another level, but summer was here and that's what I was gonna enjoy.

6

This summer turned out to be one of the best thus far. The vacant lot had expanded to the beach, Silverstrand Beach, a stretch of sand about eight tenth of a mile between two jetties nationally known for its waves and territorial behavior. We called it the Jetties and it was for locals only. I was involved with the territorial mystique of being a second-generation local. We would ride bikes, walk or have somebody's mom drop us off. Our daily mission became to get to the Jetties because that's where it all happened. Our mischief had turned to more crime than prank, and with the pecking order becoming more concrete. Showing up on the Strand that first day, I was taken aback by some of the people there. I'd heard stories about these legends, and wasn't sure if they even existed. Seeing them for the first time was monumental.

There was Dudey Wares, The King, in person. The Pierdon brothers, Jimmy and Ronnie, these two brothers would argue among themselves all the time sometimes coming to blows, but when a third party intervened, they would get double trouble on their ass for getting between family. The Lupien brothers looked like a small, medium and large version of the same person, and if my memory serves me correct they all had the same chipped tooth in the front. Also Butch Powers, Tommy Sange, and Bennie Tee were there that day also. Bennie Tee was a thick Samoan whose name was notorious and infamous everywhere. Charlie Fotatoea was standing next to Bennie, thinking to myself a Samoan and a Hawaiian together that's unheard of. But that tradition didn't dictate their world. These two guys were tough; no they were double tough. In the neighborhood, we would always talk about who would win the fight between Bennie and Charlie and always backing your winner with arguments on why. But the next day you might have a completely different view on who would be the victor.

Although some were in the water catching waves and others were standing on the beach, I could see the group within the group. Dudey had his back to me, and the width of his shoulders seemed to partially block the sun. These guys were not kids they were grown men, muscular, tan, with a calmness that comes only from massive confidence. Being in earshot, I heard Dudey telling how he fought some sailor that past weekend and how his opponent had him wrapped up in a face-to-face bear hug.

Bennie calmly asked, "Well, what did you do?"

Dudey proceeded to say how he bit the guy's nose.

"Completely off?" Bennie then said.

"I don't know, but I felt my teeth coming together," Dudey said back grinning at Bennie.

So far our little fights would cause red skin or a black eye at worst, but these guys were animals, so naturally I wanted to be like them. I didn't receive the nodding glance of acceptance that day, my first day at the Jetties. Besides I had my own crew, David Melborn, who in his own right was tougher than most of us and looked older. He would have to bring his birth certificate when he played Little League baseball since other parents thought he was older because he was able to grow a full beard at fourteen. The reason he could fight better was that his dad would drink and come home hitting his mother. David would get involved, taking the ass whipping instead to protect his mother. But after some time he became better at fighting, after all he was fighting a grown man, and turned the tables whooping his dad's ass. We became good friends and remained that way for years.

Others were Steve Deerington, who always thought for himself, never got caught up in a lot of our situations and Gary Shankland, who turned out to be a real nut, doing anything on a dare. These people defined my life, and who I wanted to be with. So, I'd find myself standing in front of the mirror in the bathroom at home practicing my right hook over and over, at times feeling like I accomplished my goal by being just a little quicker than the guy in the mirror. Doing push-ups, I wanted to grow overnight. But mostly, I wanted to establish a name for myself on Silverstrand.

Still having to do my chores I would zip through them to create more beach time. We would all just hang out at the beach, and being able to tell people you were on the Jetties with the legends of Oxnard became surreal. Some of the crew went surfing, with others and myself just hanging out, but as I would stare at the ocean, that surfing thing seemed like something I could do. Being athletic, how big a problem could this be to learn? I would watch for hours. The local surfers made it seem effortless, the paddling out, the turning around and with a couple of strokes, they were standing on a stick on top of the water. This baffled me, but at that moment, that's all I wanted to do.

With surfing came a new language and a whole set of unwritten rules. You didn't just borrow somebody's board, surfboards were sacred, and so I set out to buy my first board. It was nine feet eight inches, heavy, red and made by Mory Pope. It was truly a pig, but it was mine. A little beat up, but for only ten dollars I was surfing. Not being good enough to surf with the experienced locals on the good waves, I had to go down the beach and go through this learning process. No schools, no teachers on how to surf, just get out in the ocean and on your own learn to surf. The best way to describe it is it's like a sock in a washing machine, the ocean is the washing machine and you are the sock. Going down the beach and paddling out, inevitably the ocean would pound me into submission. A lot of people never get past that first couple of days and any progress is very slow. It required a set of motor skills that I'd never put together before all at once, but I was determined and like everything else I don't quit.

Everything was an attempt at first: attempting to stand up, attempting to catch a wave, attempting to put my right foot forward searching for balance. And then hope. Having my right foot forward made me a goofy foot. It's a term that was created from the Mickey Mouse cartoons, when Goofy would surf his right foot was forward hence the term, goofy foot. It seemed natural to me, so that's the way I learned. But the truth of the matter is, more waves break to the right, not left, so this would put my back against the wave instead of facing it. Making surfing for me even more of a challenge.

But I would show up on a daily basis carrying my pig Mory Pope and get in the water. All the radios were fixed on 1520 KACY on the AM dial, Wilson Pickett, Otis Redding and Martha and the Vandellas had us *dancing in the streets* and we were focused on one thing, the beach and surfing. Showing up in just trunks and a T-shirt, no towels, no shoes, no sunscreen and spending all day at the Jetties doing what we do. I noticed it was the same people every day, no outsiders ever. Whenever I would see a car cruising with boards strapped on top, slowly Dudey or Butch would turn their heads squinting from the sun looking at that particular car, then it would speed up never to be seen again. Silverstrand was territorial to the fullest degree, and not knowing then what I know now, the old crew was grooming us to pass the torch of ownership. The sole right to the waves at the Jetties, and heir to the throne was not an easy task. So in the summer of 1965, we watched diligently and imitated our beach going teachers. There were times when non-local surfers would show up, get out of their car and without verbal exchange got their heads slammed against the windshield sometimes breaking it and beat down horrifically. Word was out, "locals only" and we meant it. I would look at the sky and think to myself, how am I so blessed to be one of the chosen few?

My life was going better than I ever imagined.

Lying to our parents about staying at each other's houses, we'd end up at the beach at night. Digging a hole in the sand having only trunks and a sweatshirt we would sleep and wait for the morning waves with our surfboards within arm's reach. Laughing and talking the night away for tomorrow could be the day the waves could be *pumpin'*, gliding on top of the oceans waves on our fiberglass sticks and getting that feeling that none of us had ever experienced.

The old-school crew and my new-school crew didn't interact that much for being on such a small piece of sand. We were separated once again by age and reputation. Once in a while Dudey would give me the nod of "hey what's up," or one of the other surf regulars would acknowledge my presence. Spending hours in the water being young, we never tired but standing on the beach after surfing it was as if a food alarm clock went off inside all of us at the same time. We were starving.

47

Somebody would always ask, "Does anybody have money?"

And then we would head to The Corner Store (incidentally that market is still there 48 years later), grab a container of milk, some Good-n-Plenty candy or this relatively new product, Twinkies. Whatever we got, we would always split, no selfishness existed among the Jetties crew. And the first time one of the old-school cats would ask you if you wanted to walk to The Corner Store, it created a step closer in your complete rite of passage. But if nobody had money, we still went to The Corner Store and stole ourselves something to eat. That was the law of the land.

One afternoon Jimmy, the older of the Pierdon brothers, a Vietnam vet as well as a recipient of the Purple Heart invited me to The Corner Store, so off we went. Jimmy was funny and eventually we became close, but on the way back to the beach we walked by a row of houses and there was a little dog outside its yard.

Jimmy started saying, "Get back in the house... go on."

Next door, there was a man working on his motorcycle, a biker type. He yells out to Jimmy, "Watch your mouth."

Trying to explain, Jimmy said, "I was talking to the dog."

"I don't care who you were talking to, watch your fuckin' mouth," said the unknowing biker.

It all happened so quick, Jimmy ran up the short driveway into the garage hitting this guy with both fists over and over like sledgehammers. I remember him hitting the gas tank on the motorcycle when missing the guys face, putting big dents in the tank. It happened so quickly. The neighbor who owned the dog came out and asked Jimmy, "Do you need something?"

"Yeah," Jimmy said, "Call an ambulance for your neighbor."

Back on the beach we could hear the sirens as we paddled back out to surf. A couple days passed and as Jimmy and I walked past this biker's house on the way to the store, I could see him in the garage, jaw wired, bandages around his head and not saying a word as we passed.

I was still wearing my hair in a pompadour but with the water and the wind rearranging my hair it now hung down and was getting lighter by the sun. From my push-ups I was getting bigger and also tan from the beach. Seemed like my mother was happier, probably because her son wasn't looking like a hoodlum any longer and eating more seemed to make my mother happy also. Mothers like you to eat a lot for some reason. This was the best summer so far but was coming to a close with high school starting next.

7

Colonies of kids gathered in various places at high school. The halls had groups of students with notebooks, by the picnic tables girls talked with each other wearing dresses called shifts, low-cut, short and gathered right under their bumps. The high school girls looked good, wearing makeup and hair done in a puffy way. In the parking lot guys were leaning against jalopies and lots of Chevys from the fifties all having one thing in common, a chrome gas cap. Their cars may look like they were ready for the junkyard, but they would always have a chrome gas cap. And there I stood taking it all in, high school. And I have to do this for four years. My mind was on the beach and the possibility of surf.

I had figured out ways to get out of going to church, but dad would never let me drop high school. So there I was, a red and white Viking from Hueneme (pronounced y-knee-me) High School. I started seeing familiar faces. There was David who we now call Melby, Steve Deerington known simply as Deer, Be-Bop, Jock and Gary. We were all starting high school and familiar faces let me know it was going to be okay. Bennie Tee walked across the campus and didn't seem like he belonged there with his size and mature look. Teachers even went out of their way to greet Bennie, coaches loved him, and he was the one person that everybody in school knew who he was. I found myself in my usual school routine of sitting in the back of the class, staring out the window, once in a while cutting my eyes when a girl would turn around and look. Classrooms had this oversize clock above the teacher and when teachers would talk I would find myself staring at the clock, I would think is it broke? The hands just weren't moving and I wanted to be anywhere but right there right then. And there was the social part of school between classes and lunch. Walking into the cafeteria took on a red carpet event and when Bennie motioned me to sit at the table with him, it was like I had finally arrived. Yes everybody, I know Bennie Tee personally.

Everybody took the same classes but you had an option of music or art, so being artistic I chose art with Mr. Hasbro. He became another teacher that I remember, having him as my art teacher for four years he had the ability to make me want me to learn. Being a good artist, I looked forward to his class. In that four years he taught us one thing over and over, that "Simplicity is the essence of good design." Walking around the class, he would put his hand on your shoulder while looking at your art project and tell you, "That's good." As funny as he looked with his checkered coat, bow tie and glasses, he was pretty cool. Other classes took on the same ho-hum boredom, another black and white film on some useless knowledge, with one kid always in the class volunteering to run the projector. We would make kissing sounds when that one student would raise his hand claiming to be a projector expert.

The girls were taking on a new dimension also, their bumps had become bigger and they were paying more attention to every detail of their dress and makeup. They became my motivation to go to school every day. Two thirty in the afternoon and finally schools out, with plenty of daylight left to go to the beach and that's what we would do. That boost of energy that comes from being able to do what you want to do would kick in finding ourselves at the Jetties again. With the season getting closer to winter, the waves would become bigger and the feeling of needing to conquer became reinforcing. My confidence level was climbing; after all I knew the right people and hung out at the right places. But the crew got smaller on Silverstrand. Dudey was rarely seen anymore and the old school and the new school were mixing, the torch had been passed. My pride for who I was and who I was becoming started to swell with each day. School became tolerable as well as do-able and it was okay also to start missing dinner with the family once in a while, with prior notice. My mom would save me a plate for when I got home.

Still lying about my homework being done and still responsible for my chores, I had figured it out. If I did the work around the house my dad would stay off me. This seemed like a sensible trade-off with more time to do what I needed to do, surf, steal and chase girls. Every song on the radio started to talk to us in a language that only my generation understood. Although we surfed, we listened to Motown. Even though the Beach Boys were out, we considered them shallow and without soul. Our music had a quality not only from listening, but feeling every word and note. Misunderstood by adults, we understood each other completely. Across the board my confidence exceeded the norm. I wasn't scared of girls; I adored them. My ability to ride waves was increasing and my skill of thievery was growing at a steady pace. I was now going into a store setting my sights on what I wanted and taking it. I had added finesse to my stealing portfolio, sometimes putting the expensive item down my pants while paying for something less expensive. And if the merchandise was big, I would walk to the store's front doors, suddenly turn around with a shocked look on my face as if I picked it up to look and forgot to put it down. If nobody was behind me or paying attention, I would calmly stroll out. We were taught to never run unless caught; running only brought on unneeded attention. Never was I confronted, never. Stealing became routine so I had everything I wanted without that troublesome time-consuming thing called a job. A job at this point would only get in the way of having fun.

Eddie Kane was the oldest member of the beach crew locals. He was in his late twenties and me and my friends our early teens, which created a big age gap. Most of us were in awe of Eddie, he was the coolest one around, not big and tough but smart. He rented a house on Silverstrand with his longtime girlfriend Mary. Hanging with us surfing, laughing and teaching us a side of life we had not experienced. Eddie was a master thief and his girl Mary was quite the cat burglar. But to us he portrayed using an angle that we had never considered, using our brains. Eddie was smart about everything. As young bucks when we arrived at the beach, we'd grab our boards and run as fast as we could to the water, paddling out and searching out the waves. But Eddie would stand there looking while smoking a cigarette, pinpoint where the waves were breaking and paddle to that one particular spot. Last in the water he would always catch the first wave, smart.

His hustle was hitting cars (stealing out of parked cars). With all automobiles having wing windows only secured by a button, Eddie would slide a slightly curved butter knife between the gap of the rollup window, popping the wing window then reaching his arm in and opening the door. Taking only money, he would then lock the car door back up; most times the owner didn't realize their money was gone. He never did it at our home beach, always out of town, and never took anything but money. He would leave stereos, jewelry, always just taking cash leaving the car like he found it, locked. This never would draw heat from the police. Mary would do the same with houses and they always had money. Rent right on the beach at Silverstrand was about eighty-five dollars a month, so hitting a few cars a week they could live for the month. He never got greedy and that was another sign of his intelligence. Eddie just wanted to live on the beach, be left alone and surf. When there were no waves or the weather was bad, he would invite some of us to his house. Putting on music that we've never heard, and telling us stories we became very impressed.

Using only cash to live was not out of the ordinary. You could buy a house or brand-new car with cash never arousing suspicion. Stealing cash and spending cash looked like the norm and Eddie lived like this his entire life. It was years later that I learned Eddie's real name wasn't Kane, it was Kaninback. He was becoming one of my first teachers on how to be low-profile.

The girls were really starting to pique my interest at this point and looking around my high school we had some lookers, with big hair, full makeup and chewing gum, they looked better than good to me. That's what school had become, planning for after school mischief and flirting. My father had been a good example on how to treat women, so I followed his path of charm and I was a kid in a candy store with girls everywhere. One of their friends would pass on the information about being liked by a certain girl and suggest that you talk to her friend; naturally I had to play the game as if I were a peacock in full fan walking around the yard. How it worked was, to try to get a girls number and call her, but I put a twist on it. If you want to talk to me here's my number, call me. I was going through the transition of confident to cocky.

One day at the high school quad there she stood, Sue Givens with her black hair ratted into a bouffant hairstyle, black eyeliner accenting her brown eyes and wearing a cotton shift dress. Two years older than myself and very very curvy. With my life of lying and stealing going so well, I figured I should bring Sue into the mix. Living three blocks from me helped my cause also, always telling my parents I was going on a walk after dinner, I would start running to Sue's house as soon as I was out of eyesight. She also babysat the neighbor's kid, so there I would be also, sneaking in the back door. Sue was sixteen and having a driver's license allowed her to borrow her dad's Ford L.T.D. once in a while. With the story of going on another walk, Sue would pick me up around the corner and we would just cruise with the music holding hands. But something wasn't settling quite right with me and then I figured it out. I should be driving my girl, not my girl driving me. With no prior experience, I got behind the wheel and off we went. With the big V-8 under the hood of the gold Ford, all over town you would see this car going fast with my little head in the driver's window.

Often in our search for waves, the Jetty crew would head out of town, going north stopping at the Ventura Point, Overheads, Stanley's, Little Rincon or Rincon. With one of the older kids driving their own car or somebody borrowing their dad's car and our boards sticking out the windows or strapped on top, you would see the Jetty crew on the coast highway. The reputation at our beach had built to a point that outsiders didn't surf there, even in the absence of the locals. Our financial bag of tricks rose to new dimensions, Eddie had taught us well. We were hitting cars now and when hungry go to a restaurant ordering too much food then bolt out the door. That was our Dine and Dash number. Often we would pull up to the gas pump and tell the attendant seventy three cents please, stations were full-service and every gas station had an attendant checking tires, washing the windshield, oil check and pumping your gas. As for the days that we didn't have seventy-three cents, we'd pull into the station and yell to the attendant, "JUST CHECKING OUR TIRES," as we pumped our own gas.

Gas pumps had a little lever on the side when pulling it down gas would come out; putting it back up automatically the pump would go back to zeros on the money meter. With one of us blocking the view from the attendant and another pumping gas while working the lever up and down, within seconds we had a full gas tank and off we'd go. They also would have locked cash boxes on the islands between the gas pumps, blocking the view again, an oversize screwdriver became a master key and with a big pop, "wah-la" gas and food money. We surfed up and down the coast of California grabbing money along the way with the Jetty motto becoming, "As long as other people have money we will always have money." We were laughing and cutting up everywhere we went.

With new homes always being built, contractors created model homes complete with cheap furniture to show prospective buyers how the housing tract and finished homes would eventually look. Backing our trucks or cars up to the model home, we would steal everything. Eddie always had new furniture.

Driving down the street seeing somebody sodding their lawn with new grass, we would come back at night, roll up the new sod and sell it back to the sod farm. There was no shame to our game, young and out-of-control, but to my parents I was a good student and surfed for a hobby. Definitely living two lives, my petty criminal lifestyle started to satisfy that adventure bone within me, and with no consequences, why would I ever stop?

Sue would want to skip school and play slap and tickle, which seemed like a good idea to me. Certain houses were known for being hangouts when people played hooky. Sometimes hiding in the backyard when the parents came home for lunch and with truant officers roaming the streets searching for us, staying out of sight was necessary. Eventually, I legitimately stayed home sick and my mother had to write a, "please excuse note" and when going back to school I got caught; my mother's signature didn't match the other thirty "please excuse notes" my girlfriend had written. So, thinking my mother's was a forgery this brought the other thirty to light. I received detention for the remainder of that school year. Receiving my first sentence of terminal detention with no parole and for the first time, my mothers and father's antennae were up. Why is our son acting this way?

My older sister has never deviated in life, never went outside the lines, so when I did, my parents were legitimately shocked. Skipping school with a girl would make my mother constantly say over and over, "Sex is not love."

I would think to myself, maybe not but it's got to be real close.

This hurdle didn't slow me on the road of life that I was on, I just needed to step up my game of slickness and that's what I did. I wasn't the only one breaking the rules. The world as we knew it was changing at a rapid pace with some of the traditional concepts becoming obsolete. The radio was playing music from other parts of the world with a major influence coming from England. The British invasion was in America and along with Smokey Robinson and the Miracles you could hear the Rolling Stones or The Yardbirds on the radio. Solo artists such as Bob Dylan or Tom Jones were changing the smooth voices we had come to know and the music became raw, edgy with the lyrics not about love anymore. Now the music was more about culture and social change. It was the sixties making the gap between generations more obvious and defined although being a part of that change created excitement. Style of dress was considered Mod, which made pretty much anything acceptable. Long hair was the order of the day, and it seemed like everyone went out of their way to look and be different. Overnight, weed (marijuana) was everywhere in the neighborhood and had everybody talking about the long-term effects of smoking it. Rumors that it caused people to become raving maniacs, or murder for no reason and not being able to control their mind.

I was now going to house parties where everybody drank, but drinking wasn't a big deal to me. I lacked feeling in control of myself when I drank, so I decided that it wasn't for me. There were also pills now, Reds, Yellows and Rainbows, which were barbiturates and gave you the feeling of being drunk, again not for me. There were white crosses, Benzedrine and everything was wrapped up in tinfoil and called a "Roll." The white crosses looked like a little package of miniature lifesavers when wrapped and you could get any one of these for one dollar. The white crosses had ten in the Roll and the others had four, all for a buck. Taking two Dexedrine pills one afternoon in school (Dexedrine is a cousin to Benzedrine only stronger), not eating and not being able to sleep that night. I laid in bed watching the clock and hearing every creak in the house, my father snoring and other sounds that probably weren't even there. I waited for the morning to come, this by far being the worst night of my life. So Dexedrine or any other -drine was added to my not-for-me list. But still having the need to hang with the crowd I would be in these parties watching other people drink and take pills, very entertaining. I noticed how sloppy and out-of-control people looked and acted, embarrassing themselves by doing stupid shit. My attraction was the atmosphere itself, the secrecy, the underground world that we had created and that I was a member of it. That was my new high.

The heavy hitters would be at these parties also, Bennie Tee, Charlie Fotatoea and others that I was learning about. Not everybody went to Silverstrand, so in town there was a whole other set of promising legends that I got to know also. Bennie would drink until drunk and then ask me to drive him around town, no problem for me. I had already completed my, learn as you drive program in Sue's dad's car. Though the car that I would drive Bennie in was older, the steering wheel bigger and the nuts and bolts looser causing it to drift all over the road. But driving Bennie boosted me up to semi-celebrity status in the neighborhood. These parties were not always a good time for everyone. Some of the things I would see was sheer craziness.

Larry Kough drove a 1956 Chevy Nomad, a two-door station wagon with lots of windows and chrome. Larry's Nomad was dark green with Cragar mag wheels, a beautiful car and in pristine condition. Once Charlie came out of a party after heavily drinking most of the night and started knocking out every window using his head on Larry's car. He then opened the door and tore out the steering wheel with his bare hands. If I hadn't seen it with my own eyes, I wouldn't be telling the story. A little while later Larry left the party and arriving at his car said, "What the fuck happened to my car... ...WHO the fuck did this?"

Someone shouted to him, "CHARLIE. CHARLIE DID IT."

When Larry heard that Charlie was responsible, he quietly went to the back of his Nomad wagon, got a pair of vise-grip pliers and clamped them on the steering shaft, started his car and drove off quietly.

There was something always happening at these house parties; at the beach and around town and I had this need within me to be there when the possibility of something happening happened. I couldn't miss a thing, what I would hear and what I would see defined my world. Sue, my alleged girlfriend started asking me why I had to go to the beach all the time, why did I have to hang with this crowd. She eventually became what's-her-name and faded from the picture. I would still see her at school and she was always asking me what's wrong?

And I would just look at her crazy, I didn't know what was wrong, I didn't know anything was wrong. I just didn't know. But I did know I was having a good time and shame on you if you didn't get that.

Our criminal mischief was consuming our lives, at school joints of weed were being passed in textbooks and school took on this meeting place for *taking care of business*. I was ditching more school hopping the locked fence to go surfing with my buds, homeroom was the only class taking attendance, and when we figured that out we were all good. One day at school some of the older kids were dressed completely different wearing these English suits and Nehru jackets. Jerry Roward was one of these kids, so I went up to him and asked, "What's going on, why are you guys dressed like this?"

He told me, Terry, Bobby and Owen and himself had gone down to Hollywood and burglarized this house rented by The Turtles, an upcoming English music group. They were now wearing their clothes and when he showed me the inside of his jacket there was a tag that read *Made for The Turtles.* I couldn't believe how cool that was, seemed like everybody was into something all the time.

At home I would just be passing through, grabbing something to eat and go into my room and turning the music on. My conversation was less and less towards my family; I couldn't relate to them, they seemed square and out of touch. Not to mention they had no understanding of me and how I was living. My mom would ask, "What's wrong?"

I would always reply, "I just got a lot on my mind."

Yes, fifteen years old with a lot on my mind, really? What did I expect my parents to think; I was trying to solve world hunger. I just wanted them to leave me alone. I was so connected to my own world, that it was causing me to disconnect from them. I often heard my mother and father talking about what they should do with me.

How about start by not asking me "What's wrong?" all the time was my mental answer.

Now, I would seldom eat with the family and any questions I usually answered with one word. I was becoming a smart ass and just wanted to go far away from my house. My father wasn't hitting me anymore, so I created an alligator mouth, even though to my father I still had a canary ass. Around town, I was considered a little tough guy, but to my father I was still his son. So, often my mouth would write checks that my ass couldn't cash. One particular dinner I recall, I didn't eat all the food on my plate and my father told me, "Eat, there are kids starving in the world."

Without hesitation, what came out my mouth next was, "Why don't you put that food in an envelope and mail it to them?"

As I was picking myself up off the floor, I thought to myself, didn't dad say he wasn't gonna hit me anymore? But when all is said and done, thinking back, I was not leaving many choices for punishment at this time in my life.

The music we were listening to was opening doors to options and I listened to music all the time. I wouldn't watch television, but at times when walking past the den, I would see my dad watching a western with Glenn Ford or his favorite television program, the Thursday Night Fights from Madison Square Garden. He would invite me to sit and watch the fights with him and often I would. My father knew boxing and football and I learned a great deal about both sports from him, we witnessed the first bouts of Joe Frazier, George Foreman as well as Indian Red Lopez. I enjoyed these times with my dad and in September we would sit and watch football together. My motor was still running very fast, so I never could watch a complete football game. Besides still going to school, surfing, doing my chores, chasing girls as well as keeping up with my lying and stealing, I was a busy boy.

My Mory Pope surfboard was getting more beat up by the day and on the weekends I would fix the dings using car bondo. Surfboard leashes hadn't been thought of yet, so losing your board in the ocean left you the one option of bobbing up and down in the water while watching your board hit the rocks over and over. From my stealing enterprise, I had enough money to order my first new surfboard, a Yater Spoon. I went up the coast to the town of Santa Barbara and with my board being custom-made (for my size), paying cash I bought my first brand new board. Hearing crime doesn't pay made me disagree that day, crime pays very well, thank you very much.

Some of us were getting cars so getting to the beach became easier. Melby bought a Volkswagen truck looking like a Volkswagen van with a truck bed.

We also had started burglarizing homes and the money was flowing. There was an affluent area on the north side of the harbor called Oxnard Shores. I burglarized a house one night there and the house belonged to Sonny and Cher, it was their beach house so it didn't have a lot of items, so I only took the rocking chair (sorry Cher). I would carry a small plumber's pipe wrench and after knocking on the door loud and long with no answer, I would put the pipe wrench teeth on the doorknob and turn. Instant presto I was in.

Another friend named Steve Winsal, whose mother worked all the time, gave us opportunity to have a daily yard sale. We would put her furniture, lamps and stereo outside in the yard placing sold signs on them, then placing the stolen items randomly throughout the yard. It was quite the racket but Steve's mother came home from work early one day, she looked at Steve and me and shook her head. That was my signal to just walk and that's exactly what I did.

One overcast morning in Oxnard as I walked on the street with my pipe wrench under my coat, I knocked on a door on J Street in South Oxnard. With no answer, I gripped the doorknob turned and soon was opening dresser drawers, looking for money and jewelry. In the bedroom as I opened a drawer there was a gun holster without the gun along with a badge. I was in a cop's house, he wasn't working that day and he had his gun on him. Panic set in. I was in this cops house uninvited. Not taking anything, within seconds I ran out of the house through the alley throwing my pipe wrench and never have I burglarized a house since.

I was fifteen now and my father strongly suggested that I get a job. The idea of a paycheck sounded good, so I started my search finally landing a weekend dishwashing job. It was at Frank's Pizza

Palace on Palm Drive; this made me a workingman.
An older Italian couple, the Luseedos, owned it. Mr.
Luseedo ran the bar area and Mrs. Luseedo sat on the
stool at the corner of the counter all day and night
making sure the restaurant ran smoothly. There was
a television above the bar and when the television
show Jeopardy was on, I noticed Mr. Luseedo could
answer all the questions. But as a couple, they argued
all the time, screaming at each other with the
restaurant full of customers. Also in the Luseedo
family, were two twin sons, another younger son and
one butt-ugly daughter. Whenever the whole family
was gathered in the restaurant, there would be yelling
and cussing at a world war level. Most the time it was
about why the daughter couldn't find a husband.
Washing dishes and listening I would think to myself,
your daughter can't find a hubby because she looks like
a man.

My job consisted of washing the dishes, pots as
well as the pizza pans; my work area was a row of
three metal sinks next to each other with gas flames
under them for heat. First, rinsing the dishes, then
placing the dishes on a rack, I would lower them into
the first sink with soap, the second had bleach and the
third was fresh water. Other aspects of my job
description were being responsible for emptying the
trash as well as to sweep and mop. I was getting paid
minimum wage, which was a dollar thirty an hour, so
on the weekends, I could be seen riding my bike to
Frank's Pizza Palace. The back of the restaurant faced
A Street, which was known as the weekend cruise spot.
With cars bumper-to-bumper, girls yelling to the guys
and guys yelling to the girls, along with the best fights
of the week it was definitely the place to be. But here I
am wearing my dishwasher apron and rolling out
trash, watching as fun goes by and even my eighteen-
dollar a week paycheck couldn't soften the way I felt
about missing out. Hearing all the cool stories on

Monday of what had happened on A Street reinforced this left out feeling. But I started to take the trash out more often, and on my cart would be apples, Italian bread, homemade lasagna (packaged individually) and beer. I would stash a bag around the corner and after work I would ride my bike home carrying these stolen food items. With some of the surf crew starting to do overnight surf adventures, the food and beer came in handy. Other kids were doing exactly the same, whenever we got hungry we would just drive up to the back door of the restaurant that one of our surf buds was working at and get handed a bag of food. Most jobs lasted about a week for everyone because when there were waves, nobody showed up for work. But being my job was at night it didn't cut in to my beach time. My dad was proud that I was working and would often say, "Save your money, you're doing good."

For me, making eighteen dollars a week, I couldn't have put a down payment on a hubcap of my dream car, so it was good that I was stealing to supplement my income.

Mrs. Luseedo really liked me as well as her three sons. Mr. Luseedo didn't like anybody and his own family didn't like him. The twin sons would come in the restaurant and start making food along with making a mess and I would have to clean it up, but always throwing me a little weed and a wink for my troubles, so it worked out.

I was smoking marijuana daily, but it was real private and a hidden ordeal highly against the law. The police could pull over your car and vacuum it and finding any marijuana seeds, you would go to jail. A couple of guys in the neighborhood went to the penitentiary for simple possession of weed. This one guy got arrested with two joints and received two years in the penitentiary, a year for each joint. As far as for harder drugs, pills or heroin (cocaine had not made its entrance on a large scale at this point in time) when busted for possession and found guilty, the police would confiscate your car and light it on fire in an open field. Insurance in the case they had missed some narcotics hidden in your vehicle. I knew this one guy named Danny who had a brand new Corvette and got busted for heroin possession, convicted the police department lit his brand new Corvette on fire, a fucking brand new Corvette!

Times were truly different, a completely different mindset, any long hair or wardrobe out of the ordinary was enough probable cause to search your person and automobile. But nothing or nobody could detour us, not parents, not school, not even the police on what we were gonna do and how we were gonna live. We started wearing two T-shirts of different colors and if the police started chasing you, simply remove one shirt and you would look completely different.

Somebody would light up a joint, you would take a couple of hits and pass it around. We pooled our money to buy four-finger lids, a bag of weed that's literally four fingers high in a baggie for ten dollars. We would roll joints the size of your pinky finger and take pride when someone would say, "Nice roll job."

The music was talking to us as a generation more than ever and we were interpreting everything in our own way. Kids were sniffing glue as well as huffing gas, which I never thought was a good idea so I never even tried it once, but others did and with that the sixties were headed for the history books. I started juggling girlfriends, setting up a rotation system that allowed me to see each girl once in a while, this would also cause the girlfriends to be happy to see me because of my often absence.

66

A&W Root Beer sponsored a dedication hour on the local AM station and girls would dedicate songs to their boyfriends. Hearing the lyrics "he's so fine I'm gonna make him mine" personally dedicated to you on the radio gave you a reputation as a playboy, and that was a good reputation to add to your résumé. But I cannot lie, once during the dedication hour a song was dedicated to me with the caller identifying themselves only, as from a friend. The song by Ray Charles was *Hit the Road Jack*. To this day I don't know who dedicated that song to me and the fellas razzed me on this one, but a dedication was a dedication, so to me that added to my playboy status.

No longer hanging at the Foster's Freeze, the new spot was Bob's Big Boy hamburger stand, on Oxnard Boulevard. Bob's sold hamburgers, milkshakes, French fries and gas, yes they had gas pumps on the side of the hamburger stand. I always thought this was strange, burgers and gas. In the parking lot they sold everything from pills to weed, even heroin, so Bob's hamburger stand seemed like a natural place where I should be. Everybody would back their cars in, running car to car and talking to each other, flirting with the girls and with people selling drugs blending into the commotion. It was truly an eclectic setting, families buying food, people pumping gas and the parking lot full of teenagers being teenagers. My father would get his gas at Bob's because it was the cheapest in town, 24.9 cents a gallon. One early evening my dad pulled in to get gas, seeing me running around the parking lot acting a fool, he pulled his big Dodge towards me, gave me *the look* and told me to get in his car. On the way home he kept asking me, "What were you doing there?"

"What do you mean?" I said, "Everybody goes there dad. We just hang out having fun."

To this he argued, "If everybody jumped off a bridge, would you?"

Not answering but thinking to myself, Dad, there ain't no bridges in Oxnard.

Having to leave with my father embarrassed me. When is dad gonna get it? I kept thinking as I looked out the window of my father's Dodge Polara.

8

I would always think about characters I knew and realize there are two types of characters; the characters you hang with and the characters you don't. Melby, Deer, Be-Bop, Bennie, Eddie and a small group of others were truly characters, but I couldn't imagine my life without them. The non-hang out characters that I knew just seemed to me were going in an odd direction in life. I pretty much stayed away from them on a personal level. Tommy Sange, for example, would drive from Hueneme High School to Oxnard High School every day when school was out with the purpose of never stopping at a light or a stop sign. This was his goal while inviting people to be passengers on the seven-mile ride. Please understand, Tommy would not stop for anything or anybody, often he would invite me but I would always decline, I just thought it was crazy. And Tommy died at an intersection while doing this before he was eighteen years old.

Then there was Tommy and Tony, two brothers that no one would hang out with, and that's why they only hung out with each other. We nicknamed them Tommy Salami and Tony Baloney. What these two nuts would do is invite people over to their house, put LSD in their alcoholic fathers wine and watch him start *trippin'*. Also not to forget the guy down the street who would hit .22 caliber bullets with a hammer. Definitely characters, definitely characters you don't hang with. So when my mother would accuse me of running with the wrong crowd, I would think of this group of non-hang out characters, not our tight little crew who were nothing more than fun-loving criminals, living life and misunderstood at most.

As I was creating controversy in my family, the sixties were creating controversy in the world. Groups like Strawberry Alarm Clock, the Young Rascals now created our music and every garage band was playing *Louie-Louie* by the Kingsmen. I also enjoyed this music but in my heart of hearts I still loved Motown, always with that smooth rhythm and blues. The beach crew was spending more and more time together and we would go over to each other's houses and eat. At all times polite to the parents. We knew how to act when we needed to, and most of the parents were good to us. I would go to Melby's or Be-Bop's for dinner, always helping their mother with the dishes and saying please and thank you, always on my best behavior. Though anybody that went to Deer's house to eat, only went once. With everybody sitting at the table, Mrs. Deerington would serve everybody and the visitor would get an empty plate, telling her son, "Steve, he's your friend, share your food with him." We thought that shit was so crazy. Once when Melby was leaving Deer's house, he grabbed a banana off the top of the fridge and Mrs. Deerington called Melby's mother to report the stolen banana and she wanted it back. Melby bought a banana putting in a shoebox to let it rot, wrapped it like a gift and gave it to Mrs. Deerington for Christmas.

On some days I would plot to have my surf crew pick me up early for the beach to get out of doing my chores. When the carload would pull up to my house, I would pop the question, "Dad, my friends are here. Can I go to the beach now?"

Dad would always answer the same, "Sure you can, after you do your chores."

All my buddies would jump out of the car and we would look like a bunch of little ants mowing, weeding and raking my yard. There would be my father with a big screwdriver adjusting the carburetor on my friend's car, making sure the car idled right. Anytime someone came over in their jalopy or parent's car my father would open the hood and adjust things. My friends liked my dad and he liked them. And I always felt that my dad liked the loyalty and the closeness of my crew and probably because it reminded him of what it was like to be sixteen.

We would travel in groups or pairs in search of waves. One summer afternoon while on Pacific Coast Highway with Johnny Starky, who drove a Nash Metropolitan (smaller than a Volkswagen Beetle), with our boards on top we were flying down the coast. Pacific Coast Highway is a winding and windy stretch of highway along Southern California's coastline with large rocks separating the road from the ocean down below. Long story short, the wind got under our surfboards and caused the car to become airborne and all I remember is seeing the ocean and the sky changing places as the car started flipping off a cliff. My mind started processing everything in slow motion, frame by frame then blackness.

After being thrown out the next thing I remember is lifting my head and catching a glance of the car going off this eighty-foot embankment. My head felt heavy so I laid it back on the asphalt. Taking a few seconds to assess the situation I decided to get up. I could move in my mind, but my body would not respond. Turning my head to the left, I could see Johnny lying in the street starting to slowly get up, but I was still unable to move. Hearing a woman's voice to my right I tried to focus on who she was and what she was saying. She had a small medical bag with her then she proceeds to give me a shot of morphine, all the while telling me how I was going to be all right.

71

She turned out to be a doctor traveling on Pacific Coast Highway behind us. None of this was making much sense and as I lie there all I could think of was my new Yater surfboard is probably all fucked up from the accident. Eventually, and this was pre-cell phones so everything was eventually, Highway Patrol showed up and an ambulance and I am on my way to St. John's Hospital in Oxnard. In the emergency room the doctors were cleaning up my wounds but I was still unable to move. My father walked in and that's the first time I could see in my father's eyes emotion, as if he didn't have full control of the situation. I ended up staying at St. John's for a few weeks rehabilitating, first the bed, then a wheelchair and finally I was walking again. A couple of girls came and saw me while I was in the hospital bringing me stuffed animals and cards.

While I was in a wheelchair, I met this guy who looked like Roy Orbison the singer, black hair slicked back, dark sunglasses at all times, in his early thirties and in a wheelchair also. He would roll by my room and talk the nurses, usually the pretty ones, into pushing us around the hospital grounds. He was cool which made my time there better. I healed completely and was back running around, surfing and creating the usual havoc in a relatively short time. My father was livid when he received the ambulance bill for seventeen miles of treatment and transport from the accident to St. John's Hospital in Oxnard. The bill was for fifty dollars and I remember him saying, "How can this be so much?"

I reminded him that the ambulance was a Cadillac since all ambulances were modified Cadillac's in the sixties, he grinned saying, "You're right, Cadillacs do have a nice ride."

Both of us now were laughing.

The sixties are remembered for so many things, the obvious ones being long hair and a different style of dress, questioning the Vietnam War, as well as the tactics of the government itself. But other contributions were made during this era that so many forget about, the skateboard being one. Everything starts with an idea and then evolves. The skateboard was no different.

In my neighborhood, probably neighborhoods everywhere, kids were figuring out a way to make skate boards by putting a roller skate on a piece of wood. Roller skates back in the day were completely steel, the frame, the wheels, even steel ball bearings. Someone always had roller skates lying around the house or you could pick a pair of skates up at the thrift store. Skates were made to go over your shoes with a form fitted heel and the front was this clamp mechanism you adjusted to the width of your shoe using a skate key. We would take apart the skate, hammer down the clamp in the front of the skate to make flat and mount on a two by four inch piece of lumber. We would use the biggest nails we could find, the more the better and we would be skate boarding. The only problem is when a wheel would hit the smallest of pebbles the skateboard would stop suddenly without warning. With time, we used thinner pieces of lumber shaping them like surfboards and everyone had one. It wasn't about doing tricks back then. Skate boarding was just about getting from here to there, creating this diluted down version of surfing. With time skateboards were perfected, but my generation started the wheels rolling.

Drive-in movies were at their peak, so we were seen at the Sky View drive-in on the weekends in Oxnard. Thursday was dollar night and as many people as you could put in the car only cost a dollar. But on weekends it was a dollar per person, so the one guy with the car would pay a dollar and we would jump the fence and hang out, running from car to car. But if you had a date you wouldn't expect her to jump the fence, so you would ask her to get in the trunk to save a dollar. Nothing says romance like asking your girlfriend, "Could you please get in the trunk for a few minutes."

Drive-in movies served a dual purpose also, when leaving we would grab the speaker boxes off the posts. Running wires from our AM car radio while resting the drive-in movie speakers on the back seat was our idea of stereo. The speakers always sounded like shit, but it was thing to do.

Back in school we were finding ways to beat the school dress code also, shirts had to have a pocket and T-shirts back then didn't. J.C.Penney Department Store with a brilliant marketing move created a pocketed T-shirt, the Town Craft crewneck T-shirt. You could buy three for under five dollars and we were all wearing them along with Levi corduroys (known as cords) and Chuck Taylor Converse tennis shoes, which would cost less than nine dollars back then. We were *styling* and the surfer look was the look to have. But you had to surf to be considered a surfer. There were always kids perpetrating being a surfer with the wardrobe but never at the beach, we called them "grimmies" or "ho-dads" and they seemed to get their ass kicked a lot.

Music was coming bigger by the day with original sounds and original lyrics. The people playing the music seemed just like us only with talent. The Fillmore in San Francisco was a big venue for these musicians; I never made it there but I did see some era defining musicians in my day. In Santa Barbara they had the Earl Warren Show Grounds, a large building with a completely open area and no seats. We would drive the thirty odd miles and see the Doors, Buffalo Springfield, and Jefferson Airplane with Grace Slick all for two dollars. Most of the time since the tickets didn't have barcodes back in the day, we would make forgeries in art class getting us in for free. Jimi Hendrix was playing one night in Ventura at an outside venue and cost a dollar, but not for me and my crew, no sir, we jumped the fence. Standing ten feet away from Jimi, I never guessed what an impact he'd have on the sixties. Another night, while walking around the show grounds in Santa Barbara and fifteen years old, a panel truck pulled over and someone asked if I wanted a ride to the gate. After getting in the truck, Pigpen was driving with Jerry Garcia sitting shotgun, members of the Grateful Dead.

More than halfway through high school I was starting to see daylight, I couldn't wait to be done with a structured environment. I just needed to be left alone to hang out at the beach with my friends and become a new and improved Moon Doggy like from the Beach Blanket Bingo movies. We were calling it free-spirited, school and parents referred to it as irresponsible. Whatever it was, it fit me.

In school the teachers started asking us about our futures, unlike so many others I had already found at a young age what I wanted to do in life. And what I wanted to do the rest of my life, hang with my friends and surf. Career counselors came to Hueneme High School one week having us take this cheesy career test. It wasn't pass or fail, but more to find out if you were mechanical, electrical, or work well with your hands, good at drafting shit like that. According to their evaluation, I tested highly in the Park Ranger category, and coincidentally so did all my friends. I didn't want to be a Park Ranger, at this point in my life I just wanted to be left the fuck alone.

Why couldn't everybody just get that?

9

My rebellion and protest had reached a new level, not protesting the Vietnam War or rebelling about equality for the masses. My protest came from a place where I was questioning authority around every corner and just simply was not gonna do anything that didn't fit my current lifestyle. My mother and father were shaking their heads at me at this point, although I was still courteous and respectful at home. I just seemed to be evolving into this strong-willed, cocky, wise-ass person with no rhyme or reason why. My solace came from the beach and my friends. The Strand was my love and I missed her when I wasn't there. My friends and I would meet there every day, sun, rain didn't matter, beach every day. Hard for me to explain, but the ocean has always connected me to something more than other aspects of life. I noticed this at a very young age, as well as now that I am older. Friendships have always been much defined in the same manner for me also, something I feel from other people, an unexplainable connection. Some of the crew was starting to get automobiles, and most of us had a driver's license. My dad had taken me to a parking lot to teach me to drive and would always comment, "You're a natural," when he was giving a lesson.

I was a natural all right, a natural *fool*. Driving at fourteen illegally had taught me to pay close attention when not wanting to get caught.

Shortly thereafter I bought me a 1955 Studebaker pickup truck, 289 cubic inch, three-speed on the column, primer gray with a chrome gas cap. Two hundred dollars, insurance wasn't mandatory so the natural decision was not to get any. The truck needed a radiator, so I picked one up at Rosie's junkyard in Oxnard for eight dollars, and with my dad under the hood with his big screwdriver I was driving. My mother considered the truck an eyesore, so I would have to park around the corner from our house. 1955 is the last year that you only needed one taillight, so I became a target to be pulled over by the police frequently. But I loved that truck and the freedom that came with it.

Cruising A Street on the weekends I felt like I finally had arrived. Although I had cruised A Street so many times before, sometimes as a passenger and sometimes in my sister's 1962 Ford falcon unbeknownst to her. Often I would overhear her talk about going to the movies on the weekend. Finding out the time and the place and with my extra set of keys I had made, I would take her Ford. After cruising and hoping to be seen by everyone but my sister, I would get the gas gauge back as close as possible. But finding the same parking place at the movies posed a problem many times. Saturday mornings at my house I would listen to see if my sister told my father about her car not being in the same parking spot after the movies. It never happened, but my sister never did pay attention like I did. Looking back I'm surprised the transmission survived my downshifting to low gear on the automatic six-cylinder thinking the people on A Street would notice the rumbling that *didn't* exist. But I had my own wheels now, and felt in my mind unstoppable.

The supply and demand of narcotics had hit the neighborhood as well; we all knew where to get pills, marijuana and even heroin. Being in the middle of a small drug deal became common, and I had my big toe deep in it. None of us ever saw the big picture of how dope got into our hometown of Oxnard. But everybody at all times had weed or some other form of narcotics, drugs becoming interwoven into our lives. One of the older cats told Eddie how we could get a kilo (2.2 lbs) of marijuana, south of the border for forty dollars, American side sixty dollars. Our little surf crew had been traveling further and further up and down the coast, north to Big Sur and south as far as San Diego and Mexico. So it was decided to get a couple of kilos in San Diego. We felt the twenty-dollar handling fee to get it over the border was worth it, and with our hair long and the thought of a Mexican prison, made that extra twenty dollars seem well worth it.

The kilos were wrapped professionally with a blue, red or white butcher paper, and then wrapped again with cellophane. The blue represented the highest grade with the white the weakest, and often we would find little rocks inside the kilo added for weight. But we were making money, so who cares. Once we got the brick (kilo) back home we would set it on a table on its side and with a serrated bread knife we would eyeball half the best we could, and cut. We could sell each half for a hundred dollars, and what came loose during the cutting we smoked. We also thought of ingenious places to hide the bricks in the car for the drive back from San Diego, like behind the seat or in the trunk, even sometimes on the floorboard by our feet. With being young comes ignorance, and we were both.

This is the beginning of the drug epidemic that we know of today, we really didn't know what to do and neither did the police. So with the police not having a clue what to do, they did whatever they wanted. On one of my trips down to San Diego, I was pulled over in Encinitas, California, the cop told me, "Boy, you smell like marijuana."

And then he proceeded to throw everything from inside my vehicle on to the street, another cop showed up completing the entire Encinitas police force. After telling me I smelled like weed, they both stated, "If ever you are in Encinitas again, we will take you to court and convict you."

At this point I assured them that I would never be in their town again or even look at Encinitas on a map, and I never have.

On another occasion I was on an innocent road trip with my buddy Rusty Groen. We were in his dad's 1964 Chevy Malibu coupe, truly a beautiful car. Pulled over close to the border the police told Rusty to open the trunk, Rusty stated, "I don't have a trunk key."

Which was the legitimate truth, but the police using a bar pried the trunk open throwing everything out in the street including the backseat. They destroyed the back of this beautiful Malibu. We were completely innocent; having long hair along with being young was probable cause in the sixties. This became the beginning of the end of our innocence.

School was taking on Gestapo like tactics as well. Our vice principal made it his daily mission to try and bust kids, grabbing textbooks out of student's hands to search, and ordering you to empty your pockets on-site. He would call the police immediately if ever he found contraband on a student and that became my cue to get smarter. I started wearing swim trunks under my pants and keeping any questionable items in the pockets of my trunks, so when ordered to empty my pockets I was under the radar. Flying under the radar was becoming my specialty.

High school started showing us health films in the gymnasium on alcohol and drugs. These films seemed so comical to us. Some guy drinking two beers and hitting a child on a bike with his car, showing him sitting on the curb holding his head in his hands in utter shame, then give statistics on how much time had to elapse after drinking to safely drive. Another one of these black and white films had a heroin addict chained to a bed screaming for a fix, making him look like a werewolf. That shit was just so funny to us. Our favorite was the marijuana films portraying these beatnik type characters smoking a joint, then looking in the mirror and their faces would melt off, or they would be on a ledge of a tall building threatening to jump, while they screamed some crazy gibberish. We would be high on weed watching these black and white movies, this irony added to our humor.

School was taking on a complete different feel I noticed. One of my classmates from English died and his desk stayed empty the remainder of the year. I would find myself staring at the empty chair wondering what happens when you die. Detectives were starting to come to Hueneme High School and pluck kids right out of the classroom, more and more this was happening. Rowen Barcelona got arrested for selling heroin for his uncle and was never seen again. The Reevez brothers brought pistols to school one day and they disappeared off the face of the earth also. Sitting in my math class one day, detectives even grabbed the kid in front of me for beating up the plastic Jack-in-the-Box clown. Fights became more brutal as we got older and the weapons started coming out. Danny Wright was a bully in the neighborhood, being held back in school a couple of times made him big and dumb. Danny would throw his weight around bulling. One night at the beach Danny started a fight with this wiry, skinny kid, and the kid stabbed Danny to death. We all were pretty happy about that.

And like school, I was changing. Living at home had become too much for me, my dad constantly on me about my hair with my mother steadily wanting to know every aspect of my life. So I decided to move out.

80

Telling my parents their reaction was different than I imagined, my dad looked hurt, and my mother looked relieved. My mother made me promise to finish high school, and I said I would. I was staying here and there. Joe Sanka's parents were divorced, so I would couch it at his mom's house. Joe had two older sisters, one an airline attendant, they were both *fine* and I used to enjoy watching them walk around the house getting dressed. Moving out was completely different than I pictured. I had always had pocket money from my little scams and angles, but being on my own, money didn't seem to stretch as far. What was I doing?

I have a good family, refrigerator always full and my parents aren't that bad. I wanted to be home, but my stubbornness wouldn't allow it. I had a point to prove, not knowing what that point was, still I was proving it!

Continuing to go to high school some of the people thought it was cool that I didn't live at home, especially the girls. This encouraged me to remain free. Yes, I was free. Free to be hungry, free to be broke, free to miss my warm bed. But it balanced out knowing the girls liked my newborn freedom. Maybe my values were a little fucked up at this time in my life, just maybe. The time frame is a little blurry, but I imagine it wasn't as long as I felt it was and I called my dad to see if I could come home. He said, "I will talk it over with your mother," and to call him back.

Talk it over?

What is there to talk over? I'm your son and I want to come home. Getting back to him, he asked me to come over and talk. My mother, my father and myself sat in their living room discussing the new rules if I were to come home. I was craving clean sheets and some good food at this point so I would agree to anything. But in my mind I was thinking bullshit...

this is complete bullshit. I vowed to myself within a short time I would leave again, this time never to return.

I needed to learn how to step up my game of stealing, not letting my lack of survival skills cloud my judgments. I'll show all of you, just wait.

Sooner than later I was moving out of my house the second and final time. My parent's reaction after telling them this time was exactly as I anticipated, my dad looked hurt and my mother looked more relieved. My mother made me promise to finish high school, and I said I would. Eric Clapton had formed a new group called Cream and with a hit song called *Crossroads* is exactly where I felt I was in life, at my crossroads. I looked forward as I always did to what was coming next.

10

Jimmy Pierdon had asked me to move in with him, and two other cats. Jimmy Glasen, who was a complete loner, who was always doing his own thing, and Mark Chopin, who on the other hand, was a true character, A.W.O.L. (absent without leave) from the military as well as using and selling heroin. The four of us moved to Ventura, California, on Seaward Avenue. Ventura is a coastal town, eleven miles north of Oxnard, with beaches, palm trees and mountains that seem to push the city towards the ocean. We were renting a two-story A-frame house next to the Sunkist lemon packing plant and railroad tracks. Rent was one hundred and forty dollars a month, breaking it down to thirty-five dollars each. It was very doable for guys who didn't work. The house set three houses back off Seaward Avenue and butted up to the back of another house on the adjacent street. Some questionable characters occupied the first house and we never talked or mingled with them. Our landlady Rosie Greebs, occupied the smaller middle house, in her seventies, outspoken and feisty. She even had her own local talk radio slot on Saturday nights; she would talk about the moral decay and drug abuse epidemic of the youth of today. And there we were, her moral decaying-drug abusing tenants living behind her. My hair was long which caused immediate judgments by Rosie, so stuffing it under my stocking hat I would sneak in from the backstreet. If ever Rosie saw me she would always ask, "Do you live here?"

Consistently I would answer, "No, just visiting."

The house itself was big with an unfinished second floor creating this nice open area, and set back away from the street gave us ultimate privacy. The only thing ever in our refrigerator the entire time we lived there was an unopened gallon can of Jalapeno peppers. The girls would come and go, day and night bringing us food, cleaning or just hanging out. And on the weekends, every weekend, we would have blowout parties usually with live music. A couple of guys from Silverstrand would show up and play their original music or some new radio tune. They were quite good; I even heard one of them became a professional musician but don't know for sure. The house created this never a dull moment atmosphere. There was always something kicking off, Mark's heroin customers in and out bringing anything from jewelry to power tools, Melby and the fellas stopping by to go surfing, along with other Jetty locals on a regular basis. Ronnie Pierdon, Jimmy's younger brother who was tough in his own right, would always have some hot merchandise for sale. We sold weed, smoked weed, making the Seaward house the house to be at for narcotics as well as to purchase appliances. Even automobile engines would come and go. Everything was stolen, and everything was for sale.

Mark seldom left the Seaward house because of his thriving heroin business and an outstanding warrant by the military for A.W.O.L. This left him all day to go round and round in heated arguments with Rosie, our landlady. Mark's hair was short from being in the service, so Rosie liked him, but Mark would always be stealing stuff from Rosie. Not stealing for profit, more a comatose induced type of stealing from being high on heroin. Mark would take her potted plants, outside furniture and if Rosie had her rugs out hanging to be cleaned, Mark would take those also. He wouldn't be slick about it either, when Rosie would come to our house looking for her stuff, the plants would be displayed in our kitchen with her rugs in our entryway. She would gather everything up and take it back to her house always asking us, "What's wrong with Mark?"

I would tell her Mark has shell shock (which is an old school term for P.T.S.D.) from Vietnam, although Mark had never been to Vietnam. Mark would take her stuff again and Rosie would come over and take it back. It was comical to watch. This is why Mark and Rosie would go round and round. But Rosie actually liked Mark in a strange and peculiar way, and they would often have tea together. Mark philosophizing about the decline of America's youth with Rosie in full agreement, all the while Mark high on heroin. Rosie never threatened us with eviction or any talk of us having to leave the Seaward house, and we gave her good and many reasons for throwing us out. I don't know if she saw something in us, or the hundred and forty bucks a month. Whatever the reason or lack thereof, I loved living in this environment on Seaward Avenue, which seemed to take on a life of its own.

With the creation of the birth control pill, "poon-tang" became more available. Good girls became almost good girls, and the Seaward house was a factory for future ex-girlfriends on a daily basis. With the four of us living there, Jimmy, Jimmy, Mark and me, our personalities were as different as directions on the weather vane, but everything always worked out. We never had problems among ourselves; I was living a life that I wanted to live, with the people I wanted to live it with. Ventura was my new playground and I could always find plenty to do. The Ventura Theater showed three movies for fifty cents, a plush movie house complete with balcony, although she had seen better days. But for fifty cents, what did I expect, or even care? Also I found a local music house called the

Back Door down on Wharf Street, a coffee shop type
atmosphere with a fifty-cent cover charge. I saw many
acts there, John Hammond, Taj Mahal and other blues
artists. Walking in the *Back Door* my first time, I
thought I had found the lost city of Atlantis, there were
people wearing sunglasses inside at night, others
wearing berets and I'm sure everybody high on
something. Through my seventeen-year-old eyes, I
soaked up everybody and everything.

The crew was changing; Deer never came
around anymore spending all his time surfing, or with
his high-school girlfriend. Bennie Tee stopped coming
to Silverstrand and got a job for the City of Oxnard
making five dollars an hour. Often we would sit
around and discuss the big loot that Bennie was raking
in, two hundred a week, what would he do with all that
money? Good money back then for sure. The Raez
brothers started working for their father at his
radiator shop, so they were seen less and less. I even
heard one of the Jetty locals was going to college. We
still had a strong nucleus, and when somebody would
drop out, there was always somebody to fill that spot. I
was selling pounds of weed to the sailors from the local
Navy Base and Ronnie Pierdon would always like to
come with me. I would charge more money since the
sailors were from out of state, like Mississippi or
Idaho; they didn't know anyone in California so a few
dollars more was a small price to pay to get what they
wanted. The reason Ronnie would want to come with
me was to learn the sailor's names and schedule and
get a layout of their apartment. Then go back and
burglarize their pads. If ever confronted by neighbors,
he would simply say Bob and Dave told me to let
myself in and make myself at home. Ronnie was a bold
and fearless thief and if ever cornered, he would hurt
you.

My favorite Ronnie story goes as follows; once
borrowing my vehicle and going to the beach to break

into cars, from a distance he was confronted by the owner of the car he was burglarizing. The owner had been practicing archery at the beach, so with his bow and arrow he shot at Ronnie. Ronnie holding up his arms to block the arrow, it ended up in his forearm. Coming back to the Seaward house, he swung open the door screaming for somebody, anybody to pull the arrow out.

These are the things that we lived for; the what's going to happen next stories. To me this was real-life shit that my parents never understood. I didn't just want to look at life I wanted to touch and experience it.

This only confirmed my decision of leaving home and my life was good. No, better than good. We didn't pay for anything that we didn't have to. Coca-Cola trucks would be at the stoplight or stop sign, Coca-Cola trucks not having side doors back then so we would just grab a case. Laughing and waving as we drove down the road. After all, what was the driver gonna do, chase us for one case and leave a thousand cases unattended?

Gary Shanklin was working driving a Good Humor ice cream truck in the north end of Oxnard. Wearing a white suit, a little white hat complete with a black bow tie, Gary would drive his aluminum Good Humor truck playing a catchy tune while selling ice cream to the neighborhood kids. We would drive around North Oxnard tracking him down, jump on the back of his truck and it was ice cream for everyone. Gary made twenty five percent of what he sold, and paid a hundred percent of what we stole. Gary would scream at us, but he was one of us so we figured he understood.

We were always hungry from surfing, running around, and smoking weed. Most of us had lost eating privileges at someone's parents' house, but we still had to eat. We would do our Dine and Dash number, or end up at a smorgasbord (all you can eat restaurant). Two of us would go in as legitimate customers getting plates of food, after sitting down others would join them. Six or seven hungry surfers eating from two plates and Melby would always bring tinfoil and wrap food to take with us. We would just eat and eat, and eat some more. And when the employers looked at us crazy, or said something ignorant the two paying customers from our crew would yell to them, "FUCK YOU, WE'RE PAYING CUSTOMERS!"

Even if somebody did call the police from the restaurant, we would be long gone before any authorities would arrive. Before the evolution of cell phones, the long arm of the law wasn't that long.

11

When the light blue Volkswagen beetle would pull in the driveway at the Seaward house, Mark would hustle everybody that didn't live there out. Tommy was here, Tommy Slizer an older kid who was a complete loner in all his illegal activities. With the Volkswagen parked, Tommy and Mark would have their screwdrivers in hand removing the headlights and taillights. I was trusted so doing anything in front of me made them completely comfortable. They would pull baggies of narcotics out of the spaces behind the Volkswagens lights. Multicolored pills, jars (1000 count) of barbiturates, uppers and condoms stretched in length and width full of powdered Mexican heroin. Tommy's thing was driving across the border to Tijuana, loading up his Volkswagen with narcotics and smuggling them into the United States. Tommy wore his hair in a crew cut, which gave him a look of being in the military, and the Mexican border wasn't like today, homeland security didn't exist. Border guards would profile for long hair and strange behavior, their only justification for probable cause. And Tommy gave the appearance of being in the military on leave having fun in Tijuana. He would bring quantities of narcotics back to Oxnard and Ventura religiously, all under the guise of a soldier serving his country. Personally, I thought this was a beautiful scheme, with his packages so much smaller than our bulkier kilos of weed and with him always working alone, it looked to me at the time as if Tommy had figured the game out. Quantity, equaling more money with one hundred percent profit going to the one man working alone and that was Tommy.

After removing the narcotics, Tommy and Mark would be in Mark's bedroom for hours at a time. Although they argued a lot among themselves, mostly about money, to me they had a bond of needing each other to keep their dope game of business going, creating this one hand washing the other hand effect.

Mark would pour large quantities of powdered heroin on a dinner plate for packaging, using number five gelatin capsules (the size similar to cold medicine capsules that you get at the drugstore). Selling these heroin filled caps for five dollars each. Often Mark would be in a comatose state when packaging the heroin. More than once as I would grab my surfboard to go to Silverstrand, on my way out the door I would see Mark in a complete heroin stupor with half the gelatin cap in one hand, half in the other while in a full nod. When returning to the Seaward house hours later, there would be Mark, looking the same way as when I left.

Ronnie Pierdon and his good friend Alex would be at our house all the time and they both used heroin. So when Mark was in this Rip van Winkle condition, Ronnie and Alex would creep and scoop out big portions of heroin off the plate. I would watch them amused by their stealing methods often with Ronnie looking over at me placing his finger over his lip smiling as he whispered, "Shhhhhh," with a wink and sheepish grin.

When Mark would awake from his lengthy nap he would immediately start screaming about the theft he thought had occurred but couldn't prove. Always asking me, "Did you see anyone take my heroin?"

"No Mark," I would always say, "I didn't see anything."

The dope fiends would come and go, day and night into our house. One of the reasons Mark never left the Seaward house is because everybody would bring him what he needed. Food, new clothes, anything at all, Mark would just have to mention that he needed something, and miraculously a short time later it would appear and be traded for heroin. Mark was truly the Pied Piper of Seaward Avenue, even when Mark would crack a joke all the fiends would laugh on cue and trust me on this one, Mark wasn't that funny. I was very entertained from all this *fiend* activity, their peculiar mannerisms, their almost getting caught theft stories, but very content in my own life from surfing, stealing, chasing tang and smoking weed.

Unlike Mark, I more fit the lyrics of a Junior Walker and the All-Stars song, *I'm a Road Runner Baby*, "...can't stay in one place too long." I was on the go always, mostly with the Jetty locals traveling up north to surf spots such as Tarantulas, El Capitan with our one group dream of sneaking into Hollister Ranch, located next to Point Conception, California. Melby, Be-Bop, Eddie along with a few others and me were constantly searching for waves and new experiences to draw from. We would fill our cars with surfboards and people and drive up the coast on Highway 101 and Highway 1, ending up anywhere we could surf. Thinking to myself many times, how am I so blessed to have this life full of freedom, full with friends?

I am truly blessed.

So on one of these surf excursions, we made a definite decision of sneaking into Hollister Ranch where the Hollister clothing line name derived from.

Hollister ranch is private property and a sanctuary for surfing the most perfect waves. Located on Point Conception, the furthest west point of land in California, the waves at Hollister are so sought after that the owners hire armed renegades to deal with trespassers. Since rules don't apply to the Jetty locals, our plan started to unfold. Finding a critical turn in the train tracks we camped out overnight. Our plan was to wake in the pre-dawn morning and throw our surfboards along with ourselves on the slow moving freight train and be in the water by sunrise. Dawn came, as we stood with our surfboards under our arms ready to jump. Be-Bop spotted the train coming and yelled to everyone, "GET READY."

With anticipation and the train getting closer our plan was coming together. But that train must have hit that curve going at least ninety miles an hour, blowing our boards and us back from the tracks.

"Fuck. We're gonna need a plan B," Melby said bent over laughing.

So Eddie, being the smart one of the crew, came up with plan B, suggesting we let some of the air out of our tires and drive on the railroad tracks taking us to Point Conception. Sounded like a good plan to all of us. So now here goes the Jetty crew, three cars driving on railroad tracks with a lookout on the hood of each vehicle to warn of any oncoming trains. Eddie yelled to me from his car, "If you see the train, get off the tracks."

"Thanks Eddie, but I figured that part out myself."

Finally there it was, paradise beyond our imaginations, Hollister Ranch. Being that Point Conception sticks out so far in the Pacific Ocean this creates a very large cove with longer breaking waves. And that day the waves were pumping like we had only heard about till then. That was one of the best days we ever had in our young lives, being with my friends to share it only magnified everything around me. I look back at memorable days like that particular one and how good they really were, but being there at the time it actually happens is always better.

12

When getting back to the Seaward house from one of my surf trips or just gone for a couple of hours, I had to catch up on what happened that I missed. My norm wasn't other people's norm, seeing the dope fiends come and go, new appliances still in the box sold or traded daily, even stolen car parts in the kitchen waiting to be sold. Coming out my room one morning I noticed a big Moose-head mounted on the wall but not striking me as out of the ordinary. Linda Murry had thrown a party the night before down the street at her father's house, who was Judge Murry. Melby, along with another degenerate local when leaving the party snatched the Moose-head from Linda's dad's house. The next day Linda showed up at the Seaward house demanding the return of the Moose-head, saying her dad was furious. Although Judge Murry was a fall down drunk, we decided it was in our best interest to return the Moose-head. He may be a drunk, but he still was a judge.

Anything went, creating this abnormal normal. Bringing a girl to the house on one occasion, we walked in and Mark was boiling his needles used for injecting heroin on the stove. Looking at me with her face scrunched she stated, "Your house is strange."

I looked at her crazy, "Why do you say that?"

The abnormal was normal and one consistent Seaward house tradition was parties on the weekend, unplanned and never knowing what to expect. Parties would kick off during the week also, but you could set your calendar on the weekends that definitely a Seaward party was going to happen. Groups of people, coming and going, music blaring and the landlady Rosie banging on our door trying to put a stop to all of it. She would show up at our door in the middle of the chaos screaming at anyone and everyone. Since people didn't know who she was they would offer her a hit off a joint or a sip from a bottle. Rosie was persistent, I'll say that, she never stopped trying to shut down our parties. The best being one night when she was trying to police the area, literally with her fists banging on this biker type guy's chest and telling him he had to leave. And this guy was big, Rosie was little, he picked her up and carried her to the closet, putting her in and locking the door.

There must've been some sort of abstract attraction for Rosie having us live there, because she never threatened eviction, never. To me I couldn't imagine living any other way. Some mornings I would walk the three houses to Seaward Avenue sipping my coffee, standing and watching the cars with people dressed up going to work. I didn't get that. Not the question of how does someone get up every morning and go to work, but the question of why?

One of the seldom times when Mark actually left the Seaward house, two guys showed up wanting to buy heroin. I answered the door, "Marks not here and I don't think he will be back for a couple of hours."

"That's okay, we will just wait," said the smaller one.

"You can't wait in the house. I don't know either of you."

"Can we wait out front on the street?"

"I don't care where you wait. You just can't wait in my house. I do not know either of you."

Through the window of my house I watched these two guys sitting on the curb for over two hours waiting for Mark. When Mark finally arrived home and after conducting business with the two they left. I preceded telling Mark the story of the two fiends sitting on the curb for over two hours waiting, then asking Mark, "That heroin, is it that good?"

"Better," Mark said with a grin, "Wanna try some?"

Up to this point in my life I treated all my decisions as if they were a science project. If I liked something I kept doing it, and if I didn't like something after trying it I would just stop. Real simple shit. I liked smoking weed so I smoked weed, not liking alcohol and pills I didn't do them anymore. With lying and stealing working for me, I kept lying and stealing. Even with my parents on my decision to leave home was made when I didn't like being under their regime anymore. So the natural scientific approach to Mark's question of do I wanna try heroin? Was a simple, "Of course I do."

Sticking out my arm Mark put the needle in and what happened next was a match made in heaven, Angels descended from the clouds above, personified by harps and horns all wrapped within an imaginary blanket of peace warming my bones. The sky was blue, the water was wet and I was high on heroin. Feeling as I have never felt before I remember thinking, I like me some of that heroin a lot!

After all Jimmy, his brother Ronnie, Gary even Melby had tried it. I was the one that had been missing out all this time and I had some making up to do. Having to walk by Mark's bedroom on the way to mine Mark would see me and ask if I wanted a shot of heroin? Standing in the threshold of his bedroom, sticking my arm out once again I would be off. This became a daily ritual. Now fully able to enjoy everything that I did during my day. When surfing, the water seemed warmer, a woman's touch seemed softer and with the heroin running through my body I became relentless. Whatever I wanted to do I did when I wanted and not having to answer to anyone.

I fulfilled my commitment of finishing high school to my mother, so I felt my mother and I were even. Melby along with Jimmy Pierdon were using heroin more often so spending time with them was always comfortable since we were all on the same page. I started stealing more with Ronnie, who was such a crafty thief and could smell money. We did some nice scores together. Another summer had arrived and my life was the best it had ever been, my sole purpose was to enjoy summer, every summer. For me at this point in my young life is how I wanted to live as well as die, during the summer doing what I wanted.

13

Jail was starting to become a reality for some of the crew. Ronnie would disappear and when seeing him again, I felt like a couple of weeks had gone by, then he would tell me he just finished doing ninety days in county jail. Time is truly an illusion. Oxnard's city jail was affectionately nicknamed The Rock, and Ventura County Jail was no picnic either I heard. But as usual I was flying under the radar and jail was not a problem for me. Gary Shanklin went to jail so often he was starting to wear a business suit every day, because when you get busted (arrested) in Oxnard you see the judge in your street clothes. Somehow Gary figured the judge would give him a break because he was well dressed. It might have worked the first time. But the problem the judge had with Gary was not his wardrobe, but the fact that Gary was standing in front of him again with another felony charge. Gary was just never right.

Even Melby went to Ventura County Jail on some chicken-shit charge for a couple of days; when he got out he had completely changed as if overnight. He stopped doing heroin, stopped stealing, stopped coming to the Seaward house. When I asked Melby, what's up? He told me the story of how being in jail for those couple of days he could see the ocean out of his cell window, he gave thought to his current life and decided he didn't want to live like that anymore. I still would see Melby at the beach, we would surf and laugh and he never treated me different even though we were going in completely different directions.

Walking in the Seaward house one afternoon Mark was putting on a borrowed suit. His best friend Steve Lars was getting married, and wanted Mark to be at the wedding. Steve's soon bride-to-be didn't share the same sentiments, she had called the police and they were waiting for Mark to arrive. He was busted for being A.W.O.L. as well as for a small amount of heroin. The soon-to-be bride theorized that with Mark out of the picture, her future husband Steve wouldn't continue to do the things that he was doing. The Seaward house was going down and this was the beginning of the end. Jimmy Pierdon moved back to South Oxnard to his mother's house, the other Jimmy slipped off into obscurity, and I moved to Silverstrand. Finding a little beach bungalow for one hundred and five dollars a month, also I moved this little filly in with me and we started playing house. I'd sworn off residential burglaries and started doing commercial burglaries. Dentist's offices in search of gold used on teeth and grabbing any medication I could find used for oral surgery. Also I was hitting warehouses, stealing meat, lobster tails and cases of alcohol. All these items were a quick and easy sale. Steaks and liquor at a good price made honest people drop their standard of honesty, even when they know the items are stolen. Funny the gray area of honesty people incorporate when it becomes for their personal gain. Payroll checks as well as personal checks were introduced into my criminal résumé, having a fresh face helped, as well as back in the day the owner of the check was the only person held responsible for lack of funds. It was beautiful, cashing checks in grocery stores, banks, and mom-and-pop markets. The Bank of America in South Oxnard became one of my hotspots. Recognizing the bank manager and knowing her name was Linda, although two grades ahead of me in high school she recognized my face but didn't remember my name. Standing in a bank teller's line with my bogus check in hand, I would give a big wave and a big hello to Linda across the bank. My teller would never ask for identification, after all if I knew Linda, the branch manager, my check must be good. It was so beautiful.

With a fatigue jacket on and not shaven, I once brought a bogus government check into another bank, clutching it in my shaking hand and shuffling along with an interpreter. I was portraying a war vet with shell shock and no identification, with the interpreter posing as my guardian. I sat there looking spaced and paranoid as the bank manager explained to my interpreter that bank policy under any circumstances is not to cash checks without identification. My interpreter pleaded for a moment as I sat there looking crazy. The bank didn't cash the check, but it wasn't for lack of my Robert De Niro like performance, only bank policy. We didn't win every time, but we won most of the time.

I put enough money together to buy my first brand new car, also my girlfriend's dad was general manager of Hal Watkins Chevrolet on the Boulevard in Oxnard. Saying he was more than happy to sell me a car at his cost, so he asked me, "What kind of Chevrolet do you want?"

"I want a Chevy Van."

He tensed up, probably because he pictured his daughter in the back of this Chevy Van, but finally got three words out his mouth, "Why a van?"

"For surf trips, camping, and general transportation," I added reassuringly.

My van had finally arrived at the Chevrolet dealership and walking into the finance office I laid cash down, around two thousand dollars. Driving off in my first brand new car was a good feeling that day and the phrase of crime doesn't pay didn't fit at that moment. I was eighteen and the sixties soon would be the seventies. And as far as I was concerned you could Xerox the sixties and let me run through them one more time, they were that good. Adding chrome bumpers along with chrome mirrors, carpet, bed and a four-track stereo system (father of the eight-track system) and replacing my old drive in movie speakers with some eight by ten Pioneer speakers, I was more than ready for the road. Needing rims I ended up one night in another Chevrolet dealership stealing a set of four beauty rims which were standard on Chevrolet sport models at the time. Everything was so right; I would walk across the street from my house and surf, do heroin in the afternoon or early evening, smoke weed and laugh with the fellas every single day. The stars and the moon had lined up in my young life and I felt unstoppable once again. After all, what could go wrong?

Being pulled over by the police in Oxnard and Ventura was becoming common, not frequent, but I knew in my heart of hearts this time would be different. It started out the usual with my long hair as probable cause. Cop number one then walks me to the rear of my vehicle telling me my taillight is out, as cop number two rummages through my van. As I'm staring at a perfectly good taillight with cop number one, cop number two yells out, "I GOT SOMETHING HERE."

Cop number two proceeds to pullout six brand new thirteen inch black and white televisions, still in the boxes. Cop number one then asks me, "Where did the six televisions come from?"

"I want to speak to MY lawyer," I said naturally and without hesitation.

Now I didn't have MY own personal lawyer at this time, and based my answer to cop number ones important question on when I would stay up late nights watching gangster flicks. I felt that's exactly what Humphrey Bogart would have said given this situation at that exact moment. Cuffed and in back of the police car, I was on my way to Ventura County Jail for my first time. With cop number one smirking in the rear view mirror looking back at me, "Your car rims caught our eye and we figured we'd give you a second look."

I just sat there looking out the window as we drove down Poli Street. I was booked for stolen property, fingerprinted along with pictures taken front and side. They set a bail; I paid it then walked to the tow yard and got my vehicle out. My first pinch and I'm sure I would be able to fabricate some story to secure my freedom. I was a good talker and when the judge hears my explanation that should be the end of it. It was business as usual after bailing out of jail, still surfing on a regular, getting high and stealing. My court date was weeks away and truthfully I never gave it much thought after being busted and paying my bail. Once in a while it would creep into my mind but I would chase it out even quicker, usually with the help of some activity that I was involved in. But, as time always does, it goes by and I found myself standing in front of the courthouse talking with my public defender that to me was more like a public offender. Pleading my case to my appointed lawyer about how "...they had no proof, couldn't prove shit and I wanted a jury trial."

I assured him my case was not going to be a problem. He looked at me funny, cocked his head, hesitated for a moment and said, "What logical or common sense story could you ever tell a jury of why you had six brand new televisions?"

That was the first time it hit me, I wasn't standing in front of my dad lying about doing my homework when I hadn't. I was going to be in a court of law lying to a judge on a felony charge. I was confident that my longevity and history of deceit would spin the judge's head insuring my freedom. Fuck, the judge may even apologize for inconveniencing me on this entire misunderstanding!

Ventura County Courthouse sits on top of Poli Street looking past the downtown section to the ocean. An extremely beautiful building made from imported granite and marble, manicured shrubbery, palm trees and flowers only enhance the courthouse's beauty. Inside, courtrooms are oversized having marble floors, high ceilings all trimmed with beautiful dark wood. And there I sat on the second floor, the Superior Court section of Ventura County Courthouse. I waited and waited, and waited some more and finally the bailiff read off a series of numbers and called my name. Standing at the podium, I evaluated the entire situation, I wore slacks and a dress shirt with my hair in a ponytail tucked in the collar of my shirt. My eyes were fixed on the judge as he read papers on top of his desk. Confident what the judge would see when he looked up, only the front of me. A well-dressed misunderstood youngster at most, with my long hair hid and nice clothes I felt comfortable with my presentation of being this misunderstood youth. The judge may take one glance at me and be reminded of his own son. His son may even look like me and be my age; all assuming the judge even has a son. This is gonna be a cakewalk I thought to myself, providing the judge doesn't have only daughters. The judge slowly looked up and asked, "What do you have to say for yourself?"

"Sir, I bought these televisions from a guy on the street who had an uncle who was liquidating his appliance store and I didn't think to keep my receipt because it was all on the up and up, Your Honor."

After hearing my own story out loud I could only think to myself, bullshit, this story sounds like complete bullshit! And although the judge didn't say it, the way he was peering at me over his glasses seemed he was in full agreement, that story sounds like complete bullshit. The judge looked back down on his desk slowly flipping through some papers, and when looking back up he stated so matter-of-factly, "Twenty days in county jail with six months probation. Next."

TWENTY DAYS I thought to myself, I can't do twenty days. The bailiff cuffed me, walking me through a door in back of the courtroom, down some steps to the jail section in back of the courthouse. This looks nowhere near as beautiful as the front. Putting his pistol in a lockbox provided outside, he buzzed the door of the county jail and the door opened. Telling me to sit on the wooden bench, the bailiff handed my papers to a guard inside the caged office area. Looking around I noticed a tattooed, well-groomed prisoner leaning on the counter of the clothing distribution area. I was looking at him trying to look like I wasn't looking. My thoughts were clouds of confusion and unorganized, I needed to focus. The bailiff then told me to grab a bedroll, consisting of sheets, clean towel all wrapped in a thin mattress, and escorted me further inside the jail. Ventura County Jail is set up in a tank system; a tank is a big open jail area having smaller cells within it. Ventura County Jail had four tanks on the first floor, four more tanks on the second and two on the top floor. The tanks on the first two floors are for general population. On the third floor, one tank is for women, and the other tank, tank number nine, is for protective custody. The bailiff handed me over to a jail guard and the guard opened tank number three. Each tank is set up with a long hall having bars on both sides. Five, six man cells on the right as you walk down the tank corridor with a catwalk on the left for the guards, all leading to a day room. A stainless steel picnic table was bolted to the floor of the day room area, which also includes an open toilet, shower, mop sink and a television sitting on a high corner shelf. Putting my bedroll on one of the top bunks of a cell, I slowly walked to the day area. The shower with a bed sheet for a curtain was running, a guy was watching television with the sound off, and two Chicanos were squatting in the corner whispering in Spanish. I was officially in jail, practicing my new technique of looking, but looking like I wasn't looking and trying to soak everything in. My head was spinning crazy and all I could think of was twenty days; I have to get through these next twenty days.

When my mind settled enough bringing me back to reality, I heard music being piped into the tank. The music group Main Ingredient was singing *Everybody Plays the Fool*, "It may be factual—it may be cruel—everybody plays the fool—sometimes..."

I paid attention to the others and imitated their moves when getting my food tray or fresh laundry, and in general how to act. Staying to myself and quiet as a church house mouse, I would just soak it all in. Prisoners would be doing push-ups in the day area and pacing in between sets. Some reading and others sleeping or just lying on their bunk staring at the ceiling. All this with background music from the local radio station being piped in the tank, and once in a while someone hearing a particular song would blurt out, "That's a bad muthafukin' jam, the police need to turn that shit up."

Having thirty people in the tank I noticed it was very important to not get physically close to someone else. It was as if people had a protective shield of air that others wouldn't enter. I would hear this new language being used, as other prisoners would talk to each other, "Just waiting for the Gray Goose on Wednesday so I can catch the Chain to the Q."

"You get a fresh Nickel?"

"No just a violation. Be back on Broadway in a hot ninety."

I had no idea what these people were saying; their language was completely different. They would say things such as, "Ain't nothin' but a jute ball," and always talking about this guy named *Sancho*.

All the while I would be counting down twenty days in my head with each meal getting closer to my release. There was a toilet located next to the shower in the day room, and if someone was in the shower and someone was using the toilet at the same time, before flushing the toilet you had to pound on the wall twice. The shower water would get so hot it would burn the one in the shower if not giving fair warning. I learned this immediately after seeing a fresh face fish not pound the wall, and the guy in the shower coming out naked and wet beating this fresh faced fish down. It was like a jungle setting and there were jungle rules with the margin of error nil. My days were picking up speed and soon I heard my name and the phrase, "Roll-um-up."

I was back on the streets, or Broadway as the jail prisoners called it.

I went back to the Jetties, telling anybody and everybody about my twenty-day jail sentence. Some didn't even know I was gone, time on the streets and time in jail don't travel at the same speed. It made me think about when Ronnie did time and be gone ninety days, but to me it felt like a week. Part of my stipulation for release was to report to my probation officer, so I did. He gave me dates to report and things that I should be doing while on probation. I only half listened since I'd never been on probation before and like everything else in my life, how serious could it be? I was back in the groove in no time, surfing and stealing, the usual. Although I did notice when I was in jail I missed doing heroin, so now that I was out I was getting high again. As far as for going to see my probation officer, I more or less went when I wanted. All this court stuff and jail stuff, it was one big inconvenience in my life and truthfully I didn't have time for my probation officer, he annoyed me. Besides what's he gonna do, put me in jail?

Standing in front of a different judge in the Superior Court room of the Ventura County Courthouse I couldn't help wondering, how did I get here again? The judge asked me, "Do you have anything to say before I pass down sentence?"

"No your Honor," is all I said.

"I'm revoking your probation and sentencing you to six months in the county jail. Next."

The six months didn't have the same impact as my prior twenty-day jail sentence. I don't know why? I just didn't care, thinking let's get all this over so I can be done with it and get on with the business at hand of enjoying my life. Being escorted down to the jail once again I found myself sitting on the wood bench. Ironically, the same tattooed, well-groomed prisoner was leaning on the counter of the laundry area. That's strange, I thought. He looked at me and said, "Back again?"

"Six months this time," I said shrugging my shoulders. He just nodded.

Saturday the police would give us clean orange overalls and on Monday, Wednesday and Friday, we received clean underwear, socks, and a T-shirt. I noticed some of the fellas would wash their underwear through the week without waiting for exchange day. There are only a few luxuries in jail, clean clothes being one of them. I would watch as the other prisoners would scrub their toilets clean enough to wash clothes, continually flushing to rinse out the county soap. Others would take the underwear in the shower to wash, and that's what I would do. Getting them as clean as possible, wringing them out as dry as possible, then sticking them flat on the smooth concrete wall next to your bunk. It may take a day or a day and a half to dry, but in jail time didn't take on the same pace as the streets.

Food was served on a metal tray and at odd mealtimes. Each shift of guards were responsible for serving one meal during their shift, breakfast was at five thirty in the morning, lunch at ten thirty late morning and dinner around four thirty in the afternoon. Lunch would be a cup of bean soup and a cheese sandwich, the soup served in a stainless steel coffee cup looking like it was right out of a cowboy movie. I was learning to decipher the language spoken in county jail and learned that a jute ball was that round mystery item on our food tray at breakfast and sometimes dinner. I also found out that Sancho is not who you want to be. Sancho is the universal name given to the guy that's with your woman when you're locked up. Everybody hated Sancho collectively; it was simply just not a good role to play in life. Sitting and watching the other convicts, I realized how personable some were, smart, funny and had a lot on the ball. It seemed at the time they just couldn't function in society, and here I sat, which made me their exact equal. I was paying attention to every detail, always remembering to slap the wall twice when using the day room toilet. I was learning other survival techniques also. My looking and not looking like I'm looking technique was used by almost everyone. Each tank had a self-appointed tank captain, not always the toughest guy, but definitely the most charismatic. I noticed charisma gets you farther than toughness, tough guys come and go but charm remains charming.

Every morning the guard would roll in the mop, mop wringer and bucket for us to clean the tank. Once in a while though the tank captain would announce to the guard for no apparent reason, "We're not cleaning the tank today."

"Yes you boys are, or we'll take the radio."

"Take the radio. Take the fuckin' television too," the tank captain would say as he was throwing the television down the tank corridor.

This didn't happen often, but when it did it got serious real quick. The guard would disappear and when reappearing would have other guards with him, and they had fire hoses. One of the guards would announce, "Anyone not involved, step to the front of the tank."

Silence, as we all huddled in the day room awaiting our fate. The fire hoses hit us, which forced everyone against the wall knocking us into each other and completely soaking everything. We would run into our cells and the water kept coming. The guards called this an attitude adjustment, and they were absolutely right. They would leave our tank, us, as well as everything completely soaked. Cigarettes (you could smoke in jail back then), candy bars, mattress, and nothing remained dry. Leaving us like this for days, our attitude would be adjusted. Trying to sleep at night with everything wet is indescribable. But I learned one of the unspoken jungle rules of sticking together. "If you're not with us, you must be against us," a very valuable survival tactic. It wasn't about agreeing or disagreeing, simply sticking together through the good as well as through the bad. A valuable lesson indeed!

The guard would bring the mop set up every morning after the soaking, but not until the tank captain gave us the go-ahead did we clean up all the water.

There was a list for haircuts and I put my name on it. My hair had been growing for years, but it was time for a new look. The jailhouse barber who cut my hair was very good, and I was pleased. Doing push-ups regularly my arms were starting to buff up as well. I started looking like the others doing time, which was my goal. Nothing like setting and fulfilling personal goals in life.

I started paying less attention to the calendar, which allowed me to become more engaged in tank activity. The storytelling and comedy filled up my days. Weekdays would fly by from all the activity of people going to court, bailing out and so forth. But the weekends, they would drag. But Saturday night definitely became the highlight of the week, for the reason of Solid Gold being on the television. Solid Gold was a music and dance show in the early seventies featuring the Solid Gold dancers. Most all of the tank would be gathered in the day room. Most of us would be showered up, our overalls rolled down tying the sleeves in front, all this anticipation for the one hour of seeing the Solid Gold dancers strut their stuff, and it was beautiful.

Taking a Three Musketeers bar and breaking it into pieces, then putting them in one of the cowboy steel coffee cups (which we would hide after a meal so as to have our own personal drinking cup), adding scolding hot water from the mop sink and slowly stirring with a brand new comb for a spoon, you would have hot chocolate to watch the show with. Picking out my favorite Solid Gold dancer, she would become my imaginary date for Saturday night. Whatever gets you through another night, right?

My personal Solid Gold dancer is what got me through.

The jailer came to me one day telling me I qualified to be a trustee. Not because my trusting nature, but my relatively clean criminal record. Very few people were in this jail without lengthy rap sheets from previous crimes. With being a trustee this enabled you to move around more, so why not?

Part of my job description was serving meals to all nine tanks. When I would get upstairs tank eight being females would want to be seen and have short flirty conversations only using their eyes. Tank nine was protective custody and those rats made no eye contact at all, they were labeled and everyone knew who they were. And a rat is not a good thing to be, being Sancho is better than being a rat, and being Sancho wasn't good at all. That was society's ladder in Ventura County Jail.

Never did they mix rapists, wife beaters, or pedophiles with general population either, for the simple reason the general population prisoners had wives and kids. Although locked up for murder, drugs or profiteering most everybody had some sort of values making women and children off limits. I would put less food on the trays going into tank nine and more food on the trays of tank eight out of general principal. I was issued khaki pants and white T-shirts to wear as a trustee with the other part of my job consisting of taking care of the courthouse's first floor. With the oversized marble hallways and offices, my job was to keep them clean. If someone would spill coffee or debris, I would be right there cleaning. My station was a mop closet, which I turned into a little office, organizing and bringing in an office chair I would sit and read while on call for any cleanup duties. Women, beautiful women would be everywhere, which made me look forward to going to work. I would cuff my T-shirt sleeves and as I slowly mopped up spills I would flex my arms whenever the ladies were around. I was nineteen getting ready to turn twenty, so a look from any one of these females would carry me throughout the rest of the day.

Not fearing jail anymore my cockiness surfaced as it always has. One morning getting ready to go to my little trustee job in the courthouse, one of the guards said something to me and I came out my mouth with, "Fuck you."

"Segregation," is all he said as he snatched me up.

He proceeded to escort me downstairs to a place that I'd only heard about until then, affectingly called The Hole. Telling me to take off everything but my boxer underwear he opened the gate of the cell telling me, "Get in."

Slamming the cell door behind me I could hear him walk off as I looked over my new surroundings. It was a six feet by eight feet concrete floor with the only thing in this cell being a toilet. Thinking to myself, I'm fucked as I could hear the usual jail noises above me although slightly muffled. I remember trying to get comfortable on the concrete floor, but it was next to impossible. Somehow this experience wasn't adjusting my attitude as it was designed to do; instead it was making me a little crazy inside. The rules of The Hole are during the day only boxers are to be worn, but at night you receive a blanket. If somehow you don't act right, you forfeit the blanket at night along with your boxers.

So, there I was naked, without any clue what is motivating me to act crazy. Trying to get comfortable now naked in the cell is not next to impossible, it is completely impossible. With a couple of days gone by

112

the jail Sergeant paid me a visit and asked, "Are you ready to go back upstairs to general population?"

"That's completely up to you, boss," I said with an attitude.

"Are you going to treat my staff civilized?"

"Do what you got to do," I said; although I was more than ready for a shower and a good night's rest on one of those thin jail mattresses. My old cell upstairs would feel like the Waldorf Astoria compared to where I was, but I couldn't make myself agree with the sergeant's request. His decision was to leave me in there for another day, which made a total of three days. Three days in The Hole felt like three months anywhere else, and I was starting to notice that father time changes depending on situations and environment.

Being released from segregation, I was taken back to my original tank. I noticed a newfound respect from some of the others, as the guard let me back in. Others had been to The Hole so they knew what I was up against. I was being looked at differently, as a standup guy with my reputation labeled solid. Also now able to speak the jail language, the Grey Goose is the prison bus, a Nickel is five years, Q stood for San Quentin, and the Chain was simply shackles and handcuffs which tied prisoners together. Getting my trustee job back along with my daily push-up routine, time was picking up speed again. Then the night came in which I couldn't sleep, tossing, thinking. Finally morning and one of the guards said what I was waiting to hear, "Roll-um-up."

I'm not going to lie and tell you that it was the song playing on the radio when walking out of Ventura County Jail that morning, but in my mind every note was clear as Wilson Pickett blurted out the words, "Broadway. Funky—Funky—Broadway."

That feeling of release that morning was beyond description, but what now?

Having my priorities in order, like always, I needed some poon-tang and narcotics. Needing money also, I decided to sell my van getting two hundred dollars less than I paid and bought a red 1967 two door Chevy Impala. When doing time in Ventura County Jail, your face becomes very familiar with the police. From being a trustee in the courthouse most of the local police knew me, so much for flying under the radar. I decided to move to Ventura to avoid the heat of the Oxnard police and checked in to the Ocean View Hotel. Which is not by the ocean, and has no view. My rented room was located right next to the manager's office. It was thirty-seven dollars a week, which included a kitchenette. Deciding on my livelihood, I would sell heroin exclusively, I had watched Mark package and distribute, so I was highly confident that I could do the same. Number five gelatin capsules only purpose was for distribution of heroin, so they became outlawed to buy from pharmacies. Heroin was being now put in penny balloons, tied and rolled and a little bigger than the size of a peanut M&M, they were sold for ten dollars. The balloons were designed to swallow when in a precarious situation, and salvaged later. In Ventura they sold for fifteen dollars instead of the ten-dollar Oxnard price, so I felt like I was on my way to the big time.

Back in the day, the police would patrol hotel parking lots checking license plate numbers to monitor criminal activity, so I would park my Chevy down the street from the hotel. I moved a little strumpet in the hotel with me and we started playing house as I sold narcotics. The manager of the hotel was a little guy and looked like he was from the Mediterranean. He wore a little stingy brim straw hat and always had mustard in the corner of his mouth. Whenever I had conversations with him I had the urge to take my

114

finger and wipe the mustard off. Every time seeing him he would comment on all the traffic going in and out of my room, saying it needed to stop. I would send my *now-then* girlfriend to talk to him, wearing no bra she distracted him enough to overlook the possible shady dealings going on in his hotel. With selling the narcotics comes other opportunities and I started moving merchandise also. With my new knowledge of antiques coming from my constant reading, I started turning a hefty profit from vintage stolen items. Basically my room in some ways, at the Ocean View Hotel was a miniature version of the Seaward house. Jail hadn't made me a smarter criminal, just gave me this not give a fuck attitude. Proving I could do time the threat of jail didn't register. I stayed at the Ocean View Hotel for over a year involved up to my eyeballs in the crime game.

Nothing happened that I could put my finger on, but my instincts were telling me that things were heating up. So I decided to get out of town and move up north to Santa Cruz, California. With no one around, grabbing my stuff I just disappeared from Ventura not telling anyone, even my flavor of the month girlfriend. I felt free driving north and nobody knew where I was, I had not even talked to my own parents in a couple years. Under the radar once again, I felt I could leave all the police heat in Ventura and Oxnard. And with my fresh face in Santa Cruz the conquering of this new town shouldn't be a problem.

During the first night of driving my mind was all over the place. No plan and not knowing anybody in Santa Cruz all I could think about was missing being fifteen years old in trunks and a T-shirt standing at the Jetties. I had literally picked Santa Cruz from looking at a map; a beach town far away from the police of Oxnard and Ventura was how I based my decision. Although I had already proven I could do jail time, I hated jail and the lack of freedom. So moving would give me guaranteed freedom.

I grabbed a hotel in San Luis Obispo that first night, and when I awoke in the morning, I felt better about my decision. I jumped on Highway 1 taking me by the ocean and the trees of Big Sur. Santa Cruz had a popular surf spot called Steamers Lane, so I pictured myself surfing there. Although I didn't have my surfboard and hadn't surfed in a couple of months, I still had my imagination, which was something that always brought me through any situation. As I drove along the coast I decided to use another alias, I would now be known as Benito Robbie. Using aliases before, this was nothing new, even once walking out the front door of the Ventura police substation using another name, false Social Security number and signing a promissory note to show up in court, I walked right out the front door with a felony charge, so beautiful. When issued a bench warrant for failure to appear in court, it wasn't me they were looking for, it was this other guy that didn't exist, O the good ole days.

Before the computer age and cameras in every corner of every building in the world, criminals had a sporting chance with the police.

I drove thinking to myself, Benito good choice, a name so abstract that it sounded legitimate. I always loved Highway 1 with the cliffs and the constant pounding of the waves throwing themselves at the rocks below. It was a beautiful morning and Benito was enjoying the four hundred or so mile drive to Santa Cruz, California. Seeing the beach turnoff signs I pulled my Chevy off the highway. Parking at the end of Seventh Street I was in Santa Cruz. Getting out of my car I was wearing bellbottoms now, a double thin cuff on the bottom, known as a Folsom cuff. My shoes were Romeos, a type of slip on leather shoe and a white

116

T-shirt. It was chilly so I slipped into my black leather jacket.

14

Being Santa Cruz is about seventy miles south of San Francisco, I noticed right away the weather was different than Southern California, where I had lived for so many years. It was definitely bittersweet; I was a stranger in a strange land. But with imagination, determination, and no rehabilitation I would be fine.

I did notice feeling lonely though, not the loneliness from being alone, but a loneliness coming from not knowing the layout of the town or anyone in it. I grabbed a hotel room my first night in this new setting, and when the clerk asked me, "Identification please."

"Don't have any," I said, letting the clerk see my hand full of money, "Would like to pay for the entire week."

He waived the identification policy telling me just to sign the hotel registration. When he turned the hotel book register around, I signed Benito Robbie. And thought to myself, now what?

My narcotics and money were running low, not a panic desperation low but the feeling of low enough to have to get my hustle on. Money and narcotics had become my security in life, and often I would stick my hand in my pocket to check the level of my personal security. And right now it was low, with nothing familiar around me I found myself sitting in cafés sipping coffee and watching. My move had not been well planned, but to turn around and drive back south didn't make sense either. I would sit, drink coffee and watch. Sure something would break, I spotted a couple of the local shady characters and striking up a conversation I asked, "Where can I get some heroin?"

They both started talking at the same time filling in words and sentences for each other. They told me how if I gave them a hundred and forty dollars for a gram of heroin, in a couple of hours I would have it in my hand.

"WHAT? I'm supposed to give you a hundred and forty dollars, I don't know you, and you want me to wait for hours also?" Looking at both of them crazy I added, "Are both of you fucking crazy?"

We talked longer and I agreed to their terms only if one of them would stay with me until I received my narcotics. The deal was set and as I was talking with my hostage, while waiting he explained to me the dope game in Santa Cruz. I couldn't believe it and proceeded to tell him how we did it down south, smaller amounts costing less and no waiting. His eyes lit up as I continued on my theory of selling narcotics. Not making the fiends wait freed up more time for them to steal, which allowed them to make money and be back buying from you quicker. I spent a couple hours with this fool and his constant talking and storytelling agitated me.

His friend finally arrived back with my narcotics and the heroin looked like Taster's Choice coffee crystals, and I insisted that they come to my hotel room with me, saying that I would take care of them with some heroin, but in my mind the reason was to make sure the heroin was real.

It was real all right, some of the best I'd ever done, which got my little brain working overtime. The profit margin on these coffee crystals grams wouldn't be enough for my troubles. So using the knowledge that I learned from the neighborhood, the ghetto is where I needed to be to get the powdered heroin that I had become accustomed to. I ended up in Watsonville and San Jose, towns close to Santa Cruz. After climbing the food chain, a process needed to buy bigger quantities, I secured a heroin connection in San Jose. Four hundred dollars an ounce for quality heroin. After bringing it back to Santa Cruz and packaging it in balloons, I could set my own price. I decided on twenty dollars a balloon which seemed like a lot even to me, but making it readily available at all times justified my pricing decision. Business was a little slow at first since nobody knew me but it started picking up. Not because I'm an aggressive salesman, narcotics sell themselves and getting the word out was my only job in this grass roots endeavor.

Looking in the local newspaper, I found the second floor of a large Victorian house to rent. One hundred and sixty dollars a month seemed a little steep but the location is why I rented there, only being two blocks from downtown Santa Cruz. I've never liked people knowing where I lived, so I would walk the two blocks to Cooper Street to deliver the narcotics. Downtown Santa Cruz is a very artsy section and Cooper Street was busy at all times. This allowed me to look like another hipster strolling through downtown checking out the shops and eating at the outside cafés. My downstairs neighbor was this girl named Melinda, she talked all the time and whenever seeing me she would ask me a list of endless questions, "Benito, where you from originally, what are you doing in Santa Cruz?"

"Originally, from Oregon and I'm here looking for work."

My phone would be ringing off the hook, and Melinda would steadily remind me of her being able to hear my phone day and night. Reassuringly I would always tell her sorry for the ringing noise, adding potential employers were calling me all the time. She would always say back, "Don't worry about it, and good luck finding work."

"Thanks Melinda. I feel like I'm going to land that dream job real soon."

In my mind I always wondered how people couldn't put one and one together.

I was selling heroin alone, eating alone and I felt more alone than ever. The world seemed bigger and I missed the Jetties and being surrounded by laughter and the simplicity that came from the surf life. One day on Cooper Street as I was on my delivery route and from a distance I noticed a face looking very familiar. The closer I got, I became sure of who it was; it was Bobby Fay from Oxnard.

"BOBBY, BOBBY FAY FROM OXNARD," I yelled down the street.

Taking a moment to sink in I could see Bobby focus on me. Then he recognized me yelling, "Holmes, what you doing up here in Santa Cruz?"

"Living baby, living," was my grinning reply.

Bobby grew up three blocks from me; although older I had always heard about him and had seen him a few times in the Oxnard neighborhood. Bobby was five feet six inches tall and only weighing one hundred fifty five pounds, but had a reputation of being able to hit like a heavyweight. With his black hair, blue eyes and sporting a little Clark Gable mustache made Bobby very handsome. I suggested we grab lunch, which he agreed. We sat there eating and laughing, talking about Oxnard and how different Santa Cruz was. For me it felt so good to find someone again I could relate with, and we talked and laughed some more before Bobby asked me, "Why you in Santa Cruz, and what are you doing up here?"

"Oxnard had become too hot with the police, so I came up here on a fluke and for the second part of your question, dealing heroin."

"Got any?" Bobby said while having this sheepish look on his face.

"Sure do. Come back to my place with me, it's only a couple of blocks and by the way Bobby, I go by Benito up here."

He didn't ask me about my new name and I liked that, in fact I liked a lot of things about this guy. Bobby and I had this instant connection, not just of trust but something deeper. Back at my place we openly discussed everything, Bobby telling me how he was on the outs with his wife and not knowing what his next move was. I told him to move in with me and start selling heroin; Santa Cruz is the land of milk and honey. I explained how my business came about and the changes I made with my twenty-dollar balloons. Suggesting he get an ounce of heroin and do the same, I would be more than willing to help him get on his feet with the money part. That's exactly what happened, and when he paid me back immediately from his first profit I was very impressed. He had the same values as I of practicing the Golden Rule. Never under any circumstances, never, do you fuck over your friends.

Bobby was a character and his humor kept me laughing. Seeing Melinda, I introduced Bobby saying, "Melinda, this is my good friend from the Pacific Northwest, and he's gonna be staying here with me. He's looking for a job as well."

"Well good luck to both of you on finding work."

Bobby was on the same page as I on how can people not know what's going on around them? We even added this to our daily humor routine, often walking around the house asking each other, "Any prospective job leads?"

"No. Not yet."

"Well, don't get discouraged, I'm sure you'll find something."

We would just laugh.

Our heroin business was thriving so we brought in a couple of guys as runners. When the phone rang Bobby or I would find out where and how many? Then one of the runners would ride his bicycle to the spot, dropping off the narcotics and picking up the money. Business became like a machine, but also very boring, but we both needed money to survive. And like most things in life, there was a trade-off for money coming fast and easy. Endless shady people who we dealt with, their wild and way out stories of no money at that moment, but in an hour they would be rich. What can possibly drastically change in sixty minutes? Nothing, that's what! Bobby and I came up with a foolproof method of dealing with credit situations. When asked for narcotics on the *cuff* or *front* we would just give them one or two balloons as a gift. This ensured they wouldn't duck you because of owing, causing them to take their business elsewhere and they wouldn't ask you again for credit. After all you just gave them something for free; it would be in bad heroin manners to ask again. But the most important reason is, they wouldn't put a dime in the phone, and call the police on you.

At night I would walk to the downtown section of Santa Cruz along Cooper Street. Often I would end up in the Catalyst, a local bar and music joint. I would meet a lot of the female local talent, noticing they were different than Southern California girls but we would still enjoy each other's company. The money was rolling in and I was tripling my money every time I would take the forty-mile drive to San Jose. But I was becoming antsier by the day from boredom. Bobby would join me downtown often, and with his good looks and Paul Newman smile he never left the Catalyst alone either. The Catalyst had a big fish tank above the bar area with a piranha in it, goldfish circled around the tank also until the piranha became hungry. I would find myself sitting at the bar staring at the piranha tank and counting the goldfish, watching and waiting for the goldfish count to change.

Although the money was good, the narcotics trade was good and Bobby was becoming a very good friend, I found myself so bored. Since being a kid I had noticed one of my main characteristics was that I became bored easily. I was twenty-one years old and the year was 1972, but for me I needed something new, something brand new. The lyrics from a Billy Preston song stuck in my head. "Will it go round in circles, like a bird, we'll fly high up in the sky—I got a song—ain't got no melody—Will it go round in circles?"

Hard to explain, but I wanted more out of life than answering a phone and watching most of the profit flow through my fingers. The more I would make the more I would spend. It was the easy come easy go theory, and selling narcotics is a daily task. I was completely tired of all the people around me that I needed to make my business work, and I'm sure they were very tired of me. The dope game is very exhausting for everyone involved. Bobby felt the same way, and we discussed alternative moneymaking schemes, excluding getting a job. With our two brains put together we came up with a solution, a solution that would not involve other people and not have to be done daily. Our agreed choice for our dilemma was armed robbery.

But what would we rob? Since we were both rookies in the armed robbery field, once again we had to put our brains together.

In the early seventies massage parlors were popping up everywhere. They were frowned upon by the local community citizens, and zoning commissions would try to close them down as quickly as they would open. But the reality was massage parlors appeared everywhere. Not talking about a massage technique from Sweden, relaxing your muscles taking the stress away from life's pressures. These massage parlors would relax your muscles and relieve the stress from the lack of sex. They were in the news daily, as the city would try to close them down. Bobby and I felt if nobody liked these massage parlors we would be doing the community a service if we were to rob them. It sure sounded good at the time. Bobby owned a .38 caliber long barrel pistol and I had my trusty .32 caliber five shot handgun. These two guns would become the tools of our new profession. Armed robbers without a clue would be our new job title, and we were on the road to retirement within our minds.

Parking my car around the corner with the engine running and bandannas to cover our faces, we looked like members of the Jesse James gang. At the entrance to these massage parlors sat the gentleman who was in charge of collecting the small cover fee. We would grab him and walking to the back area, we knocked on every door demanding the girls along with their clients into the hall. Bobby became this maniac as he tossed around commands, and demanded all the money. I would look at Bobby in amazement with his animated gestures and take control attitude. Bobby was a good actor indeed. We would collect all the money putting it in a pillowcase, and then Bobby

125

would shout, "I KNOW THERE'S MORE, GIVE IT ALL TO US, I KNOW THERE'S FUCKING MORE."

During this first robbery everything slowed down and went frame by frame, as if I were watching a movie in very slow motion. Commanding everyone to stay put and give us time to escape, we would ensure their total safety. Running back to the waiting car we drove back home. My mind was playing tricks on me as I was thinking I heard sirens, and every car behind us looked like a cop. But it was all in my mind and we ended up back home safe. Dumping the pillowcase on the bed we sorted out the money and in counting it totaled less than nine hundred dollars. To me it seemed like a lot of work, four hundred dollars and some change each. Also I noticed I was relatively calm during the actual robbery, but once at home I was sweating profusely. Bobby's voice brought me back to the here and now, "We did it, we did it Holmes."

I nodded my head in agreement, but deep inside I knew I had just crossed a line that I could not uncross. It was less than a week and I found myself doing another massage parlor robbery. The take was a little more than the first robbery, but far from any retirement amount. At home sitting across the kitchen table from Bobby I relayed my concerns of stress and lack of money from these two robberies. Two robberies in one week that's not good, we need to talk about an alternate plan. Bobby was in full agreement as we discussed options on what we would rob next with neither of us ever saying it wasn't a good idea to rob at all. We were both young, and with youth comes confidence and invincibility, even to the point of one small part of my insides thinking I was the ghost of John Dillinger. I also noticed I slowed down on my spending, hoping to put the next robbery off as long as possible.

My appearance has always been very deceiving, looking relatively calm on the outside but with my engine inside revving past the safe limit.

Supermarkets, Bobby and I fully agreed would be more lucrative but need more planning and we were both up for the challenge. I sat in parking lots for hours, along with Bobby watching the movements inside the stores of management, customers and clerks. The big glass fronts would cause a visual problem during the robbery from anyone driving by, and the number of people inside the market created a crowd control problem as well. We would sit in parking lots and watch, with the glass fronts in our favor now allowing us to locate the safe along with the manager's schedule for opening that safe.

With the motivation of more money and parking the still running getaway vehicle, we scurried across the parking lot to the entrance of the supermarket. We were going to attempt our first supermarket job. Pulling up our bandannas at the last possible moment so as not to arouse suspicion we entered the supermarket with guns drawn. As Bobby directed the manager to the safe, I kept clerks and customers secured. This first supermarket robbery felt to me like it would never end, time just stopped and with the open glass fronts I felt the entire world was watching. Now with Bobby holding the moneybags we backed out of the store slowly, turning in the parking lot we tried to walk instead of run, once again not to arouse any suspicion. I noticed I was calmer now compared to my first robberies and would engage in full conversations with Bobby as we drove away.

"It went well. I think we did all right, don't you?"

"Absolutely, we got what we came for, *their* money!" Firmly Bobby stated breaking the ice.

This time after pouring the money out of the pillowcase we netted almost six thousand dollars, better, much better I thought. We spent money like there was no tomorrow and at times I would think that there was no tomorrow. Nice restaurants, over tipping, clothes, pretty much anything we wanted. We had in our pockets more money than most people made in half a year, and now we knew where to get more. Also I would find myself giving to the less fortunate with visions of being a new age Robin Hood. Adding money to an established cockiness created a far cry from the young kid that was satisfied with good waves and sunshine at the Jetties. I had created this state of no rules, and I was the governor.

When reaching in my pocket and feeling my money knot diminishing, Bobby and I would rob another supermarket. The robberies becoming smoother with experience and the needle moved lower on my inside stress detector. We traded in our bandannas for ski masks, which only added to our bold and brazen approach. Reading the newspaper or watching the news the robberies were only reported as two masked men, a Mutt and Jeff team (expression for tall and short use by the police). With my cynical sense of humor I once went back into a supermarket I had robbed, recognizing the female cashier from the robbery I chose her line to buy my cigarettes. She was cute, so I asked her out on a date. We ended up going to a local nightclub with live music. As we sat there listening to the band all she wanted to talk about was how she was involved at being at the business end of a gun in an armed robbery. As I sat listening I would just nod my head and tell her the most important thing was that she was okay, and it wasn't her money that was taken. I was breaking all the unwritten rules of robbery, which at this time I was ignorant of. Cocky and spending money like a lead singer with their first hit record, committing robberies in the town I lived while using my own automobile, and most of all guilty of being twenty-two years old.

Bobby and I received a tip on a jewelry storeowner that would make large cash deposits on the last Thursday of the month. After closing his store he would use the night deposit drop at this one particular bank. We decided that would be our next score, and waited for the last Thursday to arrive. According to our inside information the moneybag would contain between ten thousand and fifteen thousand dollars. We figured it for an easy hit-and-run, waiting in the shadows by the bank deposit we would draw our weapons forcing the jeweler to lie down, and off with the bag we would go. Easy money, money which had our names written all over it, and we waited for the last Thursday.

We pulled up to the bank leaving my car running close by, but not too close. Pulling our ski masks down from the knit hat position and with our pistols tucked in the waistband of our pants, we waited in the shrubbery located by the night deposit. There wasn't much of a moon, which created more darkness in our favor. Bobby and I had hashed over and over the details of this robbery, so as we squatted quietly in the bushes our only communication now were from looks or eye expression. Waiting, we heard a car finally pulling up, right on time I thought to myself. I was making myself ready with mental preparation as I glanced over at Bobby hopefully doing the same. I was finding out when I would visualize over and over what was going to go down, it would go down exactly like I visualized. It was working in the supermarket robberies...it would work here also. Hearing the engine go off of the nearby car, I squatted griping my pistol between my legs.

"THIS IS THE SANTA CRUZ POLICE, THROW YOUR WEAPONS OUT, SHOW YOUR HANDS AND SLOWLY WALK OUT ONE AT A TIME."

My first thought was FUCK, and then my brain told me I hadn't done anything wrong. Unless squatting in the bushes, wearing a ski mask and holding a pistol is illegal?

Well I learned in Santa Cruz apparently it is, as more police surrounded Bobby and me. Different faces and voices of the police were asking me the same question at the same time, "What were you doing at the bank in the bushes?"

"I want to speak to my lawyer," I calmly said, as I heard Bobby saying the same.

As the police put me in the back of the squad car, I looked over seeing my Chevy still running. It was well tuned and quiet so the police never noticed my car. But as I stood there glancing, my heart told me I would never see that car again.

Brought to the Santa Cruz police station, I was once again fingerprinted with pictures front and side. The police officer then told me I wasn't being charged with anything at this time but being held on suspicion. Suspicion, nice I thought to myself, because I've never heard anybody serving time on sheer suspicion. I will be back out on the streets in twenty-four hours, forty-eight hours max. Keep in mind these are my thoughts, not the thoughts shared by Santa Cruz County. Bobby and I were escorted to one of the tanks similar to Ventura County Jail; only difference is Santa Cruz County Jail cells surround the day area. I made my bed from the bedroll given to me and lied down on my bunk. Bobby was in the same cell and we would only discuss our situation quietly with each other. Nice thing about Bobby was, we shared similar values, and privacy was first and foremost.

130

Looking around it was the usual jail atmosphere, music piped in and everybody looking like they weren't looking. One prisoner was tattooing another using a sharpened staple connected to a pencil with thread from a bed sheet wrapped near the end holding ink that was made from burned Bible pages mixed with water. The ink from the words on the pages would meltdown, adding water created tattoo ink. I thought this was very creative; the tattoo looked like shit but a very creative method. In the day room was also the usual with people doing push-ups, sitting at the table writing letters and doing whatever. But I was being held on suspicion; I didn't have to worry about getting comfortable.

While I was laid up in Santa Cruz County Jail awaiting my release, little did I know a series of events were unfolding creating a domino effect that would impact my life. During one of our first robberies Bobby's bandanna slipped down off his face for a moment in one of his animated rants. And with the detectives showing the victims a photo lineup, Bobby was identified. Because of the Mutt and Jeff stature of the two-armed robbers, this made me guilty by association and I was charged with two robberies. My mind stutter stepped when I realized I won't be counting days in my head or even months as before, this could be a serious amount of years in the penitentiary, the California state penitentiary which has a reputation of bloody and unforgiving. I didn't have knowledge of the law and the loopholes that consist within the law. But after talking to my court-appointed lawyer, along with given a high bail, I once again needed to put on my thinking cap because I wasn't going anywhere. My lawyer explained to me a preponderance of evidence clause. This in layman terms means, we know you did it and don't have much evidence, but you prove to us that you didn't do it. I didn't know where to start but I did know I had to fight

harder than my lawyer. After all, I'm the one facing
time not him. The court system is very complex and
concrete and nothing about the law is understood.
Every motion, every objection needs substantial facts
to back any arguments you may have, and I was a
little light in the argument department on my
innocence. But the other prisoners in my tank were
more than willing to give me advice and guide me
through this process so I could regain my freedom. As
I'm listening with this one saying that and that one
saying this, I'm thinking to myself, you guys can't get
yourself out of jail, how are you going to get me out of
jail?

My inner voice kept telling me when listening to
these generic lawyers, no thank you, I can do bad all by
myself. But like anything else in life you get used to
your surroundings and I was doing my push-ups,
joking and becoming a respected member of tank
number two. Because of Bobby's and my charges we
moved up on the respect status scale and were looked
up to by some of the other prisoners. With not much
time passing I was soon throwing around the little
clout that I had. Making sure we watched Solid Gold
on Saturday night and showing the fresh face fish how
to make hot chocolate from a Three Musketeers bar.
But on my insides something was growing, that little
seed of defiance that was planted by me years ago
seem to flourish in this jail environment. I adopted
this attitude of perseverance and resistance, never
showing emotion. I somewhat pictured myself as *Cool
Hand Luke*, from the movie starring Paul Newman. It
became a game of who had the stronger will, the
guards or me. You can never break me and you will
never see me sweat. From my daily push-ups and age
I was growing and carried myself as a man, or as I
thought a man should be. Bobby was doing the same
and together we made ourselves known in Santa Cruz

County Jail. You messed with one, you messed with the other.

The court process is long and drawn out and I found myself waiting up to forty-five days in between court appearances. When finally going to court the guards would transport you to a holding cell until your name was called from the court docket. At seven thirty in the morning I would be transferred to the holding cell for a one thirty in the afternoon court appearance. The holding cell consisted of nothing more than benches and a toilet. I would find myself sitting on the bench and just thinking about everything from my past to my unknown future. With no books or magazines to read I would just watch the traffic of other prisoners going to court. Some being sent to the state penitentiary, others were receiving only days in county jail. It was the widest of varieties and there I sat stuck, with no idea on what was going to happen next. Sneaking cigarettes and matches in the seams of my orange jumpsuit I would be smoking in the holding cell, a definite rule violation. But for me rules didn't apply, I had my own two rules I now lived by.

Rule one: fuck all rules.

Rule two: refer to rule one.

This attitude that I adopted along with this testing of wills aimed against the guards got me sent to tank four. Santa Cruz County Jail didn't have a segregation cell per se, so tank four was their solution to problem prisoners. Bobby was right alongside me and we made ourselves comfortable in this new tank, and the people in my new surroundings were on a slightly different level compared to the other parts of the county jail. They were people that had been to prison, people that were going to prison, with everybody showing full respect to each other. This seemed like where I should be, I had enough problems with my robbery charges I didn't want to hear from some other prisoner that was doing three days how the oatmeal was cold. I'd gotten myself into a serious jackpot and making the oatmeal hot wouldn't fix my problems.

I continued to do my push-ups along with others in the tank, Bobby was very strong and we would do up to three hundred, sometimes four hundred push-ups a day. But one guy stood out more than anybody I've ever seen in the push-up department. His name was Richard, and every night he would do ten sets, one hundred push-ups in each set equaling a thousand done all in fifty minutes. It was amazing to watch; I had never seen anybody do such a feat of strength. Richard wasn't muscular either instead he was of lankier stature with extraordinary tendon strength. The police left us alone more as members of tank four also which was fine with me and although I didn't know what exactly was going to happen to me in court I kind of had a general idea.

With not much evidence against me, I decided on a jury trial for both robbery charges. It didn't take me long to see the way this trial was headed. I pictured in my head what the jury would see. A young man sitting at the defendant table with a lawyer, dark hair slicked back with a well-trimmed Fu Manchu mustache while dressed in an orange jumpsuit staring straight ahead with no emotion. Also I had a clear thought on what the jury may be thinking. They (the prosecution) may not have overwhelming evidence of these two robberies but he's guilty of something and doesn't need to be in our neighborhood. When the judge asked, "Young man, you have anything to say before sentencing?"

I had nothing, what could I say? Everything just seemed surreal as I stood and stated, "No your honor."

I was found guilty of two counts of 211 in the California Penal Code, armed robbery.

"On the first robbery charge, I sentence you to one year to life. On the second robbery charge, your sentence will be law prescribes, five years to life, both sentences to be served in the California Department of Corrections. Next."

My body didn't go numb and my thoughts didn't become scrambled as the bailiff escorted me back to the holding cell. I was at a point in my young life that nothing or nobody could detour me from my self-appointed gangster role. As for my sentences, in California the years to life means if and when they decide to grant parole you have a lifetime of parole. But at that moment that was not my main concern, first I had to get the years done from my sentence, I'll worry about the lifetime parole later. Getting back to tank four as the guard locked the gate behind me one of the fellas asked me. "What did they give ya, Holmes?"

"They smoked me. Gave me law prescribes, with a life top."

"Damn Holmes, that's too bad."

I had learned more of the jail language and began using it in my daily life. So when I replied,

"Ain't nothing but a *jute ball*, see you on Broadway or the other side, in a hot minute."

Although a jute ball is a mystery item on your food tray it can also be referenced in other ways. So all I was saying is that I was young and the time would go by fast and I would get out or I would be killed in prison (the other side). We all called each other Holmes or Homey, an honorary title when not using someone's name. So if I hadn't been successful in life's tribulations up to this point and was to die that day, I would at least be known as articulate in the jailbird community.

I continued to live in the county jail until I was to catch the chain on the Grey Goose to the state penitentiary. Although my time was running I still just wanted to get this all behind me so along with others and Bobby I waited for transport. Bobby had received the exact same sentence, creating this ironic sense of comfort for both of us. Lying on my bunk at nights I would try to imagine what prison would be like? From the stories and the actual scars on some from stab wounds I knew over all it wasn't gonna be good. Bobby and I vowed to do whatever it took for us to stay alive, whatever it took! Bobby had become a good friend and I never cared about another human being as I did until then. He had the characteristics of loyalty and honor and our bond was closer than ever as we prepared to be transferred to the unknown.

Funny the transformation that takes place in the human body as it kicks into survival mode. Animals in the jungle as well as animals everywhere use instincts to survive by identifying the predators and not becoming the prey. I found myself studying people more than usual and would create violent scenarios in my mind and solving them. I was determined to not be disrespected in prison, which would lead to an altercation. And from my understanding all altercations ended badly for one of the parties, often death. It wasn't about toughness anymore; there were weapons involved. Instead it was about smarts, cunningness and the ability to react quickly in any situation anywhere and at any time. I basically had to remove that part of my brain which thought about consequences and react when needed, without any hesitation. Hesitation would only get me killed. Someone had passed me down a book to read called *Papillion* by Henri Charriere. Papillion, French for butterfly, is about a man accused of murder and his struggles. Accumulating fourteen years in the prisons of French Guiana and South America, Papillion's personal freedom was his daily goal. He was the only man ever to escape from Devil's Island by putting coconuts in a net and floating on the ocean for days to escape. This book became my blueprint for doing my time and the handling of situations that may arise. I would lay on my bunk reading for hours, making my mind free to join Papillion on his adventures. Once again I heard the words, "Roll um up."

But this time it wasn't to go out on Broadway. Cuffed and shackled complete with belly chain connecting everything I was on my way to the northern guidance center of the California Department of Corrections via the Grey Goose. The bus was full with every color, every race and with everyone's face looking disheveled. There I sat with Bobby a few rows behind me taking the trip to the state penitentiary. My eyes said goodbye to the outside, as the bus rolled north.

My mind went into a time warp and I thought about my past once again. I was beginning to miss the simple life on the Jetties more and more. I also evaluated my past couple of years and the direction my life was headed. With all my illegal activity I still wasn't financially ahead, what was I doing wrong?

I had lost my voice also. Just waking up one morning ten months prior and my voice was gone. I was only able to speak at a very low volume. Others couldn't hear me and I would have to repeat myself over and over which caused me not to speak much at all. Bobby had got used to our lack of verbal exchange but the other part of the world must've just viewed me as a mute, or a very quiet person. The ladies really liked my new demeanor though, quietly talking or not talking it all. The ladies, I forgot about them. The *tang* I had taken for granted wasn't going to be around for a while. With that thought and the screeching of the air brakes from the bus my mind was brought back into reality. I looked up, and was at the back gate of the state penitentiary.

This place was massive, groups of prisoners gathered in the oversized yard area with concrete buildings everywhere containing cellblocks all wrapped in a double fence with razor wire along with gun towers on every corner. What the fuck have I got myself into?

The back gate slowly slid open, as the guards of the two adjacent gun towers watched from their platforms holding weapons. The bus then crawled along a small stretch of road stopping at one of the back buildings. Glancing over my shoulder I looked back at Bobby moving my head in a half shake. I sat there with my eyes darting around until it was my rows time to exit as we formed a single file line outside the bus and walked to a door in the direction of the guard who was guiding us. Once inside the Receiving and Discharge (R and D) part of the prison we were instructed to sit on benches in a holding area. Bobby sat next to me on the bench not saying anything, and I remember the noise. Noise created by hundreds, maybe thousands of people in the yard and cellblocks yelling and talking all at the same time, but not necessarily to each other. It created a buzzing sound. Glancing around I noticed guards along with some prisoners involved in individual tasks that seemed to have purpose. The combination of noise and activity formed this enormous machine making a noticeable, almost touchable prison environment. The others along with myself in the holding cell were the only parts not contributing to this machine, as we sat there quietly waiting for our next command.

R and D was a series of humiliating and time-consuming hoops to jump through. I just wanted to go to my cell and lie down. Exhausted from the bus ride along with my mental time traveling, all I wanted to do was take a nap and wake up from this bad fucking nightmare. But losing my freedom meant I lost my way of doing things, which made me even more resistant. The northern guidance center is only a stop off on the way to a prison destination decided through observation and evaluation. The prison itself is separated by a series of cellblocks, one side being the mainline for convicts designated specifically there, and the other side, the guidance center. I was taken to the guidance center section and given a cell on the third tier of the cellblock. Bobby was placed in another cellblock, which looked the exact same. Although we were separated in our living quarters I would be able to see him on the yard, or in the movie house. Each cellblock had its own chow hall (cafeteria) and barbershop including a day room area. The prison was like a city and each cellblock was like a smaller city within the big city, everything coming together to make this madhouse of noise with ant colony like activity.

Four handball courts, a baseball diamond, two basketball courts and a weight area known as the iron pile, this made up the yard in the guidance center. When I wasn't confined to my cellblock or cell this is where I would be, on the yard. I had endless energy and would run, hit the iron or be playing handball. Bobby would meet me out on the yard daily and we did everything together. The weights were all welded onto the bars and dumbbells so prisoners wouldn't kill each other with the loose weight plates and the weights would jump at forty to sixty pound intervals, which caused you to get strong quick.

Once again the pecking order was in effect and very noticeable on the yard. Little red weighed three hundred and thirty pounds and big red weighed three hundred and fifty pounds. Both were painted solid red and when anyone bench pressed either one of these the yard would take notice. Richard, the pushup king from Santa Cruz County Jail bench pressed little red three times on his first day in the yard, Richard was just one very strong person. Bobby had superhuman strength also, only weighing one hundred and fifty five pounds he could still keep up with the big boys. I was strong but my claim to fame was my endurance. I could run for miles and miles, hit the iron pile and play handball and still not be tired, even in my single cell at night I would do push-ups. I just turned twenty-three years old and felt like the California Department of Corrections was testing my mental, physical and other aspects of who I really was. I always found a way to win and being in prison, I would find a way to win there also.

The chow hall had four-man tables mounted to the floor with the seats mounted to the base of the table. I was starting to see how everything was welded and connected everywhere, trying to cut down on the already existing weapon problem. Lining up in single file and grabbing a food tray, prisoners would serve food onto your tray. They would fill each of the tables individually in the order of the food line and this caused the line to shift and juggle to ensure sitting with your own race and circle of acquaintances. Extra guards made their presence known in the chow area for better control of this highly volatile area. Any altercation taking place in the chow hall had the potential of exploding and guards paced on the catwalks above holding their carbines ready. This place was tight with security, but still could never stop the violence and murders that took place there.

During my first week in the day area, where they would lock us in until all the silverware and metal trays were accounted for, I stood against the back wall waiting. Two Chicanos were assaulting another Chicano, as one held the victim the other was stabbing him, over and over the knife was going in his chest until you could literally see the life leave his body. No guards rushed in, and no one in the day room got involved either. I watched and then slowly turned my body away so as I looked completely oblivious to the murder I just witnessed. I wasn't alone, the whole day room was doing the same as guards told the assailants to put down their weapons and step away from the body. All of a sudden a siren sounded and we were shuffled back to our cells. Later that same day as we were put into the day area after our next meal, I looked over at the area where the man was stabbed to death and it had been completely cleaned up. There was no trace to be seen of what had happened hours earlier. That early evening on the yard seeing Bobby I never said a word. That's just the way it was in the penitentiary, if it's not your business don't make it your business.

Prison is best explained as a jungle complete with animals of prey and the rules become jungle rules, only making sense in the jungle. Everyone has enemies including me, not from people I knew, but because of my race or where I'm originally from. California has had a war between the North and the South for as long as I can remember. The color of your skin or the location of your hometown is reason enough to your enemies, like I said jungle rules.

California had also implemented trailer visits, another attempt at controlling a non-controllable environment of violence. Married prisoners could get a three-day trailer visit every ninety days with good behavior as a motivation. Their wife and kids would be dropped off at the trailer on Friday afternoon and would have to leave on Sunday. A picnic table set next to the trailer and a small fence complete with razor wire created a yard area. From my cell on the third tier I could see one of the trailers out my window. On the weekends I would find myself staring down at this trailer and wishing that was me in there with a woman. I was missing me some tang, and all over the prison was the generic variety of tang. Thank you, but no thank you, I'll just wait.

Standing in front of my cell one afternoon on the third tier of the prison block I waited to be locked in. Leaning over the rail I looked down as one of my Homeboys was looking up at me, his name was Rufus. Prison has a commissary store for buying cosmetics, snacks and other various items. Snacks are known as zoo-zoos and wham-whams with ice cream being one of the premier treats in prison. Rufus yelled up to me, "I'm going to the store, want anything?"

"Ice cream," I said back down to him.

But with my voice being almost nonexistent, Rufus couldn't make out what I was saying. He screamed back, "WHAT?"

"Ice cream, I want an ice cream."

"Muthafuka, what do you want?" said Rufus grinning. "I can't hear you, STOP WHISPERING."

Long story short, the next morning when I came out of my cell and was walking down the tier, some of the fellas were giving me the usual what up nod, and calling me Whisper. It stuck that fast, literally overnight my new name became Whisper.

I knew a Mule, a Reno, a Cool Breeze even a Bo-Bo. Nicknames were very common; after all we had nicknames for each other growing up on the Jetties. So now everywhere I went and when introducing myself, I was known as Whisper. Bobby never called me anything else after that day, it just stuck.

Politicians were always on the side of one issue or another when it came to prison reform. Over population, rehabilitation or cutbacks, always something involved with changing the current prison system usually to make themselves look better. But during this time of my incarceration the main issue was integrating prisoners back into society. I was transferred from the guidance center to a medium level joint (prison) in the middle of the state. I was glad to get out of the guidance center. The state's objective for my placement through evaluation and observation was to serve my two sentences concurrently doing the mandatory minimum. If I showed change along with good behavior the state was trying to avoid sending me to a super max penitentiary for a long length of time. My age along with my lack of longevity in the California penal system made me a perfect candidate to make some politician get reelected. Bobby was right along there with me, and the way we figured it we had two or two and a half years left on our sentences. There were two other murders while I was at the guidance center, so if some politician wanted to look good on the ballot, I was more than a willing guinea pig. This new facility seemed to lack some of the urgency of dying young and this was just fine with me. When lying up in my cell, I couldn't help but to think about life, my life to be accurate. I didn't like living imprisoned, and I was positive I would not like dying in prison either. Unexplainable is the only way I can explain watching someone murdered. My first thought always was glad it's not me. My second thought, glad that it wasn't Bobby or someone else I knew and liked.

I had been locked up for a little over a year now. Things were relatively uneventful with me only receiving one major write-up (rule infraction). It'd been a particularly hot summer and I, Bobby and three other prisoners had climbed the ladder to the water tank inside the prison. Swimming and smoking weed inside the tank, we cooled down and enjoyed the summer afternoon. On descending down the tower ladder we were spotted by one of the guards and the

143

prison whistle blew for an emergency count. Standing by our bunks guards came by checking for inmates with wet hair. Bobby was the only one that wasn't busted out of our crew because of his short Irish hair, which didn't look wet even when it was.

The four of us were taken to the local county jail and charged with an infraction from the Health & Safety Code. The state trying to say this water was used for drinking and we had contaminated it, the truth was this water was for fires and had nothing to do with being drunk. The three others pled guilty and were taken back immediately to the prison facility, as for me I never did things the easy way. I demanded a jury trial, which made the district attorney look at me crazy. Also I demanded the water to be tested, which would make me only guilty of swimming in the water not contamination of it. My court appointed lawyer was looking at me crazy by then. I have no idea what makes me tick sometimes; I just have this streak of defiance and insubordination.

The judge became upset with me for making a mockery of the court system and without a plea or trial he gave me a hundred hours community service upon my release. Yeah right, that's gonna happen!

Thirty-eight years later and I still owe that county a hundred hours of my service. Defiantly hardheaded is definitely part of my chemical makeup.

As for Bobby, always scheming and conniving with a silver tongue that could talk a bulldog off a meat truck, had a money plan of his own. Bobby was in contact with this little filly and talked her into delivering us narcotics. Not the usual visiting room smuggling routine, but a creative plan that would ensure everyone's safety from creating a new felony. With an archery set she would shoot an arrow over the double fence with the package (narcotics) secured to the arrow. Ingenious I thought. Having someone mail the narcotics to her house she would then drive to the facility at night and become the long lost daughter of William Tell. With Bobby working in the recreation yard he would be able to retrieve the package before the yard was open to general population. We were selling joints of marijuana for a dollar with the package sometimes containing heroin which we would share with the fellas or trade for commissary.

I was still running and working out along with getting high so the time was just rolling by.

One evening as I was walking in the cellblock a guard stopped me saying, "You and Mr. Fay are being released in two days, right?"

"Sure boss, we are being released the day after tomorrow."

The fact of the matter was we weren't, the truth was we were being transferred to another prison. I just thought this guard was fuckin' with me.

I found Bobby on the yard and relayed my conversation that I just had with the guard. Bobby also knew we were due for release from that facility, but with the stipulation of being picked up by another jurisdiction to finish serving our sentences.

My little gears in my brain were working and so were Bobby's. We both went back into the cellblock and approached this particular guard. Picking his brain, we asked him if he was the one in charge of our release paperwork. He replied he was and would be the one dressing us out and giving us our kick out money. The state of California would give you one hundred dollars at the time of your release, called kick out money. Bobby and I then went to his cell and discussed how we could take advantage of this guard's oversight. Maybe, just maybe this guard hadn't flipped further through our files; if he had he would have seen on one of the pages in bold red letters, HOLD FOR TRANSFER. Being a hard case created a bigger file, which worked in my favor that day, but still with everything a just maybe.

The next night we approached the same officer telling him we had a small favor he may be able to help us with. Playing on the fact that he was a man along with his self-perception of being a good guy we stated our business. Bobby and I took turns explaining our dilemma of being locked down for over a year with both of us suffering from lack of tang, reminding him that he spoke of our release the night before and this is where the small favor from him would come in to play.

With usual kick out time between eight in the morning or nine, we further stated we had a couple of ladies picking us up at midnight the next night, and officially one minute after twelve would be considered the next day. Naturally we would sign our papers that night reading the appropriate kick out time in the morning, also adding it would be our little secret, just the three of us.

His look was distant, so I stated one more time that he had Bobby's and my word that nobody would ever know. We didn't want to push so I added as we walked off, "Think about it boss, just think about it."

The next evening dragged, one minute my mind would tell me I was going and the next minute my mind would tell me it's not gonna happen. I was torn between excitement and frustration. I wanted to go back and talk to the officer some more, but Bobby and I agreed we shouldn't badger him. We took our best shot and now it was time for the chips to fall where they may.

Bobby got a message to his girl and arrangements were made for her to be in the parking lot with her headlights on, this would make our story to the guard plausible. Bobby also instructed her to bring somebody else with her to cover all our bases on looking like two ladies were anxiously in wait. We told no one of our plan, but when no one was around I would grab Bobby by the shoulders and sing in his ear the lyrics from a Allman Brothers song, "I got to run—to keep from hiding—only got one more silver dollar—ain't gonna catch me no—ain't gonna catch the midnight rider."

He would look at me, and with that Paul Newman smile of his we would both snicker.

Lockup time the next night finally came and I sat in my cell trying to relax. It would be a couple more hours before I would know the outcome of our plan, as well as my fate of that night.

It was now a few minutes before midnight and I could hear the mechanism in my door move from the officer pulling the lever at the end of the tier. This is really happening I thought as I tried to remain calm and not tip my hand as this guard was involving himself in Bobby's and my plot of escape. Upfront in the guard's office we signed proper papers, as well as a form stating we both received a hundred dollars. The guard only gave us fifty dollars each but I was okay with that because as far as I was concerned everybody was on the hustle with some scam or the cutting of corners, only difference between them and me was I got caught. I also made a point to tell this officer, "Thanks boss, I always knew you were different than the others."

"Good luck to you two. Don't hurt those ladies that are waiting for you."

"You know how we do it boss," is all I said as I strolled out the front door.

It was hard to walk slowly in the parking lot towards Bobby's girl's car and I kept elbowing Bobby, as we got closer to our ride to freedom. The girl had brought her brother as the other member of our alleged double date. What did I care though, I was free and it felt real fucking good. My escape didn't have the flair of Papillion's coconut raft off of Devil's Island, but it was good enough to get my young ass free that summer night.

15

Then came the usual now what? I didn't own a car and only had a few bucks to my name from selling narcotics in the prison facility. I'll figure out something, I always do I thought as we drove away from the joint towards the lights of the city.

That first night we stayed at the girl's house and when we awoke in the morning she told Bobby she had a boyfriend and we couldn't stay there. Fuck I thought, I'm not going back to jail because of some jealous boyfriend.

Bobby and I discussed how we needed to get out of there quick and in a hurry. I shaved off my mustache in a weak attempt to throw the police off my trail and hadn't felt this way since running away from home for the first time, the feeling was desperate and my words were to the point, "Bobby, we need to get out of state and figure something out."

He nodded his head in agreement.

Without a car, without much money we were dropped off at the freeway onramp on our way to parts unknown. Bobby and I would take turns sticking out our thumb in an attempt to hitch a ride and dozens of cars sped by with only a couple slowing down to give us a long look. This is not good—this is not good at all. The girl had made us sandwiches, which we ate in the first twenty minutes of standing on the side of the highway.

Eventually a car stopped and picked us up and gave us a ride to the next onramp, and then another car did the same. It was three in the morning and we hadn't made it even close to being out of California. We were cold, hungry and pretty much without a clue and I felt I was stuck between the proverbial rock and a hard place. By early morning we ended up in the truck stop in Bishop, California. After throwing some water on my face and rinsing my mouth out, I didn't feel good but I felt better. I had always envisioned myself as this outlaw going against the grain of society but at that moment I felt trapped and not like an outlaw at all, more of a bum. Unshaven, hungry and tired I could only picture what others must be seeing when looking at me. But I needed to snap out of it and once again get my thinking cap on.

We didn't even know where we were going and we didn't care. Our philosophy was keep moving because a moving target is harder to hit.

Finally Bobby with his silver tongue talked this lone girl into giving us a ride and in exchange we would help her out with gas. She was driving this little pickup truck with a camper on the back, and I volunteered to lie in the back, giving her and Bobby more room in the cab upfront. Although she agreed she was very apprehensive of the two of us riding along with her, but after a few miles she was okay. Being worn out I closed my eyes and listened to the miles of highway under the tires causing me to fall asleep. When I opened my eyes Bobby was now driving, and the two of them were laughing as they listened to the truck radio. She introduced herself as Cindi, with an "i" and looked more comfortable now than when first picking us up.

Bobby had a special way about him making others feel comfortable, and Cindi was very receptive to his charm. Every time we would stop for gas Cindi would insist on paying. Although we agreed on splitting the gas bill for the ride she would pay. Putting up a superficial argument, Bobby and I would let her win saying we would get it the next time. But she didn't care about all that, she felt safe and protected with us as we traveled on Highway 80. We all did agree though that Bobby and I would buy all the food and drinks.

We were low on money, real low. So when we pulled into these one horse towns that only had one gas pump and selling only a couple of food items, one of us would keep Cindi occupied outside and the other would go in the store area to steal. I thought to myself as I walked out of the store one time, I've become quite a gangster, taking beef jerky and bologna sandwiches, yes quite the gangster.

We traveled through the entire state of Nevada, the tip of Utah and when we were in Wyoming Cindi asked me, "Where are you guys going anyway?"

"Where are you headed Miss Cindi?" I said back with a question answering a question.

"A small town on the outside of Lincoln, Nebraska, to see my parents."

I said, "Cool, you can drop us in Lincoln we are on our way to Iowa."

Bobby and I had no idea where we were really going but this sounded good at the time. With all of us taking turns to drive, California was getting further away and I was really enjoying the scenery, the mountains of Utah, the openness of Wyoming and Nebraska. Grass covered the hills with cattle grazing, cornfields everywhere, and I was starting to feel better by not thinking of where I was coming from but where I was going to. I always liked the adventures of my life and with Bobby as my road dog made it even better. He, like me, wasn't a complainer and we laughed our way across the country on Highway 80.

Dropped off at the University of Nebraska in Lincoln, we said our goodbyes to Cindi, thanking her and wishing her good luck. I needed a shower and shave as well as Bobby also. Sneaking into the University shower, we ended up with the Nebraska Cornhuskers football team coming into the locker room as we cleaned up. It was spring training and nobody really knew everyone, so Bobby and I meshed into the situation and adding football jock lingo. We were naturals.

Shortly we were back out on the highway looking for a ride out of town. After a couple of short lifts we found ourselves on a two-lane highway surrounded by cornfields somewhere in Nebraska. Without a map and before the innovation of cell phone tracking devices, there we stood with corn everywhere and not a car in site.

The asphalt was hot under my feet and I keep shifting my weight from one foot to the other, and I was hungry again. It was no different for Bobby, and he ran off into the cornfields to grab a couple of cobs of fresh corn. As boring as this may seem, with our comical perspective on life and not give a fuck attitude things seemed pretty good at that moment. I felt like a kid again with an overwhelming sense of freedom, not necessarily freedom from jail but from life. Bobby returned with fresh corn and after giving me a couple of ears he took a bite of his, immediately splitting the kernels all over the road.

It turned out to be feed corn, which is solely grown for cattle, something neither of us knew. We were both bent over from laughter and would've looked comical to anyone watching, but there was nobody around for miles. I have no idea how much time went by as we stood on the side of the highway but it was probably more than two hours and less than four. Hot and tired we continued to stand there. What else were we going to do?

Just as things seemed at the most hopeless of points of this continuing hopeless situation, the sky all of a sudden opened up and it started to rain. Not the rain that I had experienced before growing up in California, but drops of rain that were heavy and would sting the skin. The sky was black everywhere I looked, and neither Bobby nor myself had seen any of this coming. It just kept raining; soaking us and everything we owned which didn't equal much. We hadn't seen a car literally in hours, but I could see the headlights of a car now. Please stop. Please stop, that's all I kept thinking.

"My name's Vern, you boys get in and get out of the rain." The voice came out from the passenger window of the El Camino. I opened the door and Vern told me to throw the bag on the passenger seat in the back and get in. Completely soaked, Bobby and I climbed in and the El Camino started back down the highway.

"You boys hungry? Come on to my mother's house with me and have something to eat. Hell of a storm, right boys?"

Vern drove fast and was very animated when he would talk or laugh. I liked Vern immediately and he gave you the sense that you had known him for a long time. Being rescued from the rain only added to my fondness of Vern. It wasn't long and we were pulling in the driveway of the small farmhouse. With Vern parking his car on the front lawn he got out, grabbed the bag from the back and yelled, "Come in the house boys."

Once inside he introduced us to his mother and told her that we would be staying for dinner. She turned and looked at us, "You boys like tomatoes?"

Bobby and I both nodded yes as Vern's mother showed us where the bathroom was telling us to get out of our wet clothes. She handed us towels, a couple of Vern's T-shirts and shorts.

After dinner Bobby and I were outside having a smoke and we both agreed these are good people. Vern and his mother are good people. Vern's mother insisted that we call her mom as we helped her clean up the dining area and kitchen, and we were sticking to our story about going to Iowa, trying to find work and get on our feet.

These Midwest people were good in the fact that they didn't ask questions, and I liked that a lot. Vern told us that he would come home on the weekends to get his laundry done and visit with his mother, he continued that she needed help around the farm and if we wanted the job it was ours. Room and board and a few dollars on the side is all moms could afford, but with Bobby and I very very low on funds, it was the deal of the century. Feed a few chickens, a cow or two along with some hogs it shouldn't be that difficult. The idea of some home-cooked food, clean sheets and not standing on the highway with my thumb out only sweetened the deal.

Mom had a spare bedroom at the far end of the house and this became Bobby's and my living quarters.

With our rubber boots on, Bobby and I would feed and water the animals twice a day, and since I was in excellent physical shape the farm life wasn't that difficult. The first week we were there mom's pig

Girdy, gave birth to a litter of nine piglets. I didn't
know it then but I know it now, when pigs are born
after about fifteen seconds they start running around
crazy. Part of my job description as well as Bobby's
was to give chase, slippery and quick and very hard to
catch these little piglets gave us a run for our money
that day.

Also in feeding the chickens there was this one
particular Rhode Island Red rooster who was mean,
purely just one mean chicken. And when putting grain
into his cage, he would peck me, and not a love peck,
but a piece of skin missing, bleeding peck. Always
with the need to feel as if I had won, I would put a
glass jar over my hand when sticking it in this
rooster's cage before feeding him.

"Ping-Ping" is all you could hear from the
rooster as he cocked his head and looked at me. I
would just stare back with a smile of victory.

Mom would continually cook these great meals
and I liked her very much. She had this peace about
her that I had never seen in another person. She was
so kind and Vern would come on the weekends telling
us how much his mother appreciated our help. I would
think about my own family, but I hadn't talked to them
in over four years. When mom would offer us money
sometimes we would take it and sometimes we
wouldn't.

In the evenings Bobby and I would walk around
the farm talking as we smoked cigarettes. We had
both put a little money away in the past few weeks
from being farm hands and we both agreed that we
were ready to move on.

When Vern came for his weekly visit and to do
laundry, Bobby and I told him and his mother about
our plans to leave. I thanked them both for being so
good to us and mom started to cry. After dinner on the

porch, I popped the question to Vern, "Do you know where I can buy a gun?"

"For hunting?" Vern replied.

"Sure, hunting. I would like to get a 12-gauge shotgun if possible?"

"What are you going to hunt, elephants?" Vern smiled.

"Squirrels," I quickly answered.

"And you need a 12-gauge for squirrels. I do have a four-ten shotgun that I can sell you."

"Fine, how about pistols, do you have any pistols for sale also?"

"You know what boys, you have been very good to my mother and it's much appreciated. I'll sell you the four-ten and just give you a thirty-eight long barrel that was my father's."

So the deal was set, and I reminded Vern that in a week to ten days we had to go. With me telling everyone Bobby and I were on our way to Iowa, I stuck to that story. Vern mentioned he could give us a ride to the highway next weekend if we were both ready to go, I agreed, and our plan of leaving was taking shape.

When Vern arrived the next weekend, he had the weapons with him, we got the financial part out of the way and had the usual weekend. Bobby and I took the shotgun out to the barn and with a hacksaw we shortened the barrel as well as the stock. Vern knew I didn't have anything against squirrels, and I'm sure Vern knew also I wasn't the avid hunter. These Midwest people were beautiful in that they didn't ask questions.

On Sunday afternoon we left with Vern as mom watched from the porch crying. Back on another freeway onramp, but this time I was well rested, calm and my belly was full. Naturally, mom had packed some food for me and Bobby to take on the road; she was one sweetheart of a lady.

Things were looking up when we arrived in Iowa in a relatively short period of time. Bobby and I grabbed a hotel for the week. The room was six dollars a week with the bathroom down the hall, these rural areas of the Midwest were desolate making the economy perfect for a couple of guys on the run with short money. We walked around town, a very small town in search of an automobile. We had a plan all right, having guns along with a disposable vehicle were pieces of the puzzle for our next big score.

16

I found a 1954 Pontiac, power steering, power brakes and a straight eight-cylinder engine. The seller wanted a hundred dollars, I gave him seventy five and I was driving again. This car ran like the wind but I had not bought it for pleasure it was strictly gonna be used for business, bank robbery business to be exact.

On our early evening walks at the farm Bobby and I would often discuss the mistakes of our past. Committing robberies in the town that we lived, using our own cars as well as the short money compared to the risk. Now we had a new plan, which we knew would take on more preparation but would hold a bigger payday. We also had knowledge of bank employees who were always instructed to do exactly what they were told to do. I had done my homework, which made me also aware of dye packs, alarm money as well as bait money. Alarm money would sit on a weighted device that when lifted would set off a silent alarm, bait money was recorded serial numbers used to connect the bank robber to the bank later. And dye packs were simply an explosive device that would stain the money as well as the person, which would also draw unneeded attention.

But with all federal banks employees having to follow instruction, none of these methods of apprehension would apply to Bobby and me. The peaceful setting of the farm had allowed my brain to kick into over drive making me highly confident in my new endeavor.

In the town in which we were staying, there were only two banks. We now had a checklist for robbery and we picked the bank that we were going to rob through a process of elimination. The money had to be insured by the federal government, for the simple fact that these were definitely the tellers and bank staff that would comply with our demands. As far as wardrobe, I would wear a sweatshirt with a hood and a bulky parka type jacket with a hood also. With a ski mask on and both hoods up this would make me look bigger than I was and with the added size I felt like I would appear menacing. Cutting out the right pocket of my parka I could secure the sawed-off shotgun against my body when my jacket was zipped. In the bank unzipping my coat the rifle would drop out creating instant crowd control and with a hole in my pocket my hand could remain on the butt of the gun at all times.

Bobby dressed very similar, and we both agreed this would confuse the Mutt and Jeff description.

Banks closing at six o'clock in the evening on Friday, we would make our appearance five minutes before. Our unregistered, untraceable car would be parked close but not in the same parking lot as the bank, and the keys would be on the floorboard and the car wouldn't be running. We had thought of everything.

Also we decided of an alternative place to meet if something were to happen, such as get shot or worse be busted. Because of my lack of voice, Bobby would do the talking, as I would do the gathering of the money. A unique voice would be just as incriminating as a fingerprint I thought. We gave ourselves one minute to be in the bank, a minute and a half at most. With our constant surveillance of the area as well as verbally going over and over every detail of the potential robbery, Bobby and I only could picture success with money signs in our eyes.

Friday came; specifically Friday evening and I started dressing for my first bank robbery experience. I wasn't nervous, I wasn't apprehensive, my ducks were all in a row and I had the visualization thing going on. I just knew it was going to all go okay with my only concern on how much money we talking about?

Bobby and I had agreed only to hit the tellers, and the teller's drawers were a mystery up to this point. Parking the Pontiac, we walked slowly towards the bank building. It was in the late fall part of the year and somewhat chilly, with our layers of sweatshirts, coats and knit hats slash ski masks we blended right in. Covering my face as I entered the bank with Bobby doing the same I walked to the far end of the row of tellers as Bobby stayed by the door. With Bobby barking orders for everyone to get on the floor, I pulled out a pillowcase from my sweatshirt pocket. Waiting for Bobby to finish his list of do's and don'ts to the bank patrons, I gathered money from the first teller, then walking down the row of tellers towards the door that we entered. Once again everything became slow motion, frame by frame. I could do my job of gathering the money, keep crowd control with my sawed-off and watch for any heroic activity from the bank's customers.

It was beautiful as I continued dragging money off the counter into the pillowcase. Then we backed out the door flipping our masks back up to the hat position, we slowly walked towards the car in the adjacent parking lot, weaving in and out of cars as we kept a three hundred and sixty degree watch of our surroundings. I climbed in the driver's seat as Bobby got in the back. We slowly pulled the car out on to the main road with Bobby changing clothes on the back floorboard as I paid attention to every traffic law known to man.

Back at the hotel we changed clothes and checked out. Wiping and throwing the weapons into a nearby lake as we drove to the salvage yard to sell the car to be crushed with our bank robbery clothes in the trunk. Using the junkyard phone to call a cab to take us back into town so we could catch a shuttle to the airport, we were soon on our way back to the Golden State. I was feeling really good, that was the easiest sixty seconds of my young life. As Bobby and I sat on the plane headed west we both had on a smirk, and a little over four thousand dollars in each of our pockets. It wasn't Fort Knox money, but after going without for a couple of months it felt like millions. Besides I knew I could spare sixty more seconds of my life when this money ran out. I had finally found a way to make easy money.

17

After landing back in California I found myself at the Playa de Sol Hotel in Santa Barbara. It was an upscale hotel located right on the beach, and Santa Barbara is one of the most beautiful cities with its Mediterranean feel and relaxed atmosphere. Slowing down for a moment my mind was bombarded with thoughts. I had just robbed a bank, fuck what was I thinking? Although I had given the robbery plenty of time for planning, I never gave much time for the thinking through process. I had just opened a new can in my life, and in that can was the federal government. I'm sure they don't like people taking their money.

I couldn't describe the bank that I just robbed or how many people were inside of it at the time, that sixty seconds although seeming longer I spent inside the bank was now just a blur. And within my heart of hearts, which is my true barometer on life, I knew I had crossed another line that I could not uncross.

Santa Barbara with its beaches butted up to its rolling hills was enough distraction to chase my concerning thoughts away for the most part. At times though I knew I had fucked up. The feds never stop looking for you and will spend five thousand dollars to track you down for stealing five dollars, so I just kept rolling around my same thoughts over and over. I was very calm in the robbery, but now I was discombobulated. It wasn't conscience, I lacked one, but more the thought of being busted and serving major time for a relatively small amount of money. Thoughts just kept rolling over and over and then it came to me as clear as the lake that I had disposed the weapons in. Nobody knew me in the state which I had just committed this robbery, with gloves and a mask on also the only problem I had was in my mind, I had gotten away clean. I needed to accept that fact and enjoy my life, and that's exactly what I started doing.

Since Bobby and I spent so much time together, we decided to go in halves on a car. It wasn't brand new being a couple years old but still a very nice car, a light metallic green Chevrolet. At night we would go to the movies or a card room and gamble, and with our love of the big screen we sometimes would go to two movies in the same day. Every meal we ate in a restaurant or café talking to everyone we met everywhere we went. Santa Barbara is known for its culture also, and I would find myself in museums and art exhibits putting on the façade of a gentleman of leisure. Although I was having a good time, I knew exactly what was coming next when my money got low enough.

Sooner than later our money got low, not dead ass broke low, but low enough we had to make a move. Bobby and I both agreed we would never get as broke as we had in Nebraska, standing on the side of the road hungry and feeling desperate. Desperate times call for desperate measures and desperation creates a bigger window for mistakes, so we were determined to stay in front of our finances. After all we had figured out a way to anonymously steal and get the most buck for our risk.

We boarded the plane at San Francisco airport on our way back to the Midwest, bringing more knowledge and confidence this time. Leaving our car at long-term parking loaded with most of our belongings, we traveled with the bare minimum. No carry-on luggage only check-in luggage containing bank robbery wardrobe and a couple of different weapons we had purchased in the Mission District of San Francisco. In 1974 before homeland security bringing a sawed-off shotgun and a couple of handguns in your check luggage was possible, and Bobby and I took full advantage of this no restriction rule. We carried no incriminating identification, traveled under assumed names and paid cash. Times were very different back then with everybody not being in everyone else's business. Although I had wanted to always live in the lawless decade of the twenties and thirties, the mid-seventies served my purpose just fine.

Meticulously as we were at planning how to rob a bank our method of where wasn't that sophisticated. Bobby and I would just look at a map; pick a state in the middle of the country and a small town close to the airport. Staying in a hotel near the airport we would then look at the classified section of the newspaper to find a car that was cheap yet dependable. All towns have banks and our thinking was the smaller the better. Less people, less hassle, this would only increase our odds of a clean getaway.

The town for our second bank heist was very small. Instead of a police department there was one officer known as a Constable whose job was to patrol more than one town, visiting a series of towns throughout the day. Beautiful I thought to myself, no police equaled no worry. The only drawback of this location was that there was only one-road in and one-road out. This created a double-edged sword. First there would be more traffic on this road and we would look like everyone else when driving, second if the Constable thought the crooks were driving to escape they would have to be on this road. I was probably overthinking everything, maybe even a little paranoid. My first bank robbery was more compulsive than thought and this robbery had more of a reality edge. But after studying the bank for a few days, I was committed.

And there sat Bobby and I in our three hundred dollar station wagon waiting for the Constable to make his early evening rounds. Right on time I thought, now we had fifteen minutes until it was five till six. During these times of waiting Bobby and I never said one word to each other. I know what I would be thinking, everything from being a kid surfing to obscure thoughts that made no sense. I had no idea what was running through Bobby's mind and never asked.

My hand on the stock of the shotgun in the pocket of my coat, mask down and complete focus, it was time to do this. This bank was much smaller than the first one I noticed right away as I entered. Only having two tellers and three customers with some guy sitting at a desk in an open office area, he could see me and I could see him so I motioned him to come out. While I'm waiting for the office guy to come out to lay on the floor with the others this old lady starts walking towards the door. Grabbing her by the arm I relayed to her, "Ma'am you're gonna have to wait till we're done."

Acting like she couldn't hear, I motioned her down to the floor pointing with the barrel of my shotgun, and even if she couldn't hear, I knew she could see. I was in my frame-by-frame mode as I scooped the money from the two tellers. This bank looked old with outdated furniture, but I didn't have time to remodel it in my mind or figure out why it was in this condition, I needed to go right then so I turned and backed out the door. The pillowcase felt light as I opened the cars back door, getting on the floorboard. It was my turn to lie in the back as Bobby drove. I hated not being able to see what was going on around me as I was taking off my parka and sweatshirt.

165

We decided, since there was only one road in and out that I would remain out of sight in the back seat until we got to our hotel. If by chance the police were giving a strong look at ongoing traffic it would appear as one person traveling, not two. Every time Bobby would slow down I would think something was wrong. My mind has always entertained me and I specifically remember one thought that passed as I hid on the back floor board, how nerve-racking it must be to be a blind bank robber and not knowing what's going on around you.

Back at our hotel room we chopped up the money. It was less than the first robbery; this is bullshit I thought as we got our things together to fly home. We left the station wagon near the airport taking off the license plates, and we had also packed our weapons and robbery attire in our luggage to bring back with us. Sloppy, I felt we were getting real sloppy and both smarter than this. I didn't have time to talk or think about it right then but when Bobby and I returned to California we agreed there would be some revising to consider.

I never could figure out where my take of the bank money was going. I was only spending money on what I absolutely needed, heroin, women along with jewelry and clothes. But sooner than later it came that time again, another bank. Bobby and I picked a state in the Bible-Belt this time. This robbery was relatively uneventful netting us more than the second but not as much as the first. It had been an Indian summer and we had looked a tad out of place with our coats, but with the time change creating the cover of darkness it all went off without a hitch. We were both enforcing our new robbery rule and disposed of everything related to the bank job.

As uneventful as this past robbery was, the next one made up for it, with a series of peculiarities and

166

odd events. It was winter once again so we settled on a state that had heavy snowfall and guaranteed cold weather. After picking the town we settled in for a couple weeks to watch, plan and execute before flying back to California. We were staying close to the Bay Area so we would use San Francisco airport exclusively. The town we decided on was more of a suburban location than a country setting, with us figuring bigger town, bigger payday.

As Bobby and I entered a random supermarket one night to shop, we noticed a big safe as we walked up. The safe was located right by the front door, and with everything glass it was clearly visible from the outside. As we were shopping the manager opened the safe to deposit the day's receipts. I looked at my watch; it was nine o'clock p.m. sharp. Bobby and I communicated with a grin as we purchased food and cigarettes. Back outside we discussed hitting this particular supermarket as a bonus, since we were staying in town to case a bank anyway, why fucking not?

Our next evenings were spent sitting in the parking lot across from this supermarket and watching. Nine o'clock would come and the safe door would open as the manager put money in. Every night, like clockwork without fail, every night. Our homework was complete on the bank and with time to kill waiting for that special Friday we executed our plan on the supermarket. Bobby donned a wig and became a customer pushing a cart up and down the aisles, waiting. My position was outside watching through the glass and waiting. Right on time the manager opened the safe as Bobby got the drop on him. That was my cue to enter for crowd control and backup.

Candy from a baby I thought as I drove off, with Bobby lying in the back. About a mile down the road police cars were coming in my direction with their sirens wailing. Too late fellas I thought as I drove off in the darkness.

We split the thirty-one hundred dollars in the hotel room, showered and slept. The next morning we grabbed coffee and breakfast at a local café and waited with only three more days till Friday. I looked around the coffee shop and noticed everybody was wearing plaid shirts, jeans and snow boots. I also noticed that nobody was paying attention to us; if they had been we might have looked out of place with our slacks, leather coats and leather slip on shoes. I didn't understand how anybody could live in this part of the country, cold, windy with the snow piled up on the sides of the roads after being plowed. It all didn't matter though I was there for one thing and one thing only.

"Whisper, Bobby I can't believe it's you," said a voice from behind me.

Slowly I turned my head to see. Tony, Tony Lofton standing directly behind me. Tony had served time with us in California over two years ago, and this whole scene took me by surprise.

"What are you guys doing up here, cold enough for ya?"

Everyone in these states that have severe cold and snow always ask you if it's cold enough. I didn't understand it, personally I think the cold affects their brains and that's why they always reference the obvious. But being taken by surprise I didn't have a good reply to Tony's question. So I said nothing. We motioned for Tony to join us in the booth and he started to do all the talking, telling us how he lived there now, got married and drove truck for a living. He continued to tell us that he had gone straight and was not involved in crime any more. "Good for you Tony," I said.

This chance meeting was very awkward for me and I'm usually the one that always has something to say, but I was speechless. No big deal though, Tony didn't push more questions on why we were there, and Tony was solid as far as I knew. After more superficial talk along with a couple of laughs Tony said he had to go, he was at the café making a delivery and had to finish his route. He did invite us to meet his wife and join them for dinner but we graciously declined. It was just all very strange and after talking it over with Bobby he agreed, very strange indeed.

I had a bad feeling and the closer we got to Friday evening, the worst this feeling got.

We exited our vehicle and slowly walked across the street and through the parking lot towards the bank; it had snowed all week and heavy snow flurries were still coming down. The sky was darker for lack of a moon and the beginning of a severe blizzard was taking shape. Opening the glass doors and quick walking I positioned myself at the far end of the bank. This bank was larger than the ones in the past, having four tellers as well as more customers in line and I was in my frame by frame vision and noticed that nobody noticed me entering with a ski mask on. Our beginning cue in the past was for me to unzip my coat dropping the barrels of the shotgun to rest in my left hand, as the hand in my right pocket held the butt of the gun with my finger on the double trigger. This would set Bobby off into his robbery rant of dishing out orders.

But my zipper was stuck and I started to panic. Across the bank I could see Bobby's blue eyes filled with concern. Shrugging my shoulders to let him know that we were basically fucked, he started walking towards me. I kept scanning the lobby as I fidgeted with my jacket zipper. Nobody had taken notice but I still wanted out of there right then because I felt like

169

we had already been in there for our allotted one minute. Bobby was now standing directly in front of me yanking on my stubborn zipper, I whispered, "We gotta get the fuck outta here now."

Bobby then turned his head side to side and said back to me, "Ain't nobody paying attention, we can still do this."

At that moment the zipper broke free and Bobby took his place back by the bank's front door. He then went completely crazy running around like a madman screaming for everyone to get on the fucking floor. I motioned for the office workers to join the others and went to the far teller producing my pillowcase. I could hear Bobby still screaming behind me as I collected money from the remaining tellers. By now I was close to the door, zipped back up and I along with Bobby backed out of the bank. Walking through the bank parking lot I had to hold the pillowcase closed with both hands while softly telling Bobby. "This is a good one Bobby, I think this is a real good one."

The snow was really coming down by now and we left our ski masks in robbery position. Looking to my left I could see a man staring at me from up top his snowplow. He had a look of unsure as we both kept our eyes locked on each other. My mind was all over the place as we crossed the main street and through another parking lot to get to our waiting car. Our plan was to drive directly to the airport that night and catch a flight home. With the supermarket robbery as well as being there for almost two weeks, Bobby and I had agreed it was in our best interest to leave town immediately after the bank. The roads were terrible with ice and snow as I creped along the main road towards the highway, I was sweating as I drove and everything just felt all wrong. With Bobby silent on the back floorboard, I focused on my job of driving the seventy miles to the airport.

170

It seemed to take forever to get out of this town. I could hear sirens in the distant background but wondered if they were just in my mind.

I pulled over by the Mississippi River, and with the shotgun and two pistols tied in a sack I threw them. We would have to drive all the way to the airport before disposing of the car's license plates. I continued to sweat and couldn't get my mind on an even keel as driving conditions worsened and I was on a slow crawl on the highway. With Bobby up front with me now I felt a little better, but neither of us said a word as we traveled down the highway. Finally I broke the ice, "That fucking zipper was fucked up, right?"

"We're good, watch the road, we're good."

We were good. Over forty miles away from the bank with thirty miles to go Bobby was right, we were good. One thing Bobby had that I didn't have was he was always cool under pressure and his calming demeanor would take hold on me and I became calmer.

There are a few tricks when driving in blizzard conditions on icy roads, and I knew none of them. We eventually did make it to the airport, wiping the car down and leaving it in long-term parking. Bagging our robbery clothes we put them in a dumpster by the hotel incinerator. Inside the airport we proceeded to the ticket counter separately for tickets back out West. All flights had been canceled because of the severe weather warnings.

Meeting Bobby in the airport bathroom we decided on getting separate rooms in the airport hotel and hopefully flying out the next day weather permitting. The pillowcase with money was in my suitcase so once in my room I started counting, I knew this was a good one, I just knew it. Nineteen thousand seven hundred and thirty five dollars, I wanted to tell

171

Bobby but we weren't associating in any way shape or form.

The next morning the sun was out and it had stopped snowing, but it was as white as far as the eye could see. Delta (airlines) was back on schedule flying and Bobby and I sat in the back of the plane with an empty seat between us containing the bank money. I ordered a can of Schweppes as Bobby ordered the same along with two airline-sized vodkas. We buckled up as the plane's engines warmed, then the plane taxied onto the tarmac. I felt instant relief as the plane picked up speed readying for takeoff while putting my seat in the back position I looked over at Bobby who was mixing his vodka with his soda. I let all my cares go from the night before and fully relaxed, listening to this elderly woman behind us read the morning paper to her husband.

She touched base on a couple of world issues on the front page, and then proceeded to read about a bank robbery the night before seventy miles away. Her husband listened as she described the bank and the robbery with Bobby and me hanging on every word. The article described two masked assailants entering the bank right before closing and leaving with an undisclosed amount of money. The suspects left the area in one of three cars, which the newspaper went on to describe. It had been twenty-five years since this branch had been robbed, adding no other information was known at this time.

Bobby and I sat there with half grins, both of us glancing down at the bag of money on the seat between us, plus I wanted to send a message up to the pilot telling him to step on the gas. I wanted to get back home fast.

Instant relief set in further knowing that we had gotten away clean, even the cars description in the paper were three for three, all incorrect. The FBI would be chasing ghosts as far as I was concerned.

Bobby's parents had settled in Oxnard and he grew up three streets away from my house. He was married at sixteen, with two kids by seventeen, Baby Bobby and Vanessa. He split with his wife shortly after Baby Bobby was born but they remained friends, and his children remained very important to him. Since I had been hanging with Bobby for the last few years, I was considered part of the family and his kids referred to me as Uncle Whisper.

Bobby had mentioned that he wanted to see his kids and I decided to go along for the ride. Landing in San Francisco we would drive the few hundred miles back to Oxnard, visit, and then go to Las Vegas to wash some of the money. This was our biggest score so far, so why not a little celebration in Lost Wages, Nevada. Before from our smaller robberies we would buy money orders to cover our tracks, but I felt we should wash every single dollar from this last bank. Cover all our bases so to speak.

Fifteen thousand dollars each in our pockets and back in the mid-seventies you could buy a modest house for that amount. But Bobby and I were not out house shopping, we enjoyed hotel rooms, traveling, and doing what twenty something men do with free money. Plus banks are on every other corner and spending a minute every few months for a nice payday is a good career to pursue. Also I calculated that this last bank job money would last me almost a year if I wasn't a complete nut with the money.

Back in Oxnard I stayed in the car as Bobby walked up to his mother's house.

Personally I didn't like being back in Oxnard, the police knew me and I was on escape. The new car and well-dressed helped, but it would just take one overzealous rookie to question me and I would be fucked.

After a few minutes Bobby returned to the car telling me Sharon (his wife) was on the way over with the kids. I then told Bobby I'd be back in a couple of hours to pick him up, it was family time and I didn't want to intrude. Also Bobby's mother would always look at me crazy as if I was leading her son down the path to hell. If she could only see Bobby when he was in action inside the bank acting like a complete fucking maniac, waving a pistol and demanding full cooperation. No mom, if your son ends up in hell, it wasn't from any help from me. But I'm sure I'll be skipping down the same road with him on the way there.

Driving towards the Jetties I started to feel more at home and my mild paranoia was leaving me. Pulling into the parking lot at the beach I just sat there staring. It looked the same but felt so different, also I didn't see any of the fellas so I just drove off after a few minutes. I had changed so much but was unaware of it until this point. Years had gone by without me surfing and almost five years had gone by without me talking to my folks, so I turned up the volume on the cassette player in the car and just drove.

Teddy Pendergrass was singing, and once again the words rang true and spoke to me, "...the more I get—more I want."

On occasion I would give thought to my life, but for the most part I would just shun the reality of the world and continue on my path of life being one good time.

I swung back to Bobby's mother's home, and Bobby and I decided to meet at Toys "R" Us to treat the kids. I had gone in halves on another car with Bobby, a beautiful Buick Electra 225, so I was now driving my

174

half of the Chevrolet as Bobby was driving my other half of the Buick. This was funny to me, I didn't own a car but owned half of two cars. My relationship with Bobby had grown into the most solid and trusting relationship two humans could have. We completely trusted each other, after all, even though we were the ones with the weapons, we were always outnumbered in robbery situations. Bobby's extra eyes and extra ears wasn't the only help that a crime partner could bring to the table. Trust, unconditional trust, would become insurance for complete safety when the odds were stacked against you. And Bobby was my friend, end of story, period. Besides, we were so much alike with our humor and not give a fuck attitude about life that often I would tell Bobby, "If you were a woman, I would marry you."

Bobby's reply would never vary, "Fuck you Whisper."

Baby Bobby and Vanessa had their own shopping carts pushing them up every isle of the Toys "R" Us, and when done filling each cart to maximum capacity, Bobby paid for one and I paid for the other.

After Bobby dropped the kids back off, I parked the Chevy at his mother's house and we both jumped in the Buick and started driving towards Vegas.

Once reaching the California Nevada state line I stepped on the gas. With no speed limit on Nevada highways I kept the Buick Electra deuce and a quarter going over a hundred. The white lines on the road became little dashes and Bobby and I sat comfortably cruising, changing the cassette player once in a while with conversation at a minimum. With me and Bobby on the same page, most of the time our facial expressions, half grins and looks, became our communication through life together.

175

With the sun setting it was dusk and the lights of Vegas were getting closer by the minute. This was going to be a business slash vacation for me. I always liked to wash the money from the banks in various ways, from traveler's checks to buying a coffee with a hundred dollar bill. It had become a little idiosyncrasy of mine to always make sure our money was untraceable. Bobby thought it was a little over the top most of the time but never interfered with me doing my thing. We pulled on to the Boulevard of Las Vegas Avenue and lights were everywhere. I couldn't help thinking to myself how a guy could get lost in all the commotion and dizziness that Vegas had to offer. On the way into town we noticed a group of Nevada sheriffs gathered around a hole in the desert where they were digging up a body. But to me this only comforted me in knowing I was a little fish in a big pond. On the strip I noticed a big neon cowboy waving, Bobby and I looked at each other and with a half nod I pulled into the Frontier Hotel and Casino. One hotel was as good as the other for relaxing by the pool, gambling and washing our bank robbery money. As soon as I stopped the automobile the valet ran up to the driver's side offering to carry any bags and park our Buick. Bobby told the valet our suitcases were in the trunk, threw him a five dollar tip but added we would be carrying the small overnight bags ourselves, which contained our guns, heroin and money. I like this shit I thought to myself, this is how I should and want to live every day of my life.

Bobby and I decided to put some money in the hotel safe and after a couple of days when we checked out, the hotel would return our money, but not the exact same money, completing the washing process of the lion's share of stolen money. We decided to put nine thousand dollars each in the hotel safe, leaving us with a few thousand each for pocket money. As soon as we both signed the receipts for nine thousand dollars,

176

upon the two of us turning around, the hotel manager stuck out his hand and introduced himself to us. Thanking us for picking the Frontier, he furnished complimentary rooms and meals for our entire stay. This was a very common practice in Las Vegas, with thousands of dollars in their safe, the hotel and casino feel it's only a matter of time before the money will become theirs. Not a chance, Bobby's and my purpose was to lounge poolside during the day, and chase cocktail waitresses at night.

Vegas in the mid-seventies was a lot different than now. Workers dressed in suits with the patrons nicely dressed also, and it wasn't a family atmosphere, no kids. With my dress slacks and dress shirt, leather coat and Florsheim shoes I fit in perfectly. The gangsters owned this town and it was quite obvious to anyone that paid attention. The best way for me to describe it is that Las Vegas was like the Vegas portrayed in the movie *Casino*, starring Robert De Niro and Joe Pesci directed by Martin Scorsese. Trust and believe me when I tell you it was exactly like that, exactly.

Roulette was my game and I would sit at the table making small wagers and killing time while watching people. Bobby liked playing blackjack, and like everything else was a maniac when he played becoming animated and getting the entire table laughing. Often I would be sitting and feel someone staring at me, then turning side to side I would eventually find a pit boss or floor boss staring at me from across the room. Gangsters in suits definitely made their presence known, but they did not have to worry about me, I knew better than to break the law in their town. The only law that I had broken in Las Vegas was not reporting to the Sheriff within the first twenty four hours of my arrival. Back then it was a felony to be a felon and not let the local law know you're in town within twenty four hours. But for me

177

that never made sense to do; besides I looked more than legit on the outside and still on escape so naturally I never reported. Fuck 'um.

Bobby and I made a point to bring a quantity of heroin wherever we went and Vegas was no exception. We would meet in one of our hotel rooms to get high, and then go about our business of gambling or chasing tang. Hours would go by and I wouldn't see Bobby but never gave it any worry, Bobby was a big boy who could take care of himself. Besides I was fixated on this brunette cocktail waitress dressed like a Roman goddess, which occupied a lot of my time with the chase. Since I wasn't a drinker I would order soda water with lime, always over tipping and adding bullshit dialogue she became somewhat interested. In what, I don't know, the over tipping or the bullshit dialogue? But soon I became the Roman gladiator to complement her Roman goddess persona. I was really starting to settle in to the whole Vegas thing, fully relaxed and enjoying my newfound wealth.

With a couple of days passing, I was in a new routine, swimming at the hotel pool during the day and searching for my Roman goddess at night, meeting up after her shift for dinner or breakfast. I was a happy man. Lying in my room one night as I was waiting for the evening's activities to begin Bobby busted through the door.

"Whisper loan me a thousand dollars."

"What's going on?" Is all I could say as I was taken by surprise of the request.

Bobby slowed his breathing down and after wiping sweat from his face and neck he said, "I lost all my money at the blackjack table."

"All your money, even the money in the hotel safe?" I was still confused to what was really happening.

"Yes, loan me a thousand."

"Sure," as I reached in my pocket, and gave him the money.

I know Bobby did everything full throttle why would blackjack be any different? You have to understand I didn't really care about the money because Bobby was my friend, and I know he would do the same for me. Probably less than an hour had passed and Bobby was back in my room asking for another thousand. This is where I stepped in and tried to slow the situation down by telling Bobby, "We don't put our life on the line as well as our freedom robbing banks, to be handing over our money to these gangsters in Las Vegas."

He fully agreed, but still wanted money even offering me half of either car for collateral or payment of the loan.

"Bobby, I don't want your half of the cars or half of anything for the money, you're my friend. I just don't want us broke from trying to get rich on the luck of cards."

I could see he was in a frenzy of gambling and I felt if he just slowed down he would be okay. What, am I a priest now? I had been there in life myself, so caught up you can't see the problem. In my moneybag I had some one dollar bills that I hadn't got around to changing out for washing purposes. So I told Bobby, "Here take this money."

It was about seven hundred dollars in ones.

That night passed with no sight of Bobby and after coming back to my hotel room in the morning I

179

called room service to order breakfast for Bobby and myself. I had the breakfast delivered to Bobby's room and after letting myself in I whispered for Bobby to wake up and that food was on the way. Opening the door so the bellhop could roll in our eggs and toast, I signed the manager's name to the check and started to reach in my pocket for a tip. That's when Bobby looked at me with a half-smile half-grin saying, "I got the tip Holmes."

After closing the door behind the bellhop, we sat down to eat breakfast together, Bobby proceeded to tell me how the previous night had become a whirlwind of gambling. After getting ahead of the blackjack demon Bobby continued telling me how he was sometimes betting a thousand dollars on one hand of blackjack. Further he said, "There was this crowd around me hanging on every card dealt."

He became in a lightweight frenzy just telling me the story of the previous night, "Not only me winning sixty-eight hundred dollars back, but I felt like James 'muthafuckin' Bond when doing it."

Bobby could always make me laugh with the way he told a story. In my mind I was doing the math and although Bobby said he was up sixty-eight hundred dollars, he was really down over eight thousand dollars. I said I was gonna get some rest and hit the pool later and asked him what he was going to do?

"Going back down to the casino, Whisper. What else?"

After a short nap I decided to stroll down to the gaming tables and find Bobby to see how he was doing. I watched from a roulette table as I noticed Bobby's chip stack dwindling. I was determined not to give these gangsters our not hard earned money. Back at my room I packed, then went to Bobby's room and packed his suitcase, calling the front desk I told them to bring the Buick around front that we were leaving. After grabbing my money out of the safe while the bellhop put our suitcases in the trunk, I went to find Bobby on the casino floor. He was damn near broke again. I grabbed him by the shoulders as I spoke, "Bobby, we are leaving now. I will give you half my money when we get out of town. Let's go."

Without protest or any type of argument, Bobby followed me to the car and we drove off from Vegas. An awkward silence engulfed the interior of the vehicle as I pulled the Buick Electra into the station to get gas. After filling up the car and tipping the attendant, we tipped everyone, I divvied up my cash and handed Bobby fifty six hundred dollars saying with a laughing voice, "Here you go Maverick."

Maverick was a sixties television show starring James Garner as Maverick, a gambler in the times of the Wild West. Many times after that throughout Bobby's and my friendship did I refer to him as Maverick, and it would always bring a smirk of remembrance from that one particular Vegas excursion.

18

I was asleep in the front of the vehicle as Bobby crossed over the Nevada California border, once again on my way back to bittersweet Oxnard. It was as if I was playing Russian roulette with my freedom going back to the town that I was definitely known in for all the wrong reasons. I had put Oxnard in my rearview mirror so many times, yet always ended up back there. And after the two of us each bought a quantity of heroin, our money was relatively low again. So much for my year plan of complete relaxation and no robbery! We decided to sell the Buick and just keep one car, the Chevrolet, we took a slight loss on the deal but since we spent so much time together one car would be sufficient.

Back on the road north, I breathed a sigh of relief and thought of nothing and it felt real nice. Talking Bobby into taking the coast highway along Big Sur we grabbed the junction of Highway 1 in Morro Bay and started to cruise by the ocean. Bobby and I didn't share the same love of nature or he never expressed it the way that I would. I was always pointing out red tailed hawks or a rare condor as we drove, the giant redwoods and sequoias started showing up further north on the sides of the winding road to once again parts unknown. We even stopped and rented horses to ride on the beach, I was amazed how good a rider Bobby was. He was very athletic and pretty much good at everything he did, the horse thing did surprise me a little bit though, and the visual contrast was very humorous. We were both wearing stovepipe style slacks, a collared dress shirt and leather loafers as visions of the dapper Wild West outlaws Butch Cassidy and the Sundance Kid went through my imaginary process of thinking as me and Bobby became one with nature.

We ended up in Scotts Valley a small resort town between San Jose to the east and Santa Cruz to the west. Life became business as usual again of doing what we wanted when we wanted and where we wanted. In the evenings we would end up at this small upscale bar slash nightclub named Mona's Gorilla Lounge. In all my young travels I had never been to a nightclub with that cool of a name, and I fit right in, lying to the young ladies in Northern California of my occupation and status. I would just make up these stories on the fly of being some son of a successful entrepreneur or land baron in the area on business. One of my favorites was selling them on the idea that I was an actor, not a leading man but an extra sometimes having a speaking role. I would describe various movies that I allegedly had roles in and more times than not one of these potential overnight girlfriends would remember me from the particular movie that I was describing. Some of these girls were more pretty than smart, God bless them.

But no matter how good these made up stories were they didn't pay the bills and it became that time again. Back in San Francisco airport Bobby and I were grabbing a flight back to the Midwest, and we picked a state that we had already hit a bank in, a different city on the other side of the state far away from the previous city that we had robbed from but in the same state. Locating the right bank, and purchasing the disposable getaway car as well as a couple of pistols was no problem, but for some reason we couldn't find a shotgun to buy. We ended up settling for a 30.06 rifle

183

and after I sawed off most of the barrel and the butt it looked completely ridiculous. The hole of the barrel looked small compared to a shotgun barrel and I felt stupid while I was practicing putting it in my coat and taking it back out imitating what I would do once inside the bank. I relayed my concerns to Bobby about my crowd control weapon not being very impressive. In true Bobby fashion and humor he stated, "We could first rob a blood bank or a food bank or even a sperm bank to see if it works if you want."

"Funny Bobby, real fucking funny," I said trying not to laugh.

But it was funny and we both were laughing as we waited for that Friday to roll around so we could take care of the business at hand. That Friday came and went and we robbed and left, and as we landed back at Frisco airport we were a little over four thousand dollars richer each. My life had taken on a new smoothness, Bobby and I never talked of past robberies and never talked about future robberies, we lived in the day and were both enjoying life to its fullest.

Most of my nights I spent at Mona's Gorilla Lounge and during the day dined in cafés and talked to strangers. Together Bobby and I would enjoy movies, gambling at Bay Meadows horse track and other spontaneous ideas of enjoyment. Life was so good, so very very good. Bobby would drive to Oxnard to see his kids at his mother's house; I went a couple of times but eventually stopped completely for a couple of reasons. One being the crazy looks from his mother and another was that still haunting feeling I would get from being in Oxnard. And although Bobby's mother's house was only three blocks from my parent's home, I never gave it any thought to go visit them. That's just the way it was, it was going on six years without seeing my folks, but that's just the way it was.

It was the spring of nineteen seventy-six with the air being cool and the sun warm, and on the radio air waves, the new style of music was Funk, an offspring of rhythm and blues. Bobby had planned a weekend with his kids coming from down south to Scotts Valley and from there they would spend family time on the boardwalk in Santa Cruz. Bobby had also taken my lead and not been going back to Oxnard as often, instead meeting his kids in small coastal towns so as to spend time with them.

With my paranoia of the police at a minimum, I found my niche just hanging in Scotts Valley. I was reading more, mostly autobiographies and biographies and since people have always fascinated me reading about Johnny Cash, the Rolling Stones, Janis Joplin or Eric Clapton put me in this complete state of relaxation.

With Bobby's mother older, he didn't feel comfortable having her make the long drive to drop the kids off for this long weekend, so he had arranged for a mutual friend of the family to drive his children up north and naturally Bobby would financially compensate him for his time and trouble.

The kids were on the way and Bobby asked me to join them in the carnival atmosphere of the boardwalk. Declining, I told Bobby I just wanted to lie by the pool, swim and read adding, "Enjoy yourself and give Baby Bobby and Vanessa my regards."

He kept insisting saying the kids would like to see their Uncle Whisper, although telling Bobby I was good and just wanted to relax, I did agree to have lunch with all of them at a local restaurant before they traveled the thirty odd miles to Santa Cruz.

The plan was for Bobby's friend, who turned out to be a minister to rent a car under his name so Bobby could stay in Santa Cruz for the entire weekend and then drive the kids back close to Oxnard to be picked back up. This would leave me with the Chevy all weekend so I planned a little trip of my own to visit Mario, who Bobby and I did time with, and I would sell him grams of heroin from time to time. I enjoyed going to his house in Watsonville because Mario was real cool and his wife would make these potato burritos that were unreal in taste. Simply just fried potatoes and some mystery seasoning wrapped in a flour tortilla, I'd never had them before I met Mario and never have had them since. Unreal in taste that's all I can say.

I packaged six grams of raw heroin individually in balloons and then wrapped them all in a piece of tinfoil. I wasn't selling narcotics regularly but once in a while I would as more of a favor for someone I liked, and with the profit of these six grams I could purchase another half ounce for myself. But this day was more of a road trip with potato burritos as my prize. I showered, dressed and grabbed my brown leather coat putting the tinfoil of heroin in my sock. I was ready to leave as I yelled to Bobby, "Ready to go?"

He replied, "Yeah," adding, "sure you don't want to go with us for the weekend?"

"No I'm good Bobby, I'm going to Mario's for a little business."

"Potato burritos?"

"You know it Holmes," I said as we started walking out the door.

We drove to the restaurant, which wasn't far from the resort in which we were staying, parked and grabbed a big booth in the back waiting for Bobby's kids to arrive. Ordering two coffees, I lit a cigarette and Bobby did the same as we just sat there with Bobby glancing out the window periodically sipping

186

our coffee and smoking Camel cigarettes. Bobby muttered the kids are here as he waved them over to our booth; Gene was the Minister's name and we all shook hands with the kids crawling all over Bobby. They were excited and Bobby seemed content also, but your outward emotions are very masked on heroin, so it's difficult to know what someone is thinking or feeling when under the influence.

Everyone ordered something to eat except me, telling the waitress that I was just going to stick with coffee. Gene sat quietly as Baby Bobby and Vanessa bombarded Bobby with requests and questions on what they were gonna do throughout the weekend. I sipped my coffee and was sizing up Gene; he was a big man but never projecting pretentiousness or coming across condescending when he spoke. He was just one of those guys that would try and help people, driving Bobby's kids hundreds of miles to see Bobby was his contribution to keeping a family together. He never asked any questions and was more on the quiet side, Gene seemed all right and I was okay with him. Although he may be a family friend of Bobby and Bobby's mother, I knew for a fact that he didn't know anything about me. Bobby and I have never told one soul of our robbery lifestyle, not one soul. And back then in the mid-seventies people didn't ask a lot of questions. But Vanessa had a question for me, "Uncle Whisper are you going to come with us?"

"No baby, I got a date."

"With a girl?" Vanessa said tilting her head.

"No. With a chimpanzee!"

Laughter erupted from Vanessa causing Baby Bobby to start laughing also, even though Baby Bobby had no idea what Vanessa was laughing at. I looked over at Gene and he was just grinning. Bobby hustled the kids off to the restroom and with Gene and myself alone at the table I lit a cigarette and paid the bill, not liking to smoke in front of Vanessa since she would always tell me that smoking was not good for me. If Vanessa only knew my other activities, heroin and bank takeover robberies she would have realized that smoking cigarettes was one of the positive lifestyle choices I had. Gene and I sat there with no conversation until Bobby and the kids came back, then we all proceeded to the door. I was the last one out as two other patrons were leaving behind me; I held the glass door open starting my walk down the sidewalk to the parking lot.

"CLICK," immediately followed by, "FBI-PUT YOUR HANDS WHERE I CAN SEE THEM."

The initial "CLICK" had got my complete attention and in my mind I knew what time it was, now other FBI agents were appearing from their crouching positions between the parked cars. One particular agent had a shotgun inches from my face yelling, "PUT YOUR HANDS IN THE AIR."

Without hesitation I answered, "I'M PUTTING MY HANDS ON THE HOOD OF THIS CAR."

I was completely focused on the barrel of the shotgun and noticed how much the officer's hands were shaking as he had it leveled at my face. Personally I'd never been at the business end of a shotgun and pictured how the bank customers must have viewed life when I was robbing them. Impressive, I thought. No wonder the robbery victims were never inclined to be heroes. Someone came up from behind me placing handcuffs on my left hand pulling it behind my back along with my right hand, and I was cuffed. I then looked over and saw the same process happening to Bobby as well as Gene. With my senses starting to work again my ears could hear Vanessa screaming as well as Baby Bobby crying. So much for family day!

I looked over to see two FBI agents taking the chrome hubcaps off our car and rummaging through our trunk and interior section. Another agent was in my face repeatedly asking what my name was. I just stood there cuffed not saying a word with the whole scene seeming surreal and very chaotic. This one agent was relentless over and over asking, "What is your name?"

I finally broke the ice saying, "You're the FBI—figure it out."

After a period of time they walked me over to a FBI unmarked car, patted me down and placed me in the back seat. Bobby was placed in another car, Gene in another and the kids in yet another car. As we drove off I could still see them looking through the Chevy searching for any bank contraband or weapons. I knew the car was clean and they hadn't found the heroin on me and at this point didn't even know my name, so I felt the playing field was relatively even to this point. Although they had taken a few thousand dollars out of my pocket held together by a rubber band, that's all they had so far, and last time I checked it wasn't illegal to have money in your pocket. This caused my mind to go into cocky mode and mentally I incorporated my usual mindset when dealing with authority, fuck 'um!

The unmarked car remained silent inside as we drove down the road towards the town of Santa Cruz, and I finally broke that silence when I asked, "What am I being charged with?"

"Bank robbery," was the agent's reply sitting next to me.

My mind is thinking WHICH bank? But I felt strongly this wouldn't be a pertinent question to ask verbally at this time. Then the car became silent again with the questions being asked and answered now only in my mind. Did they find our weapons, was a fingerprint left on one of our throwaway cars or was I identified by my unique voice even though I had only spoke a short sentence in one bank when telling a lady she couldn't leave during the robbery? Also no one, and I mean no one, but Bobby and I knew about the banks, not to mention we'd never hit a bank in California, so what the fuck is really going on? My mind had a series of legitimate questions, but no concrete answers. Maybe, just maybe, the FBI were barking up the wrong tree and this was no more than some ironic set of strange coincidences that landed me in the back of this unmarked FBI car sitting next to this agent who claims to not even be sure of my name. Optimism was quickly overruled by reality and I knew that they knew that the right person was sitting in the back of that FBI car on the way to the FBI building.

After parking the car in an underground facility, I was escorted up some stairs to an office in the FBI building. Numerous agents were running in and out of the office door talking among each other and producing paperwork flipping through the pages showing each other pictures and information. I sat in a chair across from another FBI officer at a desk, silently taking it all in. The agent at the desk started to speak, "We know everything so tell us what happened."

I simply said, "If you know everything then you don't need me to tell you what happened."

Another agent came up to me holding a picture of me next to my face, which only seemed to reaffirm to him that they had the right man. I had no idea where Bobby was, Gene or Bobby's kids. I just sat there quietly watching as this circus of FBI agents entered and would leave the room without organization or a definite pattern. All I could think about was the balloons of heroin in my sock that I needed to get to so I could swallow and take them to my next stop, which

190

at this point I was very sure my next stop was jail. They were using a variety of tactics trying to extract any information from me, playing good cop bad cop, having an agent come in snapping a ten dollar bill saying it was a match from the bank, even telling me that Mr. Fay next door had told them everything. I just sat there quietly knowing all this was a lie since I had personally exchanged all the bank bills and knew the solid character of my friend Bobby. I asked if I could take off my leather coat and then one agent snatched it out of my hand feeling the lining of my coat telling me to strip off the rest of my clothes to be searched thoroughly, looking for any money band wrappers from the bank or any type of incriminating evidence.

Now I stood there on the cold tile floor only wearing my red matching tank top, boxers and socks, still only thinking how I can smuggle this heroin into jail with me. Since they were only looking for weapons and bank paraphernalia I felt confident they could see that there's no possible way I could be hiding these bulky items in the rayon material of my underwear. Then I hear, "Remove all your clothes, even your underwear."

This was probably more for humiliation than evidence gathering but I still had to comply. I cupped my thumb into the top elastic of my sock and removed it, leaving the heroin still in the sock. I then removed my other sock, my tank top and finally my boxers placing them all in a small pile in the corner of the office. I am thinking to myself there is no fucking way some Quantico trained FBI agent is gonna touch my underwear and search it, there's just no fucking way, but one did. He shook my tank top then he shook my boxers and when he shook my sock this rectangle package of tinfoil went sliding across the tile floor. All conversation and movement in the office stopped as one agent picked it up slowly and started opening it.

They all gathered around as if some magical genie was going to appear out of the tinfoil and grant them evidence and a confession. It had taken me longer than usual for my usual arrest response, mostly in an attempt to find out what my opponent had against me, but now it was time.

"I want a lawyer. And can I get dressed?"

I was transported to Santa Cruz County Jail, once again, and booked on federal armed bank robbery charges. Fingerprinted with pictures front and side, the feds started exchanging paperwork with the local county police while the teletype was busy producing more information about me. An armed supermarket robbery warrant showed up from out of state, California had placed a hold on me saying I owed them the remainder of a five to life sentence along with a one to life. I was also charged with escape, which they were now calling a *walk-off*, probably to save the embarrassment of the dumbo guard that had opened the front gate of the prison and let me and Bobby leave. The bank carried a hundred thousand dollar bail, the supermarket twenty thousand dollars with the hold from California having no bail and the creative walk-off no bail. I was past fucked, they weren't gonna put me in prison they were gonna put me under the prison. And for some odd reason I wasn't charged with heroin possession, which didn't feel like that much of a relief at that time.

Bobby arrived shortly thereafter to the Santa Cruz County Jail booking area and was given the same fingerprint and picture treatment. He was also hit with the same exact charges and bail amounts as me, and from across the room I whispered as loud as I could, "The kids they all right? And what they do with the Reverend Gene?"

"They cut Gene loose and he's got Baby Bobby and Vanessa."

"Good, that's good," I said with a sense of relief.

After hours and hours of interrogation tactics, booking and waiting for all the agencies involved getting their paperwork coordinated I was exhausted. Waiting for the booking procedure to be finished on Bobby I put my head in my hands and waited some more. It was close to midnight when Bobby and I were finally let in the door of disciplinary tank number four and as the guard closed the gate behind us he made a point to tell us, "Sleep well fellas."

That's when I realized how exhausted I really was, too tired to even tell the cop, Fuck you.

This ordeal of being arrested by the feds had taken over eleven hours so as Bobby made up his bed sheets on the lower bunk, I did the same on the top bunk across from him in the same cell. We agreed to talk in the morning and my mind was empty of all thoughts as I closed my eyes and drifted off.

The clanging of cell doors and guards yelling "BREAKFAST" woke me as my eyes focused to the surroundings that were oh so familiar, tank four of Santa Cruz County Jail. I grabbed my metal tray filled with powdered eggs, toast and mush from the tray slot and sat myself down on the stainless steel bench connected to the stainless steel table in the day room. I looked around at the same old shit before eating; it was as if I had never left this place. I could see Bobby in line waiting to grab his tray so I decided to wait a little bit more so Bobby could join me. Nothing had changed, maybe the faces of the other prisoners, but it was still definitely the same overall shit. They were still even piping in music from the local radio station and on that first morning back the song was new and very apropos, the group was Ace and their hit song was called *How Long*. "How long has this been going on—we knew this could happen to us any day—how long has this been going on— how long?"

Good fucking question I thought to myself as I started eating my powdered eggs with my metal spoon.

Because of the lack of privacy created by the other prisoners Bobby and I decided not to talk to each other about our laundry list of charges. After breakfast I laid back on my top bunk trying to find a starting place to unravel this mess that I had created, plus my body was not feeling good from the lack of heroin. I imagine Bobby was physically sick also as I looked down and saw him lying on his bunk with a towel over his eyes. Our status in tank four was teetering on the higher echelon because of our numerous felonies, federal charges and the severity of our crimes. But all that didn't matter; I was just lying there staring at the ceiling. I felt as if I'd been shot at and missed, and shit on and hit.

Just as I was drifting from the state of sleep and consciousness a guard came to the gate and told me and Bobby, "Get ready. You're going to court."

The United States Marshals wrapped us in eight pounds of chains and put us in back of their marshal's car and started driving us east. They relayed to us we were on the way to San Jose to appear in front of a federal magistrate, which is nothing more than a fancy name for a judge. We were to be arraigned on our federal charges and enter a plea. Already this federal legal process seemed more complex than any state or county system that I had been involved in. Arriving in the federal courthouse in San Jose we were escorted to one of the courthouses many courtrooms and placed in the jury box waiting for the magistrate. When the federal judge entered the courtroom everyone stood including Bobby and I, we were individually asked to come up to the podium and enter a plea on the armed bank robbery of the Security State branch bank. And the words rolled naturally off my tongue, "Not guilty... Your Honor."

As Bobby entered his plea of not guilty I was sitting back in the jury box with my mind finally getting some answers. I now knew which bank they were charging me with, not the how but at least I knew now which bank. We were both going to be appointed federal public attorneys since we were both considered indigent. The FBI was holding our money as evidence, our car status was unknown at this time and indigent seemed like a sophisticated word to describe our situation, more accurate of a description I would think would have been dead ass broke and completely fucked. My attorney arrived at the jury box handing me his business card and telling me he would come see me later to discuss my case. When Bobby's attorney introduced himself as the one that would be representing him, Bobby peered over the jury box petition and quickly stated to the attorney, "You're unacceptable as my lawyer."

The attorney look surprised asking, "Is there some conflict of interest....or some particular reason you don't want me to represent you?"

Bobby looked the lawyer right in the eye, "Your shoes, your shoes are all scuffed up. If you don't care about your own shoes, I know you won't care about me."

Although Bobby was being completely serious it was very funny to me, and as I smiled I realized it was the first time that I somewhat laughed since this ordeal started. We were then driven to the San Jose County Jail having to go through the complete booking process once again, fingerprinted with pictures front and side and placed in an orange jumpsuit and thrown into one of the tanks. This county jail was nicknamed the Snake Pits and it fit, extremely filthy as well as extremely violent. Bobby and I were separated and I now wasn't talking to anybody ever. Every time the feds would take you to court they would then place you in another county jail and since I still wasn't feeling physically tip-top this process became a pain in the ass. Not to mention our personal property we had in the previous county jail would get left behind with the promise of it catching up with you at some point. But at this point my only property was a few sheets of paper consisting of court documentation, at twenty-five years of age this is all I owned, all I had to my name was a few sheets of paper.

I laid up in the Snake Pits for a few days with no attorney visit and my name was called out again for another court appearance. And once again I was in the back of the marshal's car chained to Bobby. It was good to see my old friend again and we were both physically a lot better. In court my dump truck of a lawyer was requesting a bail reduction hearing. Bail reduction?

Why, I had three holds from the state of California, so it didn't matter what my bail amount was at this time on the out of state bank and supermarket robberies. But I did know that I wouldn't be going back to the Snake Pits after court, I would be taken to another county jail and this time we were on our way to San Francisco County Jail for a preliminary hearing. Bobby and I still couldn't discuss openly any sort of game plan since the two marshals were in earshot in the front seat only separating us by a wire screen. So for the sixty odd miles north to San Fran, Bobby looked out one of the cars back windows and I looked out the other as we traveled. Busted, disgusted and definitely could not be trusted that's how I felt, but physically and mentally stronger my fight was coming back and I was getting back to my *defiant good ol' used to be.* Looking out the window I would see landmarks that were familiar from my travels in northern California, and the memories of freedom raced through my mind, but with every movement of my body I could hear the chains rattling, keeping me grounded in reality.

Soon we were in the downtown section of San Francisco in the six hundred block of Bryant Street consisting of enormous buildings, skyscrapers and high-rises. Pulling in the back of the county jail I couldn't help but think what a monstrosity of a building this jail is and at this time the population of prisoners in San Francisco County Jail was over six thousand. As full size black and white buses with tinted bared windows were being loaded and emptied with detainees going and coming from court, the two US Marshals led us into the back door to a series of elevators. Coming out on one of the upper levels in the booking section was a complete madhouse with lines of prisoners who were in various positions of locations waiting to do paperwork, get fingerprinted and pictures taken. The marshals proceeded to unlock our ankle shackles, handcuffs and belly chain that had connected Bobby and me together for the ride. The noise within this facility was phenomenal, talking, screaming and yelling all making this a complete institution nightmare. I was put in a line to be strip-searched and the gentleman in front of me was a black man in his mid-sixties with prosthetic legs connected above the knees. When the line moved making it his turn to be searched the officers had him strip down completely naked, remove both artificial legs and sit on the linoleum floor. He didn't look human at this point, more like a blob of flesh with his face having a look of dehumanizing humiliation and sadness.

Where the fuck am I, I thought?

It felt like I had slipped into the twilight zone and when it was my turn to be searched I stood there stern with my muscles tensed trying to balance out the humility of the room. This simple process of being dressed out, paperwork, fingerprinted again and pictures front and side also again took hours. I was then led up to a tank upstairs in the high-caliber section of this county jail. Separated from Bobby I was placed in a tank of thirteen other prisoners extremely ethnically unbalanced making me the only white boy. I grabbed the only open top bunk putting my sheets on the plastic jail mattress, jumped up and sat on my bed sizing up the environment. Nobody talked to me and I wasn't talking to anyone either, only receiving glancing looks in my direction once in a while.

The feeding process was very barbaric; at chow times officers would slide in fourteen trays, a loaf of bread and fourteen apples or some other fruit. Some prisoners, usually the bigger ones who were back in county jail from the penitentiary for various legal reasons would grab two trays and walk to the small day area tables and nonchalantly eat both trays of jail food. I would sit at the end of one of these tables distancing myself as much as I could from the others and slowly eat. I could see a couple of inmates sitting on their bunks without a tray of food; this happened every meal to the same inmates. They would go days without eating or saying a word about it and the only ones who cared less if they ate or not were the officers themselves.

Other officers dressed in riot gear complete with helmets waving nightsticks would patrol the long corridor separating the rows and rows of the tanks, which would face each other. Anyone yelling to another tank or waving their hands and arms through the bars would get hit as these officers known as the goon squad would walk by. That was the goon squad's eight-hour shift in San Francisco County Jail, walking

198

the endless corridors and levels of jail cells hitting people with their sticks.

At six o'clock in the evening they would roll in a black-and-white television on this rickety stand complete with rabbit ear antennas and the picture was never clear but the volume dial would work fine, and someone would always crank it up all the way. With every tank having a TV on full blast the noise level was indescribable and at nine in the evening they would roll the televisions back out and you could almost hear yourself think again.

For as noisy as it was at night, it was quiet in the early mornings, and as soon as the small day room door would slide open I would be in there doing my push-ups and pacing. Most everyone went back to sleep after breakfast, but with me never being one to sleep much, I would be in the day room every morning religiously. Only one other prisoner would be there consistently also always sitting at the end of the table writing or reading, although never speaking to each other we sometimes gave each other a half nod as a communication of acceptance.

Five days had passed and I had never uttered a word to anyone, I'd eaten every meal and I never got hit with a goon squad baton all due to my understanding of who I had become. This was a very primal environment with the one primal instinct needed, being the need to survive, and I was doing just fine in this jungle of concrete and steel.

On the morning of the sixth day, a guard came by telling me I had court after breakfast and to be ready. Since I have had no communication with Bobby, I felt that I would probably see him at court or in the holding cell waiting for court. Two guards escorted me to the lower level of the jail to an oversized holding pen, and as I was waiting to be let in the steel gate, I could see Bobby sitting on a bench in the back.

"Nice fuckin jail, right Bobby?"

"Yeah, real nice," as he patted me on the shoulder.

I sat down on the bench with Bobby, far away as we could from the other prisoners with this being the first time we had a chance to talk one-on-one since the FBI had snatched us up. So, quietly we discussed everything from our car, how the feds found us, what evidence could they possibly have against us and finally how we were going to get out of this major jackpot.

Bobby told me that he had spoken on the phone to the minister Gene to check on his kids and apologize for involving him. Gene relayed back to Bobby the FBI after a few hours of questioning, released him with no apology, the keys to the Chevy and Bobby's children. Bobby added that Gene said it was the most exciting thing that ever had happened to him, but felt it probably wasn't as exciting for us.

You got that shit right Gene, I thought to myself.

We decided the next time Bobby spoke to Gene he was to tell him to find a way to get the pink slip (California car title) to us and we would sign off on ownership to him. I'm sure the Reverend Gene would think of us as pretty good boys for doing that, but truth be told it was insurance in case the feds had a notion to confiscate our car permanently since we couldn't produce proof of buying the car with any means of legitimacy. Now for the next business at hand of our robbery charges, Bobby and I still had no clue on how we got busted or why.

We were not due in court until the afternoon court docket which started at one o'clock, and it was only seven thirty in the morning, so Bobby and I sat there on the wooden bench of the holding pen cutting it up with conversation and humor trying to pass the dead time away.

A little after noon we were taken to an elevator traveling up to one of the federal court rooms and instructed to sit in the jury box. There were two bailiffs, one civilian sitting in the back of the courtroom reading, and Bobby and I waiting for one o'clock, and as I looked around something seemed very odd to me. With summer close, all the courtroom windows were open and didn't have screens or bars. It felt very odd like you could run, jump out the window and be on the sidewalk in the middle of downtown free before anyone could lay a hand on you. Then I thought about the elevator ride, which had taken us twenty-six floors up, so my mental escape plan never materialized past my mental blueprint.

Slowly the courtroom started filling up and we were all instructed to stand as the judge entered and the court calendar started. I had to enter another plea of not guilty and was appointed federal legal counsel and the same process applied for Bobby. Sitting back in the jury box I was soon approached by a man in an ill-fitting suit and after stating his name and that he would be representing me, he informed me that the federal prosecution had offered an eight-year deal to plead guilty to the bank robbery today. Eight years, on what evidence went through my mind? I further stated to my federal mouthpiece that there had been no hearings on evidence or disclosure, probable cause and to this point I had only spoken to one lawyer previously with his only interest being a simple bail reduction. My federal lawyer gave me a funny look when I completed stating all these facts, a look of me knowing a lot about the law for being so innocent. He then explained to me federal law, which is completely different than state law. When pleading guilty involving a federal plea bargain the defendant can do so in any state in the United States, but if the defendant chooses a jury trial the defendant has to be tried in the state that the crime was committed. He added, if I wasn't going to accept the eight-year plea deal the federal government would start extradition proceedings. Now he asked, "It's your decision, what would you like to do?"

Thinking for a minute I said, "I would like to discuss this matter with my crime partner, excuse me counselor, I mean I would like to discuss this with my codefendant, Mr. Fay."

"I'll give you two some time to talk, motion me over when you're done," as he tapped Bobby's lawyer to come with him and give us some privacy.

Alone, the first thing I asked Bobby was how his lawyer's shoes looked? Bobby smirked and we both agreed there is no way we were gonna take eight years sight unseen plus eventually having to face the supermarket robbery charges in the same state as the bank charges. We wouldn't be able to avoid the inevitable of ending up in a state court house in the Midwest. We were starting to form some kind of game plan and prioritize our felonies in order of importance. If convicted on the bank it carried a twenty-five year sentence, the supermarket robbery carried a twenty-year sentence and the two California sentences started to seem small in comparison, as we had almost two years served on those sentences. Finally as for the walk-off charge we weren't even sure if such a charge did exist since thus far neither Bobby nor I had seen any paperwork on it. And trust me on this one, the legal system documents everything and so far no paperwork existed on our escape or my heroin possession. Things seemed to be looking up to me because of my imagination working overtime but in the real world this was just the beginning.

Standing up in the jury box, I waved my lawyer back over, "Mr. Fay and I decided to waive extradition and want to be granted a fast and speedy trial as guaranteed in the United States Constitution. You make this happen, thank you."

I noticed my lawyer shaking his head during his entire walk back over to Bobby's lawyer.

Back in the holding pen Bobby and I waited for a couple of hours till both our lawyers showed up holding extradition papers. It was explained to us if we were to waive extradition proceedings, the eight-year deal would be off the table and we would be transported to the state where the bank robbery was committed and the federal courts in that particular state would conduct the federal proceedings. They added, by waving our right to fight extradition, no deals were being promised within the jurisdiction of *that* state's federal court. Finally ending with, "Do you fully understand the agreement that was explained to you, if you were to choose to waive your rights to an extradition hearing?"

I signed my papers and Bobby signed his.

I was placed back in my tank just before that evening's meal. I was extremely tired from this long day of mostly waiting with only a few minutes of actual court business. After eating I climbed on my bunk to lie down and be done with another day, in the morning I was back in the day room doing my push-ups. My only job now was waiting to be transported out of state. As I was doing my morning workout routine the usual other prisoner was sitting at the end of the table reading, I was surprised when he opened his mouth to speak, "My name is Brazil, what happened in court yesterday?"

"My pleasure, Brazil, they call me Whisper, I'm being transported out of state for trial."

"Hope for the best and expect the worst, Whisper."

"I will."

That was the extent of my conversation in San Francisco County Jail before being told, "Roll um up."

19

Out of my jumpsuit and back into my street clothes, while I was getting dressed I noticed how wrinkled my slacks and shirt had become from constantly changing back and forth and stored in these county jails, but what could I do these were the only clothes I had. Bobby was getting dressed across from me and we looked at each other without expression.

Although the two new marshals looked unfamiliar, the road that we were on was very familiar, it was the way to the San Francisco airport and since I had taken this route many times, I recognized everything around me. And now with rain coming down hard along with a heavy wind off the San Francisco Bay the Ford Crown Victoria pulled into the Delta departure section at the airport. One marshal opened the back door to let us out and the other one drove off in the federal Ford, naturally Bobby and I were wrapped in chains, shackled and cuffed. I immediately noticed people giving a double take when looking my way but quickly we were escorted to a detainment holding area within the airport lobby. It looked just like a jail cell complete with bars, a bunk and a one-piece stainless steel toilet-sink. Seems everywhere I was going lately conveniently there was some sort of cell to put me in. The other officer was back now and both of them stood outside the cell instructing us how to act once on the flight. Their plan was that we would remain chained until we boarded the plane and once on the plane the cuffs, shackles and chains would come off because of federal law that restricts prisoners flying in restraints. Finally, I thought to myself a law that works in my favor.

So in the middle of the airport in the middle of the day two marshals are escorting me as I hobble the long-distance to the boarding gate. Bobby is directly to my left as anyone and everyone is stopping to stare, mothers are grabbing their kids, and husbands are pulling their wives closer and the only thing I notice is this white-haired old lady giving me a look as if she feels sorrow and pity for me. I wanted to shout out to her, "You think you feel bad for me, imagine how bad I feel for me," but of course I didn't I just kept hobbling until I got to the Delta departing gate. Once on board we shuffled to the back of the plane and all the hardware came off. Told to sit next to each other, I slid into the window seat with Bobby right next to me leaving the aisle seat unoccupied. The two marshals reiterated that they still had their weapons on them and for us to remain compliant before they sat directly behind us. And after both marshals were seated and with the plane starting to move, one had to make it a point to lean forward and tell Bobby and I not to attempt any escape from the plane.

My immediate thought was with the plane moving where were we going to go genius, run up to first class and hide?

Almost four hours had passed and as I looked out the window I noticed the plane starting to descend and everything looked beautiful down below, the little green trees, the matchbox type cars going in every direction with all the houses seeming so small from my aerial view. We had just flown over two thousand miles and the town below looked like a little village made from children's toys. This beauty was short-lived as the plane landed and taxied, stopping at the terminal. I recognized this airport also from my past travels as I was chained again, taken off the plane and turned over to another set of US Marshals who put their chains on me after the first set of marshals removed theirs. These J Edgar Hoover types are very thorough, that's one thing I was learning as I was transported to yet another county jail. Fingerprinted, pictures front side, and once again I was laid up waiting to enter a plea of not guilty in another federal courthouse, this one being in the Midwest.

The next morning after another not guilty plea in the federal courthouse, Bobby and I were picked up by a county agency to go enter a plea on the supermarket robbery. These two officers had none of the characteristics of the United States Marshals that had been transporting us here there and everywhere. They looked like they were right out of Andy of Mayberry and as we drove I noticed two manila envelopes in the front seat of their squad car. The top envelope had my complete name on it and the dollar amount of three thousand eight hundred and seventy-three dollars and some change; I assumed the other envelope had Bobby's money in it. This was the money that the FBI had taken as evidence and it got me to thinking. Even though I was cuffed and chained, I pointed with my lips to the front seat and Bobby seen what I seen. He gave me a look of what now and how?

As we drove the manipulation part of my brain kicked in and I was looking for an angle to get that money, then the one police that was driving said, "If you boys try to run, I'm too fat to chase you, so I would just have to shoot you. We both don't want that do we boys?"

The question seemed rhetorical so Bobby and I remained silent with my mind in high gear. As we got further away from the big city the countryside became more beautiful with every mile, massive farms, red barns, old Victorian style farmhouses and cattle grazing on the tall grass. Although I'd been to this state once before, I couldn't appreciate its beauty during the winter, it was truly magnificent. Then it hit me and I blurted out, "I sure am hungry. Have you boys eaten lunch?"

The fatter of the two fat cops then asked, "What did you have in mind?"

I went on to explain about how Mr. Fay and myself had been eating jail food for the past couple weeks and we sure could go for something different. Further explaining that was our money in the front seat and I would gladly buy us all lunch before we get to the courthouse and jail, and especially before our money gets put in our property to be later put on our books (books is a term used when the jail holds your money for you to spend on commissary, cosmetics, food products and such). Continuing, I suggested that they pick a restaurant since they knew the lay of the land and shortly thereafter we were pulling into a little country diner. "Order anything you want it's on me," I said.

Naturally Bobby and I had to stay in the car as one cop ate then coming out with our food the other cop went in and ate. This took a little time but that is the one thing that I seemed to have plenty of at this point in my young life, lots and lots of time. With part one of our plan successful, all I could hope for was that they would remain oblivious to the fact that the money in the front seat was going to be used as evidence. Looking at Bobby he half smiled back at me knowing what I know, cops like free stuff and fat cops like free food, all we could do now was hope as we kept riding with our bellies full through the beautiful Midwest farm lands.

The Red Earth County Courthouse in which we pled not guilty to the supermarket robbery and received another court-appointed lawyer was extremely small. The exterior was completely brick with large pillars in the front and inside in the only courtroom everything was wood, the tables, and chairs, bench, even the jury box seating with everything polished to a high gloss.

When the afternoon court proceedings were finished we were walked, not driven to the county jail, which was built on top of the sheriffs living quarters across the street from the courthouse. I felt I was in a bad Western movie and charged with cattle rustling or being a horse thief as I walked chained through the courtyard to the steps of the county jail.

Once inside the sheriff office everything looked like a step back in time, outdated file cabinets along with old worn out office furniture all crammed into one small office area. Then it was the usual again, fingerprints and pictures front and side and when given our paperwork the money showed up being on our property voucher. Maybe things were starting to look up? But in my heart of hearts I knew this was not true, I knew I was fucked but didn't know how fucked I was since I was still unsure of any incriminating evidence the federal government and Red Earth County had on us.

We stayed in Red Earth County Jail that weekend and this was the first time that I realized what a big hole I was in. I needed to put on my legal thinking cap and come up with some questions if and when my lawyer ever showed up. Bobby and I devised a plan to get rid of the lion's share of our money sending it home to his mother so she could disperse it to us when needed in small amounts, this along with signing the ownership of the car away would eliminate questions by the authorities of having a new car and a large amount of cash with no visible means of support. Naturally I donated to Bobby's mother a portion of my money trying to stay in good standing with her.

The Red Earth County Jail had a maximum capacity of sixteen people and this was a refreshing change from the constant noise and chaos of the other county jails. And on our first weekend besides Bobby and me there was only one other prisoner, a young skinny longhaired kid charged with possession of marijuana and we immediately nicknamed him Stick-Man. The feeding in this county jail was unique also with the sheriff's mother cooking all our meals and then delivered to us by a dumbwaiter. Often she would ring the bell and I would pull the rope and a there would be a note from her asking what we would like to eat? We talked another sheriff into going to the Piggly Wiggly market down the street to buy us zoo-zoos and wham whams, cosmetics, cigarettes, magazines and any other thing that we desired. It's as if I had died and gone to county jail heaven.

But on Monday the US Marshals transported us to yet another county jail located in a big city. This particular jail had more Plexiglas than bars and I had a little narrow window that overlooked the Mississippi River from my eighth floor cell, the Plexiglas window created an illusion of my freedom only being two inches away. I would constantly stare at the river watching the many barges push their cargo north and south throughout the day, and in the early morning with the steam rising from the muddy river I would see people rowing these long, pointed skinny boats. Later I learned this was a sport called Sculling and I would wish I could be one of the people rowing up and down the Mississippi. While daydreaming I would also hope that nobody had found that bag of guns that I had thrown so casually when hastily leaving this state previously. I was still in the dark about how they had tracked us down and why they had gotten onto us? But

210

with my federal disclosure of evidence hearing coming soon I should get all the answers.

Finally seeing my federal lawyer he stated that we should consider a plea bargain with me firmly emphatic about a jury trial, I also asked him to investigate the how and why of my arrest relaying to him that he worked for me now and I have some questions I need answers for. At this point my lawyer didn't seem to care for me much, but fuck him and fuck a plea agreement since I haven't seen one shred of evidence incriminating me. Starting to read the beat up and small selection of law books having to be supplied to me legally, I was looking for any loophole to freedom. After my evidence hearing Bobby and I were taken to another county jail and being bounced all over the state was getting really old, also I found out the only evidence against me were thirty-three witnesses, all the people, employees as well as customers within the bank at the time of the robbery. I was completely overwhelmed with where to start digging myself out of this hole combined with the guards and even some of the prisoners treating us differently because we acted and carried ourselves differently than these local yokels. I knew it would be next to impossible to change the guards' points of view, but as for the prisoners, with a couple of horrific ass whippings the other prisoners got in line. Facing forty-five years one's attitude can become questionable and Bobby's and my attitudes became extremely questionable with a hair trigger of tolerance.

One morning pacing in the catwalk area, I noticed a young prisoner hanging in his cell by a homemade rope made from a bed sheet, immediately I called out to Bobby. With me lifting the body to get the weight off his neck, Bobby jumped up on the top bunk and untied the bed sheet from the steel vent. The police came charging in, grabbing Bobby and I, cuffing us and screaming how we were animals. Calmly

211

Bobby explained to them how we were saving this kid's life and ended his explanation with a big fuck you. They weren't buying it so they locked Bobby and me into our cells. The kid explained to the police that we had gotten him down and after thinking about it, he really didn't want to die. The police still kept us on lockdown status pending further investigation. The kid turned out to be doing only ten days and just thought he couldn't handle it, coming to our cell and thanking both of us we immediately nicknamed him Hang 'Um High after one of Clint Eastwood's western movies. In a couple of days the police without apology or gratitude let us back in general population, and Bobby sometimes bored would make these short bed sheet ropes and throw them in Hang 'Um High's cell when he walked by. The kid would laugh and we would laugh and within a couple of days Hang 'Um High got a cellmate who was also doing ten days and he was liking the idea of living again realizing ten days would pass.

But I was tired of all this variety in these bullshit county jails, and the variety of the guard's bullshit mentality in these jails also. I thought I had found something useful in one of the law books I was reading, so I called my state appointed attorney. I had him file what is called a writ of habeas corpus for Bobby and I, guaranteeing we would be held in Red Earth County for the remainder of our federal as well as our state trials. Bobby and I were immediately transferred back to Red Earth County with the understanding that after every court hearing, federal or state, we would be housed in Red Earth County Jail. Finally I thought to myself, some solace in this crazy confusing situation that I had gotten myself into.

I started getting answers to my how and why from my lawyer, and I was taken completely back by what I was finding out. The chance meeting in that Midwest café with Tony Lofton was the root of why I

212

was arrested. According to my lawyer, Mr. Lofton after seeing me and Bobby went home that evening and told his wife of our freak encounter. When the local news aired the story of the supermarket and later that week of the bank robbery, his wife questioned him on if he thought it could be his two former prison mates committing these robberies? Tony must have been hen pecked into submission and grown a conscious, so he eventually decided to call the FBI and give them our names as possible suspects. I don't know if it was the metamorphosis of change in his moral values or the five thousand dollars reward he would receive upon apprehension and conviction, but he definitely put the FBI on to us. Personally I suspect it was the money. As for the other part of my question on how did they track us down? After the FBI receiving our names they simply followed the movements of Bobby's kids, which inevitably lead them to the restaurant in Scotts Valley.

All I could think of was what are the odds? A series of events that with all the planning in the world I couldn't have avoided, really what are the odds? Oh yeah, I had another thought also, that I wish Tony were dead.

But after the smoke had cleared from my angry brain, I realized all the evidence against me was only circumstantial and there might be a way out of this jackpot yet.

After all parties involved realizing we were demanding a jury trial on all charges, it became like a carnival sideshow with deception, magic and state and federal clowns all around us. Learning if we let the federal government prosecute us first it would be to our advantage so that's what we did. First we were driven over eighty miles to the federal building and separated for a physical lineup so the witnesses could view us individually through a one-way glass. When

213

Bobby arrived in his viewing room he was in a wheelchair claiming he had fallen in the holding area and couldn't walk, this was to throw the witnesses off any height identification. Beautiful I thought, why didn't I think of this? The entire lineup lasted almost six hours and neither of us was identified even once by the thirty-three witnesses, and I noted to my lawyer, "All the others in my lineup with me have light blue eyes and I have very dark eyes, shouldn't you say something to the prosecuting attorney?"

He said nothing as he wrote something in his notebook. That was my first clue to where my lawyer gets his paychecks from, the federal government. Part of the lineup process was verbal and I had to read out loud off this five by seven index card, "I want these-I want those-give me these-give me those."

And even another portion of the lineup we were furnished ski masks and had to wear them as we went up to the glass to be viewed.

But still no one picked me as the one who robbed the Security State Bank, and no one picked Bobby either. If anyone was keeping score I felt as if we had won the first round. Also not being able to produce any weapons or bank money, all the feds were left with were pictures of the two suspects inside robbing the bank. I had personally seen these pictures, and if this was the evidence that the FBI were going to convict on, you would then have to charge the entire United States Olympic Ski Team with bank robbery since the assailants were wearing ski masks and parkas in the robbery. My cockiness was resurfacing and this cat and mouse game that I was involved in with the federal government would completely occupy my mind. But after a couple of days of federal game playing I would be laid back up in Red Earth County Jail for long periods of time waiting for my next federal court date. It would be the usual doing my push-ups, reading and jail hijinks and because of low crime in this county not many prisoners were brought to this jail leaving at times Bobby and I the only ones in there, once even for over a two-week period. Summer had arrived in full force and it was sweltering, I would find myself taking cold showers up to three times a day to break up the time and once in a while we would get visits from detectives trying to pin other crimes on us trying to clear their unsolved cases. Although we had robbed two banks in the neighboring state, one two states over and one down south, nothing they were trying was sticking.

They even tried to charge me one time with robbing a Kentucky Fried Chicken with an axe. Usually I would never speak a word to the detectives but this time I couldn't resist as I told him, "I would never put a hatchet to the Colonel. That would be un-American!"

With the heat being daily turned up by summer Bobby's and my temperament became stretched to the limit. One evening as we watched the news on the little black and white television propped on a chair in the common area, it was reported a man was arrested for hurting a twenty-month-old baby and possibly sexual assault. The news went on to say the man's name and that he was being held in Red Earth County Jail. Only one other prisoner was brought in that day and he had gone right to his bunk and had been sleeping the entire afternoon, so after this news story immediately Bobby showed up at the side of his bunk telling him to wake up and asking him his name. After Bobby insisted loudly a couple more times this guy finally woke up. Bobby then asked him his name and what he was in jail for? Although his name did match the man on the news he stated his charges were nothing more than a big misunderstanding by the local police as I stood by the cell door watching and listening. Bobby firmly raised his voice saying, "You have to leave, you can't live in here with us."

"Leave?" The guy said confused, "I can't leave."

"Muthafucka you have to leave... NOW."

After three attempts of begging the jail officer to be moved, the sheriff then looked over at Bobby and I and then back at the man telling him, "You're in jail you can't leave, and sometimes you have to pay for your sins."

In Bobby's mind that was the green light for vigilante justice and Bobby clocked him with a right hook knocking him out on his feet. Bobby kept hitting him, the body, the head and back to the body. The guy was positioned against the cell wall and Bobby was so close the child predator couldn't fall, so the beating continued knocking out two of his teeth and making his face into hamburger. Finally on the ground Bobby and I dragged him to the shower throwing him in unconscious and turning on the hot water, he awoke for a split second and Bobby added, "Stay in there."

We heard the shower being turned off as we sat back down on our homemade couch made out of jail mattresses to finish watching the news. Later we ate dinner and went to bed and I drifted into a peaceful sleep.

In the morning as I opened my eyes three sheriff officers were standing around me with one telling me to get up. As I was being cuffed behind my back I could see the same was happening to Bobby in his cell, then we were both escorted downstairs to another jail cell that we were unaware of that was adjacent to the Sheriff's office. The watch commander came to our cell door telling us they found an inmate huddled in the shower bloodied and scared and did we know anything about it? I said nothing but Bobby volunteered some insight, "Boss, some people don't adjust to jail very well."

The watch commander then turned around and left.

Long story short two weeks went by, no towels, no sheets and no shower and in the summer's unforgiving humidity lying on plastic jail mattress only intensified our rage. On the sixteenth day Bobby received a lawyer visit and on his way back being escorted into this makeshift segregation cell he bolted from the officer and grabbed a can used for change by the coffee pot, filling it up with scalding coffee and now holding the escorting officer hostage with the hot coffee. These past months of trial and county jail were making both of us a little crazy and it was Bobby's turn to be crazier as he was only trying to get the guards attention on humane treatment for us with clean linens and daily showers. To my surprise these tactics worked and we were given clean sheets and showers with no charges filed against us. Gotta love these small towns, and after another week we were brought back upstairs after the predatory piece of garbage was gone. As for the officer that gave us the green light to do what we did, the only times that we would ever talk to him was only to say, "You're weak. Fuck you."

This is how Bobby and I passed the summer.

The state trial became a series of postponements as they were waiting for the feds to make their case against us. We would still have to periodically show up in the state courthouse, but all in all it seemed to me that the scales of justice were tipping in my direction. Outside the leaves on the trees were turning yellow and red and it was fall with the air coming into the cell window cool and sweet, and it would remind me of California. I missed being young, being free and in general I missed the beauty of the coastline of the Golden State.

A trial date was set to pick a jury of my peers on the bank robbery charges, a jury of my peers, I thought? These people didn't look like me, talk like me or act like me, but according to the federal government these were my peers. Although they had the right bank and the right person in court, it's not what you know it's what you could prove and my confidence was very high. Dreaming of a not guilty verdict because to my unknowing eyes they lacked any evidence of substance, what they did have was only hearsay evidence from an assumption that the rat Tony Lofton, who's only motivation was profiteering off the reward money subsequently causing him to dial the phone on a hunch. They had no receipts and no paperwork whatsoever tying me to this Midwest region during, before or after this particular bank was robbed. With the state charge of robbery of the supermarket there only evidence seemed to hinge on the federal government's evidence and this created to me reasonable doubt. Now if I could just get the jury to agree, I should be walking out both of these courtrooms unscathed. And as for the charges in California, I figured I would jump off that bridge when I got to it.

Now with the jury picked I daily sat at the defendant's table watching everything unfold as the same scales of justice started tipping towards the prosecution. One morning the United States prosecuting attorney brought in a shotgun and a couple of pistols laying them on a big table and telling the jury that these were the weapons from the bank job. Furthermore he continued by saying a little six-year-old girl had found these weapons with the shotgun loaded and the safety off.

FUCK, where do they get off with this crazy stunt?

218

I had personally dumped all the artillery from the Security State heist into the Mississippi River. The only way that these weapons could be mine and Bobby's was if this little six-year-old girl was scuba diving and somehow miraculously attached the barrel back onto the shotgun. This shotgun in the courtroom wasn't even sawed-off. I thought to myself, I would be embarrassed for myself, and for all the bank robbers in the world, if I brought a full-size rifle to a bank robbery, it would just be too awkward and clumsy. Two FBI agents sat in the courtroom totally collaborating the prosecuting attorney's story, which completely angered me, and I attempted to throw a chair at the two agents. Not my finest hour as two bailiffs wrestled me down to the ground then taking me out of the courtroom, when returned I was in restraints. Now I knew exactly how I looked to the jury, like a guilty madman. But as the trial continued more lies surfaced from the FBI and prosecutor opening my eyes to the real facts of the case. Yes, it's true, I was lying every time I spoke in court, but for some reason I didn't think the agencies representing the good guys should lie, to me that was cheating.

The prosecuting attorney called a sudden recess in court proceedings and I was escorted out of the courtroom and down to a holding cell in the courthouse. With all this court mumbo-jumbo I had no idea what was going on next, but waiting had become a virtue for me as I sat on the wooden bench. In about an hour and a half time my attorney showed up at the holding cell bringing me some news, "The government will give you ten years if you plead guilty."

Then I asked, "What about Mr. Fay? What about the supermarket? What about the charges in California?"

Bobby and I had been given separate trials for what they were calling conflict of interest, so I would never make a move without consulting with him. Bobby's trial was still in jury selection, so my input on how they were acting in court could be detrimental in our decision. I asked my lawyer if I could have a meeting with Bobby along with both of our attorneys. He left and shortly returned saying the prosecution had no problem with Bobby and I discussing the plea deal offered. Shortly Bobby came walking up to my holding cell and behind him were our two poor excuses for lawyers. The deal was laid out by my lawyer and Bobby and I walked to the back of the cell to discuss it among ourselves privately, and on our return we sat down on the wooden bench and I said to the attorneys as they stood, "We will take the ten years if the supermarket sentence of time wasn't one day over ten years, and the two California charges were thrown in also with everything running concurrent. And we want everything in writing!"

Bobby was taken back to his holding cell and the two attorneys went in the opposite direction, I lay down on the wooden bench exhausted closing my eyes. I was tired, but couldn't fall asleep with my mind all over the place. Ten years was better than forty-five years in the big picture but it was still ten years and everything seemed to stop around me with the lyrics of a Bobby Fuller Four song stuck in my head, "I fought the law and the law won—breaking rocks in the hot sun—I fought the law and the law won."

My eyes opened to the sound of the holding cell gate being unlocked with my lawyer walking in with some papers containing the information on my plea agreement. After reading it I signed the next ten years of my life away with my lawyer explaining that Bobby was doing the same in another holding cell within the confines of the courthouse.

Transported back to Red Earth County Jail we now waited for our next upcoming court date to complete this plea agreement promise. Back in the county lockup Bobby or I never gave it a second thought to our decision and it became business as usual as we waited. Finally the day arrived in which we were taken to state court to receive our next ten years with the judge asking, "Were either of you promised anything in exchange for pleading guilty to robbery in the first-degree in Red Earth County?"

I answered first, "I was, Your Honor. I was promised a maximum sentence of ten years in the Department of Corrections to run concurrently with my federal sentence."

This judge was not happy with the federal government making his hands tied as a judge on any sentence passed down to me since the maximum sentence he could give was equal or less to the federal sentence, I knew it and he knew that I knew it. The federal prosecutor had made this deal without the state's prior knowledge and the federal government wasn't that pleased with the states jurisdiction either for bumbling the alleged evidence money because some overweight cop was hungry. But having these two agencies of the law in conflict was little consolation for me since I was the one receiving state and federal time. He asked the same questions to Bobby and Bobby's answers were the same as mine.

The judge then asked me if I had anything to say before sentencing.

"I do, Your Honor, I think *probation* is appropriate in this case."

The judge had no sense of humor as he sentenced me to ten years and a fine, stating the fine would equal the amount of money taken from this supermarket safe. Immediately I said, "Your Honor the deal that I struck with the federal government definitely states that you cannot give me a harsher sentence, and besides you can't punish me twice for the same crime."

He came back with, "Son you got it all wrong. The fine is your only punishment, the ten years is to isolate you from society."

Quickly I spoke up, "I'm not your son."

Then a lightweight argument erupted between the judge and me. I stated that the supermarket was claiming a certain amount of money taken which was thousands of dollars more than the actual amount and only the robber would be the one to know the exact amount for sure. Although the actual amount was in the thousands, but not as much as the supermarkets claim, I felt the ball was in my court and I could decide what this bullshit fine would be.

The smirking judge then asked, "Well, how much was in the safe?"

I covered the microphone at the podium and softly spoke to Bobby, and we came up with an amount that we could both live with since we had no plans of ever paying it. I relayed this message to the judge, "The amount from the robbery was fourteen hundred and fifty dollars, Your Honor."

He didn't like it but fuck him; if the supermarket was gonna lie about the amount for insurance purposes then why shouldn't I lie. Besides no self-respecting criminal should tell the truth under oath!

20

Now my only job was to wait, and I was getting extremely good at waiting with no clue or idea of what was next. I did notice the Red Earth County Jail sheriff's treating us different after our sentencing, almost sympathetic or maybe empathetic, whatever it was it was different. Bobby and I had brought excitement to this small town jail and maybe it would be missed, or they realized how much time had been stacked against us, seeing us as young and not that bad. Some of the guards even wished us well and suggested we turn our lives around when we get out. That would've probably been a better suggestion before all these robberies I thought but the reality of it was I wouldn't have heard any suggestion of positivity, doing what I want when I want had been my personality my entire life thus far and now it was time to pay.

The wait was less than two weeks and on a sunny day in late autumn, we were instructed to gather all our property to prepare for transport. The United States Marshals had arrived. Wrapped in chains Bobby and I were tethered together by a long belly chain and put in the back of a government car with the usual warning of no funny business. The marshals started driving south towards the center of the country, and Bobby as well as I had no inkling where we were headed and didn't ask. There was no conversation or interaction between the four of us in the car, and I stared out my side of the car with my mind without any tangible thoughts as my eyes soaked in the countryside. I knew that my eyes were going to be the closest form of freedom for a while.

After a couple of hundred miles the marshals booked us into a small county jail somewhere in the Badlands of the Dakotas, this particular jail was despicable and extremely dirty. These small off-the-beaten-path county jails would contract the federal government to house prisoners when in route and this one was downright nasty. No mattress or linen and there was no shower even in the day room where Bobby and I ended up sleeping on the concrete floor with a roll of toilet paper for a pillow. In the morning the marshals picked us up along with another prisoner, and now the belly chain tied us altogether. He was some hillbilly that wanted to talk and ask too many questions, such as my charges and how much time I received. With about fifty miles of questions passing I finally simply said, "Do me a favor Holmes, and shut the fuck up."

He never said a word the rest of the day until we dropped him in some obscure city in one of the Great Plains states. That evening was the same as our first, with another beat up small county jail for our resting place, but on the third day one of the marshals after looking at our files turned around telling us that one of us was designated to do their time in Leavenworth Penitentiary and one of us was going to be sent on to McNeil Island.

Exchanging glances with Bobby I thought to myself how we weren't going to spend the next decade together, something I had never thought of, also where is McNeil Island? I knew where Leavenworth was; everyone did because of its infamous and notorious historic reputation. Leavenworth was often referenced in movies and television crime dramas and simply known as not a good place to be. Without asking or without any conversation we continued driving down the highway, which passed through a vast wasteland of livestock grazing and rolling hills.

I could see American Buffalo wandering as we turned off the main highway onto this long paved roadway leading to a building of massive size and grandeur with the sign on the side of the roadway reading United States Penitentiary Leavenworth Kansas. Once the car stopped, parking directly in front of the prison, that's when I could see how big this place really was, and it kept getting larger as Bobby and I hobbled up the oversized steps into the prison itself. We were hurried through the rotunda area into R and D, receiving and discharge. There we were stripped of our street clothes and given wrinkled khaki pants and a khaki shirt, instructed to put our street clothes along with all of our personal belongings into a box to be sent home. I didn't have a home, so Bobby said to put his mother's address on the box, and as I finish writing the address of Oxnard, California, I realized how far I was from anything familiar to me. Bobby and I were the only ones in R and D at this time and still the paperwork, fingerprinting and picture process seemed to go very slow. Bobby was issued a number of 89758-132, and I was issued my number next in the sequence, 89759-132. The first five digits is your personal prison number with the last three after the dash representing the location and region that you received your prison number. 132 simply represented Leavenworth Penitentiary. It was now past chow time so we were given bag dinners consisting of two sandwiches, an orange and two cookies along with a small carton of milk. After the prison guard was through with his part of the receiving, a convict took over issuing us jail soap, toothbrush and toothpaste, along with a double-edged razor and some shaving cream. We were also given three sets of underwear and undershirts, socks, a prison coat and penitentiary boots then escorted to an orientation housing section located under B block. Being locked in my single cell that night I couldn't help notice how old everything was, Leavenworth being originally a fort in the year eighteen twenty-seven and becoming a prison in nineteen thirty it to me looked as if it had not changed any since being built. Even my cell located under B block was originally a horse stall used for government mules and workhorses, this place was definitely petrified with age.

In the morning the cell doors were un-racked at six, but I had been up for over an hour washing up, shaving along with my morning constitution on the toilet. Six thirty and the main cellblock was cracked open allowing us to go to breakfast. Having to wear a collared shirt buttoned up and tucked in we were instructed to walk along this thick painted yellow line in the main corridor towards the chow hall. Although the corridor was the size of a two-lane highway it was still very crowded with some prisoners on the other side walking the opposite direction also on a yellow line. This place was like a little city with everything so grand in size and so obviously old that I felt like I was in another era. My first impression when walking into the chow hall was of racial divide and while standing in line in my wrinkled receiving clothes I could feel the eyes upon me, but it wasn't my clothes causing the looks but more because I was a fresh face fish. So along with Bobby, I stood in line waiting to grab my tray and eat breakfast. After being served our food Bobby and I sat in the area that seemed to be neutral, and as we ate I kept my eyes focused on my tray. This place was crazy and how did I know? Because of the vibrations of tension that anyone paying attention could easily feel.

"I'm Donny, Donny from Sac town," as he reached out and shook my hand then turning doing the same with Bobby. Although Donny was from

226

Sacramento, the north and south feud was low key in the federal system while people from all over the United States as well as Alaska and Hawaii were thrown into this melting pot of prisoners being held in federal penitentiaries, so the representation is more by state rather than region. I liked Donny immediately and so did Bobby. But I could tell he was wound up tighter than a three dollar watch with the look in his eyes unmistakably wild, and for some reason the prison issue clothing seem to look better on him than most, and along with his jet black hair and well-trimmed pencil thin mustache he was very groomed and handsome.

After breakfast the three of us sat on Bobby's bunk cutting it up with conversation and laughing for over two hours reminiscing about being in California, and nobody at any time asked the other one how much time they were doing or what they were convicted of. That's just the way it is, this subject never really comes up for the simple reason you don't want to remind someone or be reminded of how fucked you really are.

The next morning I was awakened at four thirty and taken down to R and D for transfer. Given a bag containing sandwiches, cookies and an apple for breakfast I then was completely stripped of my prison clothing, searched and given a fresh set of prison clothing. I waited in the bullpen with other prisoners until we were chained and loaded onto a bus. As we boarded the bus you stated your full name as well as your prison number, and were offered a pack of Camel non-filter cigarettes or Kool menthols. The bus itself was relatively nondescript having no prison logo on the outside, only heavily tinted barred windows. Inside having two guards in the front area with one driver, all separating us from them with a steel mesh petition. In the back on the driver's side of the bus was a steel mesh cage containing another officer with all three prison guards having weapons. Two canisters were secured in the back area, one with coffee and one with water and a bathroom lavatory area in the rear. As we rolled down the highway, the bus would sway and react to every bump and dip in the road and being chained only made the ride that more uncomfortable.

Looking around I could easily separate the seasoned long-term traveler convicts from the newer riders. I use the restroom only once and decided to limit drinking water or coffee to avoid ever using it again, shackled and cuffed with a belly chain makes the simplest tasks a major project. When eating the sandwiches provided or drinking any beverage, I would have to bend my upper body so my hand and mouth would coordinate. Having to do the process of unzipping to use the restroom on the constant moving bus you had to almost be a physics graduate. I would watch and notice how some of the bus veterans never used the restroom, and I assumed this was from body control, and with my personal goals a priority I wanted to be the best convict I could be. I gave it a shot by mentally telling myself to slow everything down internally and it worked, so I started enjoying an afternoon cup of lukewarm coffee with my Camel no-filter cigarette along the seemingly endless bus ride that first day on my way to McNeil Island.

Fourteen hours on the road and finally we were pulling into another federal prison to be housed, getting off the bus was the morning sequence in reverse of stating your full name, prison number and returning what was left of your cigarettes back to the guard. Taken into that prison's receiving and discharge section I stripped off all the prison clothing from the morning, was searched and given a fresh different set of clothing and escorted to a segregation cell. I had managed to bring a fresh pack of cigarettes with me by stuffing them in my boxers when exiting the bus, not everyone smoked on the bus but every prisoner would take a pack so the smokers would end up with two. This enabled me to create giving back a partial pack while keeping a full pack on my body, and when switching clothes after being strip-searched you had a chance at grabbing the fresh pack from your previous clothing if the guard wasn't looking. This may sound like a lot of work, but if you're a smoker, a pack of cigarettes in segregation is a luxury item. While in transit we were unable to go to commissary or receive mail, so the attempt to get over on the police with a simple pack of smokes to make your stay more comfortable was always worth a shot.

In the early morning hour while still dark outside, the process to get ready for another fourteen-hour day of riding the bus began again. This was repeated for every day we traveled, and the only change was the amount of time that we might stay in a particular prison while we were waiting for the next bus. Sometimes overnight, sometimes two or three days or even a week, but we were always isolated from the main prison with the bare necessities of amenities. And although there was a radio on the bus, all this seemed to do was cause the racial differences to be more apparent. The whites insisted on country music, the black's rhythm and blues and the Hispanics wanting something in their native language. In a weak attempt the guards would try to pacify the busload by allotting equal time for each style of music, this never worked and there was always somebody screaming some slur about the guards being bias. All I would do was stare out the window on my side of the bus, seeing endless and endless miles of open space with the terrain ever-changing as we entered or left another state, from Oklahoma down to Texas and across New Mexico, Arizona and California then north through the state of Oregon into Washington. The bigger states of Texas and California would take us more than one day of traveling to get through, and when we were driving in California I couldn't help really feeling my lack of freedom since I was in my home state and could only look and not touch. This entire trip had taken over three weeks to get from Leavenworth, Kansas up to McNeil Island located in the Puget Sound of Washington state. My body was tired from all the bag lunches, fourteen hour travel days and being housed in various segregation cells with no outside exercise, but I was now at my destination, the federal penitentiary for the west coast region at McNeil Island. All I could think about was this country song that I kept hearing over and over as I traveled northwest on the prison bus, the song was by Crystal Gayle and the title said it all, *Don't It Make My Brown Eyes Blue.*

I couldn't help thinking to myself, yes Miss Crystal Gayle it definitely does make my brown eyes blue.

With no moon, it was a very dark night as the bus stopped where the road met the water, and we sat with the only noise that of the bus engine. I could make out the silhouettes of pine trees all around with everything looking very wet. The guard opened the steel mesh gate in the front area, and I exited along with the other prisoners stating my name and number as I stepped off the bus with another guard at the head of the dock shaking our cuffs as a security measure. I walked down the dock onto a tugboat style ferry, took a seat and waited with my thoughts for a quick moment wondering how did I get here? Sitting at the southern part of the Puget Sound on a boat and going to a penitentiary that was located on an island, is this really happening? As the ferry left the dock I could see a perimeter of lights in the far distance which I was more than sure was going to be my destination, but the small boat was headed in the direction to the far right of the lights, this I found out later was because of the extreme currents of the Puget Sound. As we got closer to the island I could start to make out large buildings inside the perimeter of lights and immediately noticed the noise I could hear coming from those buildings. Even though the sound of the boats engine was very prominent, the closer we got to the island the prison noise started over ruling the ferries motor. This was my new home and instantly I had contempt for this place, but I was stuck. No, I was more than stuck. I was completely fucked. I could remember the advice that this older convict named Buddy had given me, and although I didn't know what it meant I felt I needed to practice this valuable piece of guidance. He had simply told me, "Walk slow and drink plenty of water."

Once again I was strip-searched and given fresh clothing along with some sheets and a blanket, boots and coat then escorted to a humongous cellblock and told, "Your cell number is 3i4, fifth tier on the far right and lock up of time is ten with lights out at eleven."

And as the guard walked off I stood there alone trying to not look new which turned out to be impossible, my wrinkled clothing, sheets, and net bag with issue cosmetics and underwear told the truth, that I was very new. Asking questions in prison is not good, asking strangers questions in prison is really not good, but I had to break down and question someone because I didn't know where I was. There were so many people going every direction with purpose and I stood there trying to pick that one prisoner that wouldn't interpret my asking as weak. "Excuse me Holmes, where is 3i4?"

"All the way up," was all he said as he kept walking pointing up to the right side of the cellblock.

I climbed the concrete stairs all the way to the top and then walked all the way down the tier to the last cell. The cell itself was pretty good sized, but after putting five sets of bunk beds along with eleven metal lockers, a small table, a couple of folding chairs and one toilet, this made the cell crowded. As I stood outside I could see six other prisoners moving around in the cell, and as one glanced at me all I said was, "3i4?"

"You from California?" he stated firmly.

I nodded my head as I slowly entered the cell and seeing one of the top bunks empty I looked at the same prisoner as I was almost asking permission to put my property on the bunk. Right before they were gonna lock our cell door three other prisoners came in the cell making a total of ten. I could hear the mechanism engaging the cell door and a few minutes later a guard came by securing the door with another lock by using an oversized brass key. Instantly after the guard passing one of my cellmates started twisting up a thin joint on top of his locker and then lit it up. A couple of others joined him and they passed the joint around as one of the fellas looked at me and asked, "Do you want a hit?"

I took a couple of hits and one of the first things that I noticed was how blatant the rolling up and smoking process was, and one of the guys must have seen my concern. After exhaling the weed smoke, he looked at me smiling, "What are they gonna do, put us in jail?

We all chuckled and kept smoking.

"Breakout some cookies Homeboy," one of them said as another asked me where I was from.

"Southern California, the town of Oxnard," and I continued, "Know where that is?"

"I not only know where it is, I've been there many times. Chiques, (pronounced cheek-ez) right? My name is Richie, Richie Rich, from Simi Valley."

As I stuck out my hand with a greeting handshake and an introduction as Whisper, I knew for a fact Richie knew where Oxnard was, since Chiques was the nickname given to Oxnard, and mostly the only people that know that are people that had been there. The next morning I was hanging out in front of the cell thinking about how high up I was on the fifth tier and noticing the catwalk directly across from me, exclusively used by the guards carrying carbine rifles. Richie motioned for me to join him for breakfast, so we both started the five-story descend to the bottom part of the cellblock called the flats. In the chow hall it was the usual racial divide and I noticed another small area that seemed to be a neutral zone. After breakfast Richie informed me that he had to go off to work in the plumbing department and I let him know that I had to go to my mandatory orientation and physical.

All the fresh face fish, including myself, sat in this oversize room waiting for our next instructions as a guard shortly entered demanding our attention. He started out stating we could only address him and other guards as officer, boss or the last name engraved on their nametags. But to us we privately referred to the guards as bulls, screws or hacks. The boss man went on to say a list of rules and regulations heavily stressing the no stabbing and the no killing of another inmate rule, adding anyone involved in violence or possession of a makeshift weapon would be prosecuted within the prison as well as prosecuted in an outside federal court. He went on to explain the inside prison court system which consisted of two lieutenants and a captain sitting on a panel and after hearing the evidence from your write-up, also known as a shot, a ruling on your disposition would be made. Also the defendant was allowed to have a guard represent them in the kangaroo court proceedings, this system screamed justice was my first thought. Continuing the guard then reiterated on the no stabbing-no kill rule nonchalantly as he finished with the hygiene and dress code of the federal system. Buttoned up collared shirt tucked in at all mealtimes in the mess hall, no beards with your mustache no longer than the corners of your mouth, sideburns no longer than the middle of the ear and the back of your hair not touching the collar of your shirt. The officer in charge of orientation then asked everyone in the room if they completely understood the rules of the institution, and nobody answered as he dismissed us.

Next I went to the infirmary for my medical checkup which was no more than a doctor listening to my heart, a tuberculosis test and questionnaire paperwork asking my physical issues. I checked off the little NO boxes as quickly as I could so I could be finished with this little bullshit physical and finally finishing up the orientation process with a mandatory psychiatric evaluation. Called into the psychiatrist's office I sat there across the desk from the doctor just thinking what a quack this muthafucker must be to have all that schooling and end up with a job in prison. The doctor asked me a series of questions ranging from my childhood to my prison experiences, and I sat there listening never saying one word back to him, not one single word as he wrote notes on this note pad. And in a sophisticated tone he stated, "I've diagnosed you as sociopathic and extremely antisocial."

As I walked out of his office I felt I needed to get the last word, "You must have some super powers Doc, being able to get that diagnosis telepathically. You should be put up for the Nobel Peace Prize."

All that orientation shit had made me very hungry and very tired and it was already time for lunch so I went to the chow hall and after eating went back up to my cell to lay on my bunk and rest, although I wanted to nap I didn't, another golden rule of survival that I already knew. The three main vulnerable places people get killed in prison are the shower, on the toilet or asleep when the cell door is unlocked. Although I couldn't see light at the end of the tunnel on my ten year sentence, I wasn't going to receive an early release through death.

Only being able to lie there for a moment because of my mind racing I headed down the five flights of stairs and through the main hallway to the yard. Since being busted I had not fully evaluated my situation thoroughly and as I walked the track on the yard I tried to make some rhyme or reason out of all this craziness. After a couple of laps on the quarter-mile track I got out of my head long enough to look around at my surroundings, the double razor wire fence gave me a view of the Puget Sound and although beautiful I didn't like it since I was able to look at freedom. The sky was grey and it had just finished raining and looked as if it was going to start up again, everything was wet and everywhere I looked, the pine trees, the distant shore everything just seemed to be saturated from the constant rain. From my outside view in the yard the cellblocks and other adjoining buildings looked old and decrepit with one overall feel being that of gloom, I could feel my fighting defiance surfacing when one of my passing thoughts was, what would Papillion do?

I made up my mind right then to become the strongest man that I could, I would run laps on this track, I would do push-ups, more push-ups than I've ever done, I would read and I would pay close attention to everything and everybody around me. A feeling of being all right came over me at the same time two things happened, it started to rain again and the yard whistle blew signaling four o'clock standing count by my bunk in my cell.

The ten of us stood by our bunks for the four o'clock count as the screw went by only stopping briefly for a headcount, and after his passing everyone just went back to doing what they had been doing. With my hands cupped behind my head I lay on my bunk and looked around at my cellmates trying to evaluate their individual personas. So far two of them hadn't even acknowledged me, and mostly only talked to each other quietly and discreetly. Another cellie of mine kept to himself writing letters to his wife constantly, and Richie had already informed me about him. He wrote letters to his wife daily, although he was in McNeil Island for murdering her; he was very cordial but very strange. And then there was Hog Head, who was a great storyteller and had all of us laughing with his personal stories. I noticed that everybody in the cell of 3i4 was from California and assumed that came from an unwritten majority rules stipulation from my cellmates.

The bell rang indicating chow and Richie once again motioned me to join him for dinner, and after evening chow he said he was going to the gym and invited me, but I declined. I would get tired quickly from just walking since I had been laid up for months in county jails going to trial as well as bussed halfway across the nation. So there I was once again lying on my bunk staring at the ceiling waiting for lights out so I could get some sleep.

21

The federal prison system uses the numbers one through six for security classification. One and two are the lowest levels and only require a no fence, no wall camp setting, while levels three and four are designated to Federal Correctional Institutions, which have a fence or wall along with gun towers and these are considered medium security prisons. Level five and six prisoners have to be housed in United States Penitentiaries; these prisons are high-caliber, high-security and considered the most violent prison setting. My classification was level five, probably because of my unprosecuted escape, use of weapons and bank hostage situations as opposed to someone slipping a note to a teller in a bank. Personally I never understood someone using a note to rob banks, what you do if the police arrive, write bang-bang on a piece of paper, crumple it up and throw it at the police while surrounded? Also I was sentenced under an A statute, meaning I would have to do a minimum of one third of my sentence before seeing the parole board. B statute means you can see the parole board six months into your sentence; this is why you often read of dirty politicians and such receiving big sentences, but being placed in camps and out in six months. This is mostly to satisfy the public that justice had been done, but this was not my case since I was considered to have violent tendencies and a security risk. So the United States Penitentiary at McNeil Island was gonna be my home for a while and I needed to settle in and survive this major jackpot. I had been a big fish in a little pond in these rinky-dink county jails but now I was a little fish in a big pond in McNeil.

Along with my level classification, I was given a prison job of tier janitor which was nothing more than a daily sweep and mop of the fifth tier in I block, along with the emptying of the large trashcan in the middle of the cellblock. The job would take me twenty minutes a day and I would be paid eleven cents an hour. But to me this was going to be perfect for what I had in mind, and what I had in mind was spending as much time in the big-yard as I possibly could.

This became my daily routine of hitting breakfast, usually oatmeal, back in the cellblock cleaning the tier then out to the yard. I would run my laps until my body hurt and I couldn't hardly breathe, then do calisthenics, push-ups, chin-ups and pull-ups then walk and think. I would stay in the yard as long as I could, never talk to anyone with no one talking to me. People would come and go for the most part with the exception of three other prisoners who were always running laps. This one Chicano would always put a small pebble in his mouth before running, another had wooden beads on a string holding them in his hand he would move one bead for every lap he ran and then there was this muscular white guy who could knock down lap after lap effortlessly. Every morning there was a guarantee the four us would be on the yard running with no interaction, and on the island it was raining, it had just finished raining or it was getting ready to rain, that was another guarantee.

When I wasn't on the yard I was in my cell reading or listening to the chaos created by this prison machine. As I learned earlier to look without looking like I was looking, I now learned to listen without seeming to appear I was listening. And as my brain cleared and my body got stronger I was more in touch with the prison environment and had become a personal gear in this nonstop running machine of prison life. Another unwritten rule in effect was if you were white, the station on your radio had to be country and western, and although I'm a Motown guy some of these country songs were relatively good. I had traded four cartons of cigarettes for a used radio and on low volume at night or in the yard isolated from others I would tune it to rhythm and blues, my first love. Cigarettes were forty cents a pack because of no state and federal taxes, so four cartons of cigarettes only equaled sixteen dollars in the commissary. Cigarettes were half value of cash so I only paid eight dollars in actuality for the radio. But trust and believe when others were around I was listening to the twang of country and western music, I wasn't going to get stabbed or lose my life because I liked David Ruffin more than Merle Haggard. And as my mind cleared even more I could see the nuts and bolts of this violent madhouse.

One day when I was putting the mop and mop wringer away next to the shower area I noticed two convicts pouring Coca-Cola on the shower floor, and I had no clue why. Later that day those two same convicts who had poured the soda stabbed another prisoner to death in that shower. The Coca-Cola when dried made the shower floor sticky and good footing for their tennis shoes while the victim was unstable because of only having shower shoes as he attempted to run. Fuck, this place is dangerous I thought to myself, and this incident had nothing to do with me so I kept it that way by never mentioning anything to anyone on what I had seen. Prison killings have a reason, but often the reason is only logical to the perpetrator, it may not make sense to you or me but it makes complete sense to the killer and that's all I needed to know. I always minded my manners around others, but there's always an outside chance of someone's brain creating a scenario where I could be the enemy and needed to be eliminated. Just something you can't factor in giving McNeil Island a daily wartime atmosphere, with the only difference from a foreign war, is you live with your enemy. Walking slow and drinking a lot of water just like Buddy had recommended, I now knew what that meant. Being hydrated and walking slow not causing your heart to beat fast you bleed slower, giving you a better chance of surviving stab wounds, but for me not being stabbed at all was even a better survival tactic.

I felt as if my body was getting stronger every day with my constant running and yard exercise and started increasing my laps on the track. One morning the big white guy who would run so easy was just entering the yard and I felt like I had what it took to keep his pace, so I positioned myself across from him on the track and started running when he did. Without even so much as a glance in his direction I made my legs stay up with his and we were running side-by-side for laps turning into miles, two miles turned to three miles, three miles turned to four miles and I was hurting but would not quit. He started running faster and as my side was cramping I still kept up, and finally after six miles, he took a half a lap to slow down and after stopping he looked over at me and all he said was, "You got heart youngster. I'm Sugar Bear, what's your name?"

I couldn't answer right away because I kept spitting and gasping for breath; finally I got my name out, "Whisper."

We walked a couple more laps then Sugar Bear said, "One o'clock, the little room on the right side in the gym."

With my side still hurting I could only give a nod of okay.

After noon chow, I made my way up to the gym area and walked into the little room on the right side of the gym. Sugar Bear sat at the end of a bench alternating curls with dumbbells and barbells, he looked up and said, "Jump in."

I followed his lead throughout his workout and maybe I matched him stride for stride that morning on the track, but there was no possible way I was going to match him pound for pound in the indoor iron pile. He was a fuckin' animal when it came to the weights. Three o'clock rolled around and we were done. "See you in the morning on the yard Whisper."

This became my Monday through Friday routine with Sugar Bear. My body hurt and I was tired all the time but I continued to show up because it all boils down to heart, the size of your heart is all that matters. I liked Sugar Bear and I knew that he liked me, mostly because I didn't ask a bunch of dumb-ass questions, and we would work out Monday through Friday religiously. Getting to know him better he told me that on Saturday and Sunday he would let his body rest and shoot dope (heroin). Naturally I wanted to ask him to think of me on the weekends and throw me a package, but that's not the way it's done in the penitentiary. When Sugar Bear told me he was forty-three years old, I was somewhat amazed because of the phenomenal endurance and strength he had, also he would always get visits in the little gym room from some of the heavy hitters in the joint. Even the couple of guys from my cell who hadn't acknowledged me would stop by to cut it up and laugh. My mind put all the puzzle pieces together. These guys were affiliated with the "powers that be", the organized, detail orientated, cunning "powers that be". While doing state time I was fully aware of the different status that some convicts had, and federal time was no different, with the California system spilling over into the federal system. Murders were very common in the

California Department of Corrections, but with the killings connected to the "powers that be" on the rise in the Federal Bureau of Prisons, the federal administration did not know how to handle this growing problem. In the late seventies the start of a violent epidemic took hold and McNeil Island was one of the sparks involved in igniting that soon-to-be out-of-control bloody fire.

I wasn't this little surfer kid from South Oxnard anymore, instead I was living in the belly of the beast and had to come to grips with what I would do, or not do to survive. This place was dysfunctional and I was a part of it, like it or not fucking like it!

Back at 3i4 I felt definitely more connected to the other fellas from my association with Sugar Bear, and one afternoon Richie Rich pointed out the locker in the middle of the ten man cell only saying, "Use it if you need it."

By every bunk is a three-foot by two-foot locker so prisoners can store their personal belongings, though we had an extra locker in the middle of the floor of 3i4 before now I never dared to ask or open it. Richie opened it for me so I could take a look inside and it contained various homemade weapons, fourteen inch, sixteen inch heavy gauge steel homemade knives sharpened and usually with a handle made from heavy-duty tape. These weren't little pointed butter knifes like in the fake prison movies that people tend to believe; after all stabbing someone with a butter knife would only make them mad. These were what you call bone-crushers and it made me feel strange inside when Richie was showing me. That night lying on my bunk I had mixed feelings, on one hand I was trusted to be shown the community weapon box, and on the other hand I scared myself on how asleep I had been for a couple of weeks to the closeness of life-and-death around me. Once again it seemed as trouble had found me and I was exposed to forces I couldn't control. But fuck it I would keep doing what I was doing by going to the yard and the gym and I should be all right. But I couldn't speed up the hands of time and that truly bothered me.

Another unusual characteristic of McNeil Island is the power goes completely off periodically and it takes a couple of minutes for the generators to kick in. And in that short time of darkness, crazy things can happen. One is people start dropping things off the tiers aiming them at the guards, heavy metal mop buckets, mop wringers or bricks taken out of the prison buildings. McNeil was originally a territorial prison built in eighteen hundred and forty-one and in nineteen hundred and four it became a federal prison, so removing a brick was easy because of the age of the buildings. The guards had little Plexiglas shelters stationed all over the prison, so when the power went off the guards would scurry under one of the shelters to keep from getting hit. It was comical, but the longer the lights were off and the guards were safe out of site different races would become the target and it would get real fucked up real quick. My first Christmas in McNeil a small riot erupted this way.

During the riot with a show of force on the catwalks holding their carbines and a couple of tear gas canisters in the cellblock the police had things under control rather quickly. The tear gas was the key to their success and I found myself with a wet towel over my head and my face in the toilet flushing it repeatedly trying to get air, it would start to work then it was someone else's turn in the cell to try and breathe using the toilet. But on the upside with the holidays bring lots of visits and lots of visits bring lots of narcotics, and bringing in the New Year with weed and heroin made everything so much better. There's a prison saying, "When you're asleep or high you're beating them out of time."

And I've never been much of a sleeper but in
December and January on McNeil Island I robbed the
federal government out of quite a few days of my ten-
year sentence.

On weekdays I was still working out with Sugar
Bear and we became very close, often he would invite
me into the cellblock for a late breakfast. Sugar Bear
worked in the bakery and would concoct this breakfast
loaf of unsliced bread hollowed out and filled with
potatoes, corn and meat. He lived in another cellblock
and had single cell status so I would have to sneak into
his block passed the hack so I could snack on this
prison delicacy after our morning run. One of the
worst shots you could receive is out of bounds in
another cellblock, for the simple fact if someone were
to get killed in that particular cellblock while you were
in there, and with the cellblock immediately locked
down during any altercation, it's hard to explain what
you were doing in there so you become a prime suspect.
But for me the risk was definitely worth the reward,
any food with a homemade flare is simply such a
luxury.

Also I quit smoking and could run for miles
without feeling tired and still trying to keep up with
Sugar Bear in the gym I was reaching a new peak of
strength, not a match for Sugar Bear but stronger than
I had ever been in life. I was smoking weed and doing
heroin as much as possible but narcotics in prison
could create a tricky situation, and many people were
killed by being stabbed or hit repeatedly in the head
with a heavy pipe from not being able to pay their dope
bill. I wasn't going to go out like that and I never
overextended myself with the readily available credit
offered.

Different prisoners had different hustles in
order to get high; some sold narcotics, or ran card
games for a percentage of the money pots. Others

worked in the laundry and would wash and press clothing for a price and kitchen workers would steal from the chow hall and make tasty sandwiches you couldn't get on the mainline. And then there were people like a couple of my cellmates along with Sugar Bear, and a few others of the "powers that be" who would receive narcotics as gifts from the prisoners smuggling in the drugs, plain and simple called extortion.

But there was one dope fiend from California who had a very unique hustle, he would hire out to murder for a large quantity of heroin. He was known as Casper, Casper the Ghost. And why he was known as Casper is because he would wear a white pillowcase over his head as he entered a cell as soon as the doors were un-racked in the morning, doing a contract hit for someone scared to do it themselves. Casper would come to 3i4 sometimes to visit and pay respects to the heavy hitters and get high, he didn't know that I knew and I never let on. The only reason I knew at all was from his mannerisms and the quiet conversations he had with my other two cellies, that wasn't that quiet, and believe me when I say I didn't want to know. The less you know about other people's dirty business the better, in case they get busted your name never crosses their mind as a witness against them and Casper *the unfriendly ghost*, your secret was more than safe with me.

Although every day was more or less the same, the weekends did seem to drag more than the weekdays. I would still go to the yard and walk, sometimes run but I wouldn't see Sugar Bear till Monday morning. He literally stayed in his single cell all weekend reading newspapers from all over the nation and doing heroin, he was the homemade food connection so he really had no reason at all to leave his cell. One afternoon he showed up at 3i4 and I was very surprised to see him on a Sunday and he was carrying with him a brand-new pair of expensive blue suede running shoes, setting the shoes on top of my locker as he only said before he turned around and left, "Whisper these are for you brother."

This is the only time I ever saw Sugar Bear on a weekend. But as for me I still had a problem sitting still and I did everything I could to find something to do. McNeil Island would show movies on the weekend in the movie house and the screen as well as the seating was the size of a theater on the streets. They would show first-run movies, and the natural selection of seating segregation would be as obvious as the chow hall, including a neutral area off to the side in the back. When the lights would go off signaling the beginning of the movie, people would light up joints and cigarettes knowing full well that never under any circumstances the guards would make themselves vulnerable by being in the seating area close to us in the dark. I would accompany Richie or sometimes go by myself, and since my face was now known I would sit in the California white section. I was becoming somewhat comfortable and the time picked up speed, but never enough since I still had almost three years more to do before even seeing the parole board.

I felt as if the federal government had put me on a shelf and now all I was doing was waiting to be taken off that shelf.

Running, working out, reading, eating and sleeping that was my life and on some days it was hard to accept for me, and I wouldn't share my thoughts of confinement with anyone since they were in the same predicament as me. It was as if I was being fed a spoon full of hate daily and on the days that it was the hardest I would take a double dose of hatred. The madness continued affecting me less and less and I was being desensitized to any humanity that I may have had before. Sometimes I wondered if that fucking quack prison psychiatrist had been onto to something when he diagnosed me, but fuck him and fuck all these ball breaking guards, I was twenty-six years old and nothing or nobody would deny me what I have to do to get back to my life on the streets.

Another weekend had arrived and I found myself sitting in the movie house watching a flick about this seventeen-year-old kid sailing around the world in a nineteen-foot boat. It was a true story and I was completely enthralled in the plot as I noticed movement in the theater, lots of movement, too much movement, it didn't feel natural and my antenna was up. I looked to my left and I could see a big clearing of empty seats and as I focused my eyes in the dark I could clearly see the reason why. There was only one prisoner sitting in the middle of these empty seats and he had about ten inches of steel sticking out the back of his neck right under his skull, without hesitation I stood up and calmly exited the movie house. Within a matter of seconds the guards noticing all the movement turned on the lights and now everyone could see as this prisoner sat paralyzed with his eyes wide open, staring in the direction of the screen and a large knife in his neck. The siren sounded and we were all ordered to get down in prone position right where we were, and as I lay there watching I could see the prisoner being carried out face down on the chicken wire gurney with the ten inches of steel protruding from his neck. Ordered to go back to our cells and lock-in that's exactly what we did, and as I lay on my bunk pretending to read, I couldn't help notice how silent and awkward everyone else was. Not one word was mentioned about the killing and that was the norm in McNeil Island. Extreme violence all around treated as if it didn't exist.

22

Richie Rich was extremely gifted with his hands and his creativity; he could make jewelry boxes from scrap wood taken from the furniture factory. He could also make picture frames and purses by folding empty cigarette packs into little squares connected with each other creating the finished product of whatever the object was. But Richie's specialty was tattooing, using these homemade tattoo guns made from a long wooden Q-tip obtained from the infirmary inserted into the casing of a ballpoint pen and at the tip the thinnest guitar string used as the tattoo needle. The art and craft department supplied the India ink needed, and the only thing missing was a small motor to be used to run the whole contraption. Since Richie was a thief like most everyone else in prison, he somehow managed to break into the warden's office stealing the warden's telephone answering machine. The prison bulls came unglued searching for that telephone answering machine, but they were searching for the wrong item since Richie had destroyed everything except the small motor that would run the recording cartridge and it could be hidden easily. And one day in 3i4 as Richie was fine-tuning his tattoo gun I asked, "Hook me up with some ink Holmes."

"What you want and where you want it Whisper."

After thinking about it I replied, "I want an old-school peacock on the inside of my left arm."

Richie let me know that that would be no problem and started to shave the inside of my arm with a double-edged razor adding, "Trust me Holmes, just trust me."

And without a pattern he started to ink on the inside of my arm free hand, we talked and laughed as he added a few smaller design choices blending into the peacock. There was an opening rose flower and in the tail of the peacock instead of the natural eyes of the feathers, Richie put keyholes surrounded by bricks. And as a personal touch, above the rose next to the peacock's head, he put a small island with a gun tower and the shaded sun behind. This he said was to represent being together on McNeil Island.

And after a couple of hours and only stopping once as a guard walked by the cell, I had my old-school peacock starting at the middle of my bicep with the feathers reaching two inches from my wrist. I liked it a lot and knew Richie wouldn't take any sort of payment, but I still offered cigarettes or anything else he needed. He only looked at me saying, "That would be disrespectful—you're my Home-squeeze fool."

Since then and even still today when I look at my peacock, I think of Richie Rich, and also how my peacock was done with the warden's answering machine motor, such a classic get over on the system story making an entertaining prison memory.

I noticed the prison guards starting to grow beards and mustaches, yet they were under the same dress code stipulation as us, and in a couple of weeks everyone found out how the ban on short hair and facial hair was lifted. So now most people were growing goatees, long sideburns and anything that would give them a personal identity. Of course I joined in and grew a goatee, but tiring of it quickly I trimmed it into a thick Fu Manchu style mustache. We were also allowed to wear more relaxed clothing when going to chow and not have to walk the yellow line like a row of ducks. And with the prison violence on the rise constantly, outsiders such as newspapers were catching wind of the rising trouble and wanted answers.

Some reporters would visit the prison and be allowed on the catwalks to see firsthand how prison administration still allegedly had control of the rumored out-of-control federal prison system. The warden as well as top ranking prison guards would do interviews with various media agencies to pacify and satisfy the public's concern. This was all bullshit since only the administration was ever interviewed and their one-sided bias answers were mostly a bunch of lies. Politics at its finest since any stand up convict would never talk or be interviewed for the simple reason of the unwritten prison code, for a convict to talk to any authority figure puts doubt in the minds of the other convicts; if you talk about anything it's assumed that you would talk about everything. Even when having to go to a guard and get a roll of toilet paper you bring another prisoner with you, so there would be no doubt on the conversation with the guard being viewed by the other inmates. Prison is like one big fish bowl and everyone is watching all the time.

On a Friday fifteen minutes before the standing four o'clock count, two officers entered 3i4 stepping directly to me and cuffing me behind my back. As I was escorted down the tier and the five flights of stairs, I thought about this one guard that was always poking jabs at me when I would be cleaning the tier, and a couple of times I *might* have made some derogatory remarks back to him. But as I sat in an office with the captain, a lieutenant, the two guards that had escorted me as well as two others in suits, who I soon learned were FBI agents, I was thinking to myself this is a pretty dramatic setting for me only having cross words with the one guard on the fifth tier. The captain started the interrogation by asking me if I knew this one or that one, and I simply shook my head with a, "No I don't know anybody."

Continuing, I relayed to the captain I came to McNeil by myself, do my time by myself and will leave by myself. Then one of the agents in the suits interrupted and asked if I knew this one particular individual and where was I on February fourteenth at three twenty in the afternoon. And then my mouth took over as I answered, "Where the fuck do you think I was? I was in this shit-hole prison, and that was two weeks ago so you pick where I was, shower, yard or my cell."

Immediately the investigating lieutenant spoke, "He's on the other side, lock him up."

And as I was being taken down some stairs to a basement area my mind spoke to me loud and clear, yes you mutt muthafukers I am definitely on the other side. One bull opened the solid steel door motioning me to get in and after shutting the door behind me the other bull instructed me to back up to the tray slot so he could unlock my cuffs. As I heard the officer's footsteps fading I looked at my new surroundings, a bunk, a one-piece sink toilet and the walls were solid steel instead of bars. I could touch both sides of the walls width at the same time, so I surmised my new home was six feet wide. This cell was known as a boxcar and with only one ten inch square Plexiglas window located on the door facing a basement wall made the cell seem even smaller. I lay down on the bunk with my body tired. I had been on McNeil for only a few months and with my constant exercising and constant mental awareness, this was the first time that I realized how truly exhausted I was from taxing my body as well as the paranoia born of violence from the state of how I had been living. Immediately I fell into a deep sleep until a guard was tapping on my door and shoving a tray of food through the tray slot. I ate fast and laid back down dead to the world. The morning came quickly and although I was well rested my body was still tired, after throwing water on my face in the sink and eating breakfast I wanted to do push-ups but my body would not cooperate, so I lay back down and slept more. This time when I woke I felt somewhat normal and the thinking process of wondering what was going to happen started kicking in. An officer came by looking through the cell door window and slipped me my lunch tray. I noticed right away how quiet these underground set of boxcars were with the only noise that of steel doors being locked or unlocked and muffled voices with all this commotion seeming off in the distance. Eight days had gone by and not one guard had spoken to me, I hadn't been charged with anything and no paperwork given to me. I wasn't even supplied with a toothbrush, razor or any sort of cosmetics. The only thing in my cell was a bunk to sleep on, sheets and blanket and a stainless steel sink to wash up in with a towel to dry with. I started daily doing my push-ups again and pacing the eight-foot length of the cell, but time seemed to be at a standstill. Then I heard, "Whisper?"

At first I thought my ears were hallucinating, then I heard it again, "Whisper?"

It was coming from the small vent above the toilet in the back of my cell; I jumped up on the base of my sink slash toilet and put my mouth close to the vent, "YO."

"Whisper is that you? This is Joey."

I couldn't place Joey at first, then he told me how he was the one that would come and visit Hog

Head sometimes in 3i4. "Oh yeah Joey, I remember you. What's up?"

He told me how he was in administration segregation for some balloons of weed and asked me what I was doing down here. I don't know is what I told him, and then he asked me if I wanted any tobacco with this whole conversation taking place through the exhaust air vents in the segregation walls. I relayed to Joey that the tobacco would be nice since I don't have shit, also adding how would you get it to me? Joey explained to me how his cell was butted up next to mine, only facing the other way, then telling me to tear my bed sheet and make a small rope with a knot at the end. He said to call him on the telephone (vent) when I had the rope made. I completed the bed sheet rope and Joey said since our cells were back-to-back with only a wall between us that he would double wrap some tobacco and matches in some saved sandwich wrap from lunch and instructed me when I heard him slap on the wall to flush the knotted end of the rope. I heard the slaps and flushed my toilet, and when pulling my rope back after it had gone down the toilet, nothing. Back on the telephone I told Joey about our unsuccessful mission, all he said was to keep flushing every time I heard the slaps. And finally one time when pulling my bed sheet rope out of the toilet there was some Camel non-filters and matches, everything tightly wrapped and dry. I immediately jumped back on the telephone telling Joey thank you very much. Since I hadn't smoked in a couple of months, when I lit up that Camel in my segregation cell it tasted terrible. But the process that I had to go through in order to smoke was cause for celebration, celebration for getting over on the guards. I sat on my bunk lighting up another cigarette from the one I had just smoked thinking about Joey's ingenious method of passing contraband to me. With the plumbing tied together it was simple laws of physics that the two ropes would get tangled, fucking genius I thought, puffing my second Camel non-filter which happened to taste better than the first.

Thirteen more days had passed and without a shower, a shave and only being able to take what is called a whore bath in the small sink, my attitude was compromised to say the least. Then that afternoon my cell door swung open with two hacks cuffing and escorting me to a room at the end of the hall. Waiting for me were two lieutenants and one captain. Sitting across from them as the two guards positioned themselves behind me, one of the lieutenants started reading my charge. He quoted from the prisoner bylaw book the number of my infraction, it was 001 and immediately I knew what my charge was. 001 is the first rule listed in the prisoner rights and bylaw pamphlet; the charge was murder of another inmate. One of them continued to read me my rights and informed me that I could provide witnesses for my defense, along with being provided a guard to represent me if I so chose. When the captain finished by telling me I would be transferred to the other side of segregation and would be allowed limited reading material, as well as approved personal property, he then asked me if I had anything to say. Telling him, "I smell like a goat and could use a shower and a shave." His only reply was that the segregation officers would get to that when they get to it, adding I was dismissed.

I was immediately escorted to the other side of administrative segregation and moved into a cell that looked exactly like the cell I just came out of, except having two bunks making the cell seem even smaller. Shortly I heard a familiar voice in the segregation hallway and it was Billy the Dog Face Boy. He immediately asked me my charges and all I said was, "Double 0 1."

His reply was short and to the point, "Fuck Homeboy!"

Speaking out of the tray slot I responded, "When can a muthafucker get a shower around here?"

Billy said on Tuesdays and Thursdays we are able to shower and shave, adding we get clean sheets and clean towel also. I thought to myself it's only Monday I'll have to wait one more day, then telling Billy the Dog Face Boy I would talk to him later if the bulls leave the tray slot open after chow. That afternoon I was able to order commissary that would be delivered on Friday, so I bought the limit of what I could have in the hole. Four cartons of Camel no-filter cigarettes, Taster's Choice instant coffee, Dove soap as well as a few other cosmetic items and some batteries for my radio that I would be receiving from my property. I was still spending the tail end of my bank robbery money and there was an ironic satisfaction from the government having to pay for my store items while doing time for the government. Not much satisfaction, but more satisfaction than none. Tuesday and Thursday passed with no shower time for me from power exercised by this one bull, for reasons unknown to me, probably because he could. On Friday with my property delivered I immediately tuned in my radio, and although the reception was sketchy from all the concrete and steel, hearing music again was my saving grace. When purchasing a radio in the federal system they immediately snip the power cord, only allowing batteries to run the radio, and my current D batteries were low. I would soak them in warm water to get the most use out of them until my fresh ones would arrive the following week. Also I used my chrome toenail clippers as a mirror to shave with in between shower days since there was no mirror, not even polished aluminum in my segregation cell often installed instead of a mirror that couldn't be broken then used as a weapon. And with music and the fresh shave I felt like I had a new lease on life, then my charges hit me and I realized I might have a lease on a new life sentence.

They cracked my cell door midmorning on the next Tuesday and I was allowed to sweep and mop my cell, and shower. Also a real mirror was mounted over the sink in the shower area, and when I looked at my reflection it looked as if Stevie Wonder had shaved me the day before. Shaving using the chrome toenail clippers as a mirror I had missed patches of hair, and my mustache looked like a drunken black caterpillar crawling over my top lip. I hurried to fix my previous shaving so I could spend as much time in the shower as I possibly could before the hacks would run me back to my cell. Out by myself for only an half hour I spent my remaining time standing in the shower with my eyes closed and imagining myself under a waterfall, or standing in the rain. My mind took me various places in nature only interrupted by the guard telling me, "Times up, back in your cell."

Having two bunks I would use the top bunk for my small amount of property and be able to hang my towel over the side to dry. I was labeled single cell status, which was good news to me since the top bunk came in handy as a storage area and I liked the privacy. Tuesday and Thursday were the days that I would look forward to for shower and fresh laundry, with Tuesday the premier day since it was the longest margin day between showers. Other prisoners would come and go and I would know a few of them from the yard or from the block. They would stop by my cell during their half-hour and we would bullshit through the tray slot and exchange whatever we had to make our stay in disciplinary segregation that much better. I had no problem throwing a couple of packs of smokes someone's way if they weren't considered a lop or a lame, two terms used to describe undesirables. Prisoners who just didn't get it and you could almost see the target on their back. If the tray slots were locked we would talk code loud through the door or vents and arrange for the exchange to be made in the shower area, also known as the rain room. A book cart would come by once a week being pushed by a guard and you were allowed one book off the cart, always having to return your previous book to get a fresh one. I settled into a routine of push-ups, reading and more push-ups and more reading. I noticed how hard it was to breathe in these boxcars, my smoking didn't help but there was still no fresh air to be had until Tuesday or Thursday when your cell door would be opened. I hated every day in segregation and I could almost feel the ticking inside me like someone had a big key and was constantly twisting that key putting pressure on my mainspring that made up my attitude.

Not everyone handled the solitude the same and within my first sixty days underground in the hole two other prisoners went to extreme measures. The first one broke his eyeglasses and cut on his wrists with the broken glass. And the other moron swallowed his metal spoon from lunch chow, and penitentiary spoons are of the bigger variety so he was serious on whatever he was trying to get accomplished. Personally I was glad when they were gone since I had enough on my mind with a murder charge and the slow progress of the disciplinary board hearing my case.

One afternoon as I was lying on my bunk I noticed a letter being slid under my door, and since I never wrote anyone I couldn't imagine who was writing me. Inspecting the letter closer it was made out to Dick N. Hand with some address I didn't recognize, but on the return address it had my name, prison number and McNeil Island's address. I put it together rather quickly after reading the first paragraph and realized the letter was from Sugar Bear. Since the federal prison system doesn't allow correspondence between federal prisoners, Sugar Bear had wrote me a letter mailing it out to a fictitious name and address knowing the Postal Service would return it to its return address. Clever I thought to myself and I started writing letters to fake locations with Sugar Bear's name and number as the return address. It was another way to break the monotony and let each other know that even though we were out of sight we were not out of mind. Other names above the false addresses we would use were Seymour Buttkrack or Peter Gazing for extra yucks (laughs).

But not as full of yucks was the kangaroo court that I was standing in front of after ninety days in Ad-Seg on my charge of 001, murder of another inmate. The disciplinary board consisting of two lieutenants and a captain let me know how the federal government had three confidential witnesses testifying against me and that I was unable to question or even know who they were. I declined representation on my behalf by a prison guard for the simple reason I wasn't going to confide in him and didn't feel that he would help me.

Long story short, I was found guilty of killing another prisoner and my sentence was one hundred percent loss of good time, which only equaled sixty days at that time. I was to remain in administrative disciplinary segregation insuring the secure running of the institution pending indictment by the grand jury in a federal court in Washington state. None of this surprised me since every one against me worked for the federal government in some way, but what did surprise me was the quickness and the matter of fact way that I was found guilty. I was led back to my cell and laid down where I finished reading my book *The Pearl* by John Steinbeck. Nothing in this crazy world in which I was living made sense so I didn't spend very much energy trying to make sense out of senseless situations. My sole purpose had become being the most comfortable that I could be and giving the most not give a fuck that I could.

Every thirty days I would have to see a small panel of officers and be asked if my stay in administrative disciplinary segregation was comfortable, and did I have any complaints. Although I had a laundry list to discuss with them I would always say nothing. I was becoming hardened and my animal characteristics started dominating my human characteristics and I would look at everything and everybody as a potential predator or prey situation.

Other prisoners would carry on conversations through the tray slots or on the telephone above the toilet, and I knew the screws were always listening and never wanted them to know my business, even though my business was no more than push-ups and getting another book off the book cart with hopes of no pages missing. Torn out pages completely ruined the storyline.

My hatred for the hacks increased daily with some of them being noticeably vindictive and lazy. At times an officer would write in the logbook that we had already been out for our shower, yet we hadn't, completely robbing us of one of our Tuesday or Thursday luxuries. Sometimes I would hear prisoners asking the hacks questions, I would think don't talk to them, they are the enemy, fuck them. Even once I heard a lame ask an officer what time it was. Who fucking cares what time it is, I have a life sentence simmering on the back burner so I could care fucking less what time of day it was. But I did notice a newfound respect from most of the guards and some of the prisoners since being found guilty of murder by the prison kangaroo court. Along with my constant quietness I probably came across as unpredictable. In reality I was just biding my time the best way I could, trying not to think of future consequences and also not thinking of the wait on the grand jury who only met three times a year. I would use my imagination to suspend time, sometimes thinking about being a kid barefoot on the beach, most other times thinking about every woman I had been with, every woman I wanted to be with and every woman I should have been with. I found a radio station that played these old radio mystery shows from the nineteen forties and in the evenings with a towel over my eyes I would lie on my bunk and be taken different places through sound effects and suspenseful plots. Johnny Dollar was my favorite, he was a private investigator that would always end up at the wrong place at the wrong time, being shot at or getting his ass kicked, but he always ended up getting the girl. In my eyes Johnny Dollar was the man.

I had created this little world in my boxcar located underground on McNeil Island. I didn't care what day it was, I didn't care what month it was, I only cared about doing the best I could with what I had to work with. When I wanted a hot cup of Taster's Choice coffee I would make what is called a bomb by rolling toilet paper over and over on my hand and folding the top and bottom into the center, then using a used small lunch milk carton suspended by some sheet rope, I could heat water. Setting the lit bomb on the lip of the toilet and wetting the exterior of the milk carton filled with water while dangling it above the flame it would boil, and when done I would flush the toilet and knock the bomb into the flowing water so the bomb wouldn't smoke. A lot of work for a hot cup of coffee but I had every minute of the twenty four hour day to create comforts by getting over on the guards. I could tell my health was deteriorating from no outside activities or sunlight, my skin was pasty white with a green tint from the fluorescent lighting and my feet hurt all the time from only being able to wear thin shower shoes or socks while doing calisthenics. Humidity had crept into my cell making the walls sweat and my towel would never dry, I would wonder if it was sunny outside since it was the middle of summer in early

August on the Puget Sound. My mind was definitely playing tricks on me and I felt as if I was mentally slipping or becoming downright crazy. But I just got up every morning and did what I had to do to conquer another day. Hearing my name on the telephone I jumped up on the base of the toilet and whispered into the vent, "yo."

"Whisper, in the rain room there's a nail in the Lemacs for you."

I wasn't crazy I knew exactly what that meant. Lemac is Camel backwards, like in Camel cigarettes and *nail*, like hammer and nail, was universal code for contraband, usually narcotic contraband and the rain room was the shower. We used nail because with the screws always listening, the word nail never made sense in any conversation.

So on my Thursday shower time I reached up feeling around with my hand until I came across a Camel pack wrapped in sandwich cellophane, and after my shower I placed it between my butt cheeks and slowly walked back to my cell. After my door was keyed locked, I stood close to the door so if the guard were to walk by and look in he couldn't see my hands as I unwrapped my gift. I pulled out a modified cut down homemade syringe and immediately a grin came over my face, next I pulled out a small piece of paper and written on it was "Hang tuff—S.B." and last but not muthafuckin' least, a rolled up small red balloon.

I waited for lunch to be served so I could get the metal spoon off my tray, and as I sat on the floor next to my door I poured powdered heroin into the spoon, added some water and cooked it lightly using matches. I rolled up small pieces of cotton off my socks as a filter for the heroin as I sucked it up into the needle. After pulling the homemade syringe out of the tail of my peacock on my left arm I instantly was high. Fuck yes

I thought as I looked up to my ceiling towards the sky, and thanked not God but praised Sugar Bear.

I didn't touch anything on my lunch tray and just sat on the edge of my bunk in total euphoria. I straightened the minimal amount of my personal belongings that I had in my cell two or three times and would go numerous times to the door window and look, even though I knew the window only looked at a wall. Staring at my walls dripping with humidity and missing paint I noticed flies hovering in the middle of my cell, I continued to watch and noticed the flies would never land only circle around the center my cell. There I sat after almost six months underground, facing a life sentence, flies that would not land with walls dripping and my future completely unknown. It would be argued by some that this was the lowest rung of society's ladder, but at that precise moment underground on that Thursday I was free.

Wire was used as an expression for information and I received a wire to find a way to get to the dentist. I complained about one of my perfectly good teeth hurting and the screw said he would look into it. A week later I was being escorted upstairs to the dentist located in the infirmary, and as I walked down the center hall I seen Richie Rich who said nothing only giving a head nod.

The prison dentist x-rayed my tooth then explained to me I needed a root canal. He started performing oral surgery, and while all this was happening the convict assistant who I did not recognize slipped me two balloons after the un-needed dental work, discreetly sliding the balloons into my mouth. I was escorted back downstairs to my cell. It was weed, and after making sure a couple of the fellas in segregation got some, I emptied out a Camel cigarette replacing the tobacco with the weed and waited to smoke after supper chow. It was another distraction to break up the time so it was good. And as I lay there high while listening to Johnny Dollar, I heard commotion from a large amount of footsteps and the rattling of chains. I could hear boxcar cell doors being opened and officers barking out commands. Then my cell door swung open with the guard telling me to get dressed and exit my cell. He proceeded to pat me down and wrap me in chains, and as he was doing so I could see other prisoners in the hall going through the same procedure. We were ordered to walk in pairs with a long chain hooked on connecting eight of us to each other, and another eight behind us and so on. We were walked onto the dock area and loaded onto the prison ferry. It was an extremely warm night and the un-breathed air was more than welcomed into my lungs, but my mind couldn't help but ask what was going on. As we got closer to the shore on the other side I could see a bus and hear the motor running, I had always heard that it was against the law to transport prisoners at night on a bus but I had found out much earlier the federal government can do whatever they want. When loading the bus we were offered the usual choice of cigarettes and a lieutenant was offering sleeping medication also, it was optional and I refused since when did a prison lieutenant become a doctor? These feds made up the rules as they went along just like me, so no wonder we didn't get along.

The long chain connecting the eight of us was removed and I sat on the bus staring out the window into the night's darkness as I heard one of the prisoners asking the lieutenant what the medication was he was passing out, and all the lieutenant said was, "They're called Good Night Irene pills, that's all you need to know."

I wanted to ask if that was the medical name or were you using layman terms you fake ass wannabe doctor, but because of common sense I didn't.

The bus headed out going south and me high on weed this entire series of events seemed very unusual and peculiar, but I settled into my seat and rolled and swayed with the rest of the prisoners on the bus filled to its maximum capacity. I could see that the inmates who had taken the medication were completely out of it; some were drooling while other's heads tipped over into the aisle area bobbing and jerking with every bump in the road. At sunrise we were crossing over the Oregon California border, and with the sun shining California looked really good to me. By late afternoon early evening the bus was pulling into Lompoc penitentiary located in central California. We had been traveling almost twenty-four hours without stopping and from practicing body control I hadn't used the restroom on the moving bus even once while the prisoners who were knocked out by the Good Night Irene medication never woke during the trip.

We were given the usual strip search and issued new prison clothes then taken to H block, or Lompoc's administrative disciplinary segregation unit. There were two tiers that made up H block and I was placed on the upper tier with these cells having bars not solid like the boxcars. I could see from the cellblock to the yard and with the sun shining on the green grass I contemplated for a moment, which was better, segregation being able to see the outside or segregation on McNeil Island not seeing anything. It all didn't matter in the big picture though since my will was not my own, and the federal government only had my body but not my mind.

Through the grapevine I discovered the reason for the immediate move of all segregation prisoners being housed in boxcars from McNeil to H block in Lompoc. Some jail house lawyer had filed a class-action lawsuit against the federal government stating that the boxcars didn't have enough air for a human. His argument was that cows being transported in

264

cattle cars had more cubic inches of air than we did underground in administrative disciplinary segregation on McNeil Island. The inmate won the lawsuit condemning the boxcars permanently with the judge ordering immediate evacuation from the underground cells. And also, so that they could be inspected by lawyers on both sides, as well as the federal judge, to ensure the boxcar type cells were empty of prisoners. The air was better in disciplinary segregation in Lompoc, but I was still in the hole and without any of my personal property I missed my little bullshit articles of comfort, especially my radio. According to the guards our property would catch up to us in a couple of weeks, but dealing with the feds it was always on their time and I was getting better than good at waiting. One night in the middle of the night when I couldn't sleep I lay on my bunk thinking a variety of obscure thoughts about my young life thus far to the background noise of other prisoner's body functions, then I keyed into a radio softly playing oldies on the tier below me. I recognized the artist as Tyrone Davis and distinctly remembered the lyrics from nineteen sixty-eight, "Can I change my mind and start all over again?"

I was only in H block for a little over two months and only have a couple of incidents that are worth talking about. First, we were allowed one half hour Monday through Friday for shower and recreation and after completing my allotted time one Monday I was back in my cell putting my soap away and hanging my towel when I heard all the cell doors being rattled. This was common in H block segregation, one prisoner would start shaking his door and everyone would join in making one gigantic ruckus, but this time it was different because all the doors started rattling at the same time. It was a 4.6 magnitude earthquake on the Richter scale and the entire segregation unit went dead silent. There was no damage to the building and the shaking lasted less than thirty seconds, but that is the only time I can remember a prison cellblock noiseless.

The second Lompoc incident had nothing to do with nature and was more self-induced with me at the helm. While being served dinner chow one afternoon the guard dropped my metal spoon when sliding my tray through the tray slot, he attempted to put it back on my tray and dropped it again then something came over me. While the guard bent over picking up my spoon for the second time, I reached out with my metal tray and hit him in the head cutting his left ear slightly. Living single cell in segregation for the last nine months had made me somewhat agitated and even though I knew better, I did what I did and I knew I had fucked up. But after the guard got hit, he didn't so much as look at me or say a word. Maybe I wasn't completely in my right mind but I still knew that was peculiar, as the screw went down the tier serving more food and still not acknowledging being hit.

I went without dinner that night and laying on my bunk reading a Playboy magazine hungry I didn't give the earlier altercation any thought. Then I heard the mechanism in my cell door moving and I knew what was coming next, so I jumped up and wrapped my towel around my jewels the best I could, then stood in the back of the cell waiting. Five officers charged in my cell at once as I threw the first and only punch thrown by me, which I don't think landed, then the five guards took over and they beat the fuck out of me. Even after I was down on the cell floor they commenced to continue taking turns beating me in retaliation for what I had done to one of their own earlier. They left as abruptly as they had entered and I stayed down on the floor evaluating what just happened and wondering how six people fit in my small six by eight foot cell. Pulling myself back on my bunk I felt my body hurting in different areas, mostly my ribs along with a chunk of skin missing on my chin, which I assumed was from one of guard's rings. It was hard to sleep that night from the pain when breathing but all in all it was just part of the game.

The next morning four guards were at my cell door telling me to get dressed, which took me longer than usual because of my cracked ribs. After being cuffed, I was escorted down the tier and down the stairs to the watch commander's office. I shuffled more than walked and couldn't stand completely upright as I entered the office where two FBI agents were waiting for me. My first thought was they sure get the FBI involved with everything that happens in prison, everything that happens with me lately anyway. One of the agents spoke up, "We are *thinking* of charging you with five assaults on five officers, do you have anything to say about these assaults?"

"What assaults? I don't recall any incident involving five officers," I said still bent over.

Smiling all the agent could say was, "Good, that's real good."

And that was the end of that, just a scare tactic by the FBI for insurance that I didn't file assault on five officers first. After all, explaining why five guards were in a locked segregation cell after four o'clock count would be harder than me explaining why I was there since I lived there. Besides I'm not a rat, and filing on the police you're still a rat, and that's gospel. It took me almost three weeks to heal from my cracked ribs and looking back this was another way that broke up the mundane monotonous days in segregation. And when that officer, who now had a Band-Aid on his left ear would put my chow tray through the tray slot we never spoke, it was just business as usual and just another part of the game.

Another summer had come and gone and once again I was sitting on a federal prison bus this time headed north back to McNeil Island, but we did make one overnight stop in northern California, which made the bus ride more tolerable. Ironically, but not surprising, after being taken off the prison ferry I was placed back in my previous boxcar cell. The boxcars after inspected by the federal judge who was satisfied that the condemned cells were empty, the feds did what they always do and that was to do what they wanted. So I became as comfortable as possible without having any of my personal property and played the waiting game again. As soon as I lay down I heard my tray slot being opened as a guard leaned down telling me, "You were indicted yesterday by the grand jury on murder charges in the town of Steilacoom. Good luck."

Good luck I thought, I don't need luck I need Perry Mason as my lawyer to beat this case since the feds hand out life sentences like candy on Halloween for murder. So I continued lying on my bunk trying not to think of this jackpot I had gotten into, but instead thinking of the holidays soon to come with more visitors bringing more narcotics. Again I had my priorities in their proper order according to importance.

Two more months had passed with no word on my court case and with no serious incidents causing me to receive any sort of write up. But in those sixty days I went to the dentist two more times and had two more root canals on the same tooth. Good dentist right? I never needed any root canal to begin with but this gave me opportunity to pick up the nail waiting for me at the infirmary that had been prearranged. One time it was weed and the other time it was weed and heroin so I beat the government out of a few more days of my ten-year sentence. But if I get this life sentence I would have to get high much more to ever have the feeling like I was robbing the federal government out of time.

Christmas time came while I was in segregation and the screws went cell-to-cell giving us our Christmas gifts, a small bag of circus peanuts, cigarettes and an orange. I also received a letter from the outside from a buddy of mine named Slurp Dog, and he requested me to put him and his family on my visiting list, so I did never thinking anything would come of it. Slurp Dog was truly a character in so many ways, his name derived from when he would talk he would get real close and spit with his words while in conversation, and the Dog part was as he said, from when he was young and his family would have company his dad would tie him to a tree out back of their home because of him being so wild. If that part was true or not I don't know, but I did know he was one tough boy and well known and well respected around Ventura. And I can contest to his toughness from witnessing a personal account once when a Dalmatian mix breed dog charged Slurp one day at the beach while we were hanging out. When the dog was in the air leaping to attack Slurp, he hit the dog with a right hook to the head and a left to the body without hesitation and with lightning speed. The dog laid on the sand whimpering as the owner came running over upset about the entire situation. Slurp calmly explained to the owner everything and I could see in the dog owner's eyes he didn't want any part of the man who knocked the wind out of his dog while airborne.

Within less than a week from receiving the letter I was being called for a visit and entering the visiting room. I could see Slurp Dog, his wife, his three young sons as well as his stepdaughter. This is the first time I noticed how sociably fucked I had become from being locked in a little box for almost eleven months. I just sat there as Slurp and his family

269

caught me up-to-date on their lives and I watched them eat endless free sandwiches provided by the prison for visitors. These were the same sandwiches that I had come to despise, but Slurp and his three boys just kept packing them away as I continued to sit with little or no conversation. I was very appreciative of Slurp's visit, but at the same time somewhat embarrassed that his family had to take a prison ferry to come see me. And the other thing I noticed as I was being escorted back to my boxcar was how disconnected I had become, and was, of the outside world.

The next thing I knew I was told to pack my property and I was going to be bussed off the Island with my destination Leavenworth Penitentiary. I really didn't know what was going on but I did know that Leavenworth now was considered the disciplinary penitentiary prisoners were sent to when they fucked up in other prisons. But I hadn't heard one word on my murder trial. My first thought was wondering if Bobby was still in Leavenworth or if Bobby were still even alive since I hadn't spoken to him in over fifteen months. We had both written one letter to each other through his mother's address but that was over a year ago, but I should know for sure soon what happened with my ol' friend Bobby.

I was back to fourteen-hour days rolling on the prison bus taking the route in reverse that I had taken from Leavenworth to McNeil over a year and a half ago. We finally arrived in El Reno, Oklahoma, and in the morning they put me on a bus going back through the southwest and up through California and Oregon towards Washington state. What the fuck was going on? And then I arrived on the stop before McNeil and once again I was put on a bus going back the way I just came. I had heard of the feds putting prisoners on the *diesel therapy* tour, and now I was one of the elite that would travel never reaching my destination until the government was ready. It was a form of punishment for being a disciplinary problem, and with my murder case pending I guess the feds considered me a problem. This took weeks, turning into a month with my holdovers in segregation cells in various prisons or federally contacted county jails. In El Reno again, which is the last stop before Leavenworth, I was put on another bus headed east and ended up in Terre Haute, Indiana, and in a few days back in the direction from the week before. This shit got real old real quick and with my body bouncing around every day it started to take a toll on my mental as well as physical well-being. I started imagining myself in French Guiana alongside Papillion and this diesel therapy was another hurdle that I would conquer and come out on the other side only that much stronger. The holdover isolation cells were dirty and dingy, but now started to feed my desire to strengthen my convict character. Once in a while someone would have some weed and I would get high while waiting for the next bus. I would also do push-ups in the evening but noticed my strength wasn't the same. Time on the bus tour seemed to drag more than when I was eleven months in that McNeil Island boxcar.

As I was laid over in Terminal Island penitentiary in California for the second time, this longhaired tier janitor approached my cell striking up a conversation. He started telling me how he was a drummer for the famous Allman Brothers band, but I only half-assed listened since you hear every story under the sun with somebody telling you how important they are. I put him on the pay-no-mind list but started listening closer when he said he was going to receive a visit the next day and bring in some heroin. I'm a gambling man and I would not have bet that any of this was going to happen, and I was more than positive he didn't play drums for the Allman Brothers and the muthafucka probably didn't play drums at all. But the next afternoon with my interest still piqued by the possibility of heroin, I stuck my little homemade mirror out the bars so I could look up and down the tier. I had found a broken piece of glass and placed it into an empty Copenhagen snuff can, and this would create enough reflection to be used as a mirror, I did not originally think of this but it was another ingenious prison tool. And as I scanned the tier I spotted my new possible heroin buddy getting out of some white overalls, which were used exclusively for visits. Within minutes he was at my cell handing me a modified syringe and some balloons of heroin, instructing me how much to prepare for him. Then sticking his arm in the cell through the bars, I stuck the needle in his vein as he was telling me, "Help yourself."

"Don't mind if I do Homeboy," I replied, as I got high also.

After a couple of more tier janitor's came by my cell sticking their arm through the bars, the long-haired prisoner returned bringing with him a photo album. He flipped open the book and there he was playing drums for the Allman Brothers. And all I said was, "I never doubted you for a moment Holmes."

He then replied, "You are Whisper, right? I've heard of you from some of the fellas."

"Really?" That is the only word I said, as I thought of my newfound notoriety. Growing up, as a kid in the neighborhood, all I wanted to be was known by the right people, and through habitual criminal activity and allegedly breaking one of the Ten Commandments, I was now known in the federal prison system. I admit I liked being associated with the fellas and identified as standup, making me one of the regulars or regs as we referred to each other. But with negative notoriety the prison guards zeroed in more on my movements and associations. But being twenty-seven years old the risk was definitely worth the reward as I lay in another nasty cell, isolated from everyone and having my name mentioned in the same sentences as other well-known undesirables while on an extended bus tour. This seemed who I wanted to be.

I would sit by the window on the bus seeing the same hills, the same trees and the same broken down trucks in the fields as I was being driven stop to stop. Sometimes I would spot the same cow as I had seen the week before looking like it hadn't even moved. Being held over in La Tuna, Texas, I was placed in an underground section of segregation and my cell didn't have running water. It had a toilet that flushed but no water for drinking or washing up. So I started my sheets and towel on fire throwing them out on the tier demanding running water. Shortly, a lieutenant was standing in front of my cell angrily asking me, "What the fuck is your problem?"

"I want water boss, the fuckin' cows have water on the prairie, and I want water too."

He said he would think about it, and within a couple hours the lieutenant authorized me getting two containers of water daily. Another month had gone by and I now had been getting diesel therapy for a little over two months and being treated like an animal I was acting like an animal. After my incident in Texas, now when I would ride the bus after they wrapped me up in chains they would place a black box over my handcuffs. It was a relatively new security measure that would limit your hand mobility even more. My only entertainment was the other convicts I traveled with, but for the most part I was glad when most of them reached their destination. Some were noisy and the lops would always be asking the bus guards questions, irrelative foolish questions like when were we going to get to our destination. Who cares what time we get there, do you got a date on the big yard or something I would think as I stared out the window. One inmate stood out from the rest as exceptionally noisy and exceptionally annoying, we had picked him up in a small county jail in Oklahoma and he was going back to Leavenworth on a parole violation. All this fool talked about was how dangerous and violent Leavenworth was; he kept on and on never shutting up. You could see the fear surfacing in the fresh face fish as they listened to his never-ending rant on the deadliness of Leavenworth. And as I pulled into El Reno penitentiary for the third time of my tour I couldn't wait to exit the bus and get some rest in my solitary cell while I waited for the next bus, and mostly I couldn't wait to get away from that loudmouth muthafucka on the bus selling wolf tickets to anyone that would listen. Personally I thought he fit the old prison saying to the tee, "The loudest one is the most scared one."

23

It was dusk but I could still see the familiar direction the bus was traveling as well as buffalo grazing, I knew I was close to Leavenworth. Finally after almost three months of touring the country I was going to arrive at my destination. Giving our name and number we exited the bus and all walked up the stairs leading to the front of the penitentiary into receiving and discharge where we were processed and stripped then given new clothing. The prisoner working R and D was very flamboyant with his T-shirt tied in front with a knot showing off his cleavage, homosexuality was fairly common in prison and trust and believe, homosexuals were respected along with everyone else. Anytime homosexuals were involved in an altercation causing death it was usually more brutal and violent than your everyday prison killings. It definitely was a crime of passion and think about the consequences, having to do a life sentence in a men's prison, which could be considered no consequences at all. After the processing we were all escorted through the rotunda area and down below B block into the orientation section that I had been housed in over a year and a half ago. Out of the thirty odd prisoners only three of us were designated to do our time in Leavenworth. Since we had arrived so late we were given bag lunches for dinner and I wouldn't know until morning if Bobby was still there, when the block door was unlocked.

In nineteen sixty-two Frank Morris along with the Anglin brothers, John and Clarence, escaped from Alcatraz never to be seen again. This escape was made famous by the movie *Escape from Alcatraz* starring Clint Eastwood. At the time, Alcatraz was considered the most secure prison in the nation, and since their bodies were never found dead or alive after the escape, they closed Alcatraz in nineteen sixty-three and sent everyone housed in Alcatraz to Leavenworth which was now considered the most secure prison in the United States. And there I sat in my once horse stall cell eating sandwiches and wishing I was anywhere but here.

When I awoke that first day and after my morning constitution on the toilet, I was washing up and shaving using the polished aluminum mirror in my cell and seeing a blur in the reflection along with hearing keys jangling I knew something was up. I went to my cell door and looking through the bars I could see the guards carrying out a body on a gurney, it was the loudmouth from the bus and his throat had been cut. I had become emotionally numb to prison killings but what struck me odd was how the killer or killers didn't even wait for their victim to leave the cellblock, instead as soon as B block and the cells were unlocked on that first morning of our arrival they rushed in slicing his throat. No one was apprehended or charged for his murder and I went back to finishing shaving as the officers mopped up the blood.

Movement for breakfast from the cellblock to the chow hall was delayed fifteen minutes because of the murder, but then as I exited B bock and outside the block door Bobby was standing smiling. It was really good to see him as we started walking down the center hall towards breakfast chow; I noticed how paranoid I was from having so many people around me and just felt like everyone was coming at me in a rushing manner. Sitting in the California white section of the chow hall, Bobby and I cut it up with conversation and he finally asked me, "What happened in McNeil with you Whisper?"

"You don't want to know Bobby."

He nodded okay as we continued to eat our oatmeal and shit on a shingle, or chipped beef on toast as it's known in the free world. Bobby looked good, real healthy with his arms blown up and his shoulders and chest thick presumably from the iron pile, and it made me realize how out of shape and pasty white I must've looked. With a couple of laughs and a little more conversation, it was as if Bobby and I never had been separated, but I also noticed I had trouble forming sentences as we spoke. He told me he had to go to work in the shoe factory and would see me at lunch, as I relayed to him I had to do more bullshit orientation paperwork and receive the talk about no weapons and no killing from some guard in my orientation class. Walking back down center hall I was so fucking paranoid, I hadn't been around people in fourteen months and I was extremely tense as I tried to look calm walking with the other convicts. As I was almost at the B block gate I heard behind me, "Whisper."

Turning around, someone I didn't know was approaching me with a box having four cartons of cigarettes, Taster's Choice coffee, cosmetics and a pair of tennis shoes.

"These are for you Whisper, some of the fellas wanted to make sure you have everything."

I said thank you and carried the items back to my cell inventorying my windfall and reading the kite (note) contained with the items. I discovered that Sugar Bear had sent word to the "powers that be" in Leavenworth to take care of me and that I was considered one of the regs. The first thing I did was put on those tennis shoes and they felt better than good, I had only been able to wear shower shoes or while traveling on the bus I could only wear the Peter Pans provided for transport. Peter Pans was the nickname for the green canvas pointed thin soled shoes provided by the federal government to be worn on the bus, in actuality they were body bag shoes used when dead soldiers were being shipped home from war. My feet felt good but my mind was very scrambled from my time in isolation, I needed to snap out of it and snap out of it quickly since Leavenworth already seemed worse than McNeil if that was possible. I would continue to see Bobby at feeding times, but until I was assigned to a permanent cell block I would have to wait to see him on the yard or any other common areas of the penitentiary.

I was eventually assigned to be housed in A block and it was nicknamed the jungle, simply because it was. Over a thousand convicts in eight and ten man cells making up one cell block, it definitely was a fuckin' jungle. B-C-D blocks were single cell staus blocks, for a total of twenty-three hundred convicts in the entire prison. Since Leavenworth had recently become the disciplinary penitentiary housing the worst from other penitentiaries, Leavenworth was nicknamed The Big Top.

The fellas got me a little job in the kitchen, cleaning the bakery after all the cakes and bread were made for the day. It consisted of me taking a fire hose and washing everything down into a drain on the floor, taking me approximately twenty minutes each day and working five days a week. My main focus was to get back in shape and after my morning job I would go to the big yard and run, it was extremely cold in Kansas in the winter and my lungs would hurt from the frosty air as I would do laps in the yard. I would get so tired and try not to fall asleep sitting on my bunk in the afternoon where I would spend my time reading when not working or on the yard. Bobby threw me some weed and it would only add to my paranoia, but I still smoked it always including the fellas in my eight-man cell. Asking Bobby who he hung with, he told me he pumped iron with a couple of California boys and Donny from Sacramento, but mostly by himself, "You remember Donny don't you Whisper?"

"The one we met in orientation from Sac town when we got our prison numbers, that Donny?"

"That's the one."

And after I asked where Donny was, Bobby stated he was in building sixty-three, the segregation unit for insubordination right now. He should be out in a couple weeks, and Donny lives in A block. Bobby continued telling me that Donny had two life sentences which kept him wound extremely tight but was a solid good guy nonetheless, and to look out for him. Finally Bobby added that I needed to get moved to C block as soon as I could where he was housed in single cell status so I could stay out of the craziness that more often happened in the jungle of A block.

Within a relatively short time I was getting my wind back from running and would sometimes join Bobby in the gym at night to hit the iron. Bobby had gotten so strong that at first he left me in the dust when we would work out. But any free time I would find myself sitting on my bunk in my cell with my back against the wall so paranoid I couldn't function, just wanting everything to slow down and the constant noise to stop. Donny got out of building sixty-three in a little over a week and we hit it off immediately, and started hanging together in A block. With my paranoia starting to fade and my brain being able to form sentences again I was back in the prison routine of trying to make time fly. I exercised my rights and filed for the Freedom of Information Act, enabling me to be able to look at my prison jacket (file), hopefully to answer some of my unanswered questions, first and foremost my murder case. More running, more reading and more laughs with Donny and Bobby I was starting to settle in Leavenworth Penitentiary. I was respectful of the fellas as well as the "powers that be" and was given respect in return, even though all around me was no-respect madness. I had adjusted to being okay with everything that I shouldn't be okay with, the acts of violence that I would hear about or often see would remind me where I was at all times.

As Donny and I were standing on the flats in the jungle after four o'clock count one afternoon waiting for chow I witnessed the most horrific murder I have seen thus far. One inmate who received visits was hired by the California crew to bring in a package of heroin, and after this inmate explained to the California boy that the mail containing the package didn't reach his house, still the California boy showed up at his cell right after count was cleared at four thirty. The crewmember not only stabbed him in the neck repeatedly, he then proceeded to slice his gut open squeezing his intestines looking for the balloons of heroin that didn't exist. The bloody inmate stood in front of his cell trying to take another step, but fell dying and by this time you couldn't tell what nationality he was, he was just the color red head to shoes. I never said a word to Donny as we walked slowly and as far away from that area as we could. Then the siren sounded and chow was late once again because of the cellblock being locked down and the cleanup. The dead prisoner's wife lived close by which was common practice for someone smuggling contraband, to move their girlfriend or wife close to the penitentiary to receive visits where they could bring in narcotics for a third or half the package. But that night his wife came to the prison to claim his deceased body and all you could hear from my locked cellblock was her shrieking screams as they rolled the body down center hall out the front door with her by his side. But the next morning as Bobby, Donny and I were having breakfast not a word was mentioned about this incident, only eye contact as if to say, "What the fuck." I knew Donny knew what I knew, and that was who had committed the murder since we both had witnessed the entire series of events go down from our vantage point on the flats in the jungle. But neither of us ever spoke a word about it to each other...never.

Running on the yard I heard my name being called over the loudspeaker and to report to the administration office immediately. Outside the assistant warden's office, I was finally called in and my file was put in front of me. My Freedom of Information Act proposal had come through, and as I flipped through my jacket I noticed pages were missing, as well as names and addresses were blacked out. But as I was reading about McNeil Island and specifically the details leading up to my prison conviction of murder, I learned why I was shipped to Kansas rather than standing trial in Washington state. The day of the murder a writer from a small local newspaper was within the prison researching a story on violence in the federal prison system. He witnessed a *masked* assailant murder another inmate and I didn't need to read any further since the suspect was described as wearing a mask I automatically felt the government's case was weak against me for prosecution in an outside courtroom. How can witnesses identify me as the killer if the perpetrator was wearing a mask at the time of the murder? Although still under indictment, I breathed a little easier. I couldn't make out the names of the witnesses against me since they were blacked out, but I did confirm what I already knew about who turned Bobby and me over to the FBI for reward money. His name was blacked out but from the information surrounding his name, I could see the region where this rat muthafucker lived, and it was definitely Tony Lofton like I had strongly suspected originally. The rest of the file was just a series of observations and write-ups made by the staff at McNeil Island, and nothing in print that I was reading was flattering. But I did leave that office with a little more hope that I might not have to stand trial in federal court in Steilacoom, Washington, for murder. But with the feds capable of pulling tricks out of their sleeves at any time, and since there is no statute of limitation on taking someone to trial indicted of murder, I didn't know anything for sure.

I quit smoking once again with my running on the snow covered yard increasing daily, and within a little over three weeks I was running upwards of five miles a day. Every few laps I would stop to do push-ups or knock the snow off the weights in the yard and work my upper body. I put in for a job change and started working in the prison laundry, the exact same laundry that George 'Machine Gun' Kelly, the notorious gangster in the era of John Dillinger and Pretty Boy Floyd, worked in when doing his time in Leavenworth in the nineteen thirties and nineteen fifty-one before dying in Leavenworth in nineteen fifty-four. The laundry building was located next to the segregation unit, building sixty-three. Robert Stroud, also known as the Bird Man of Alcatraz was sentenced to death by hanging for killing a guard in front of eleven hundred witnesses in Leavenworth in the early nineteen hundreds, but because of his knowledge of birds he was given a stay of execution and studied his birds in building sixty-three. They knocked out a wall giving Stroud two segregation cells to study and have his canaries and other birds as he wrote numerous books on bird behavior, with those books still used to this day. Ironically, the Bird Man never had birds on Alcatraz like history and movies that were made about him lead people to believe.

Two Puerto Rican nationalists who tried to kill President Truman in nineteen fifty and later convicted in nineteen fifty-two for wounding three White House police officers in the assassination attempt were still in Leavenworth with me. And with all this history around me I didn't want my name etched in the archives of Leavenworth Penitentiary. Fuck this place, and I had passing thoughts of dying as an old man in prison or worse, dying as a young man in Leavenworth by someone else's hands. The brick buildings were un-remodeled and looked old and dead, and often I would see people's names carved into a brick with the date from the thirties or forties attached to the name, fuck this place I would think to myself, fuck dying here.

My hours in the prison laundry were from eight in the morning till one in the afternoon with forty minutes for lunch, and it paid five dollars a month. It was near the end of wintertime and I still had plenty of time to run and work out. My job description was to fold bed sheets, four thousand six hundred sheets to be exact, every week. But the system that they had for folding would only cause me to actually work three hours a week. I still would have to be in the laundry area for the hours of operation, but with so much free time I would play dominoes, smoke weed and read magazines. Only three white boys worked in the laundry of over thirty workers, and with racial divide everywhere there was always the respect level and no matter what color you were as the saying goes, "Everybody bleeds red."

Freeman is the term used to describe the bosses who work the prison industries, they are like guards with radios and keys but they wore gray uniforms to work. One of the freemen in the laundry was an older red-faced miserable potbellied white guy, and the other was black with a baldhead and we would refer to him as Saddle Head because his head looked like a horse saddle, but not to his face of course. I minded my business and did my job so they left me alone for the most part. Bobby worked in the shoe factory, which made all the shoes for the military, and Donnie worked in the furniture factory making furniture for various government agencies. But I would see Bobby at every chow time, and Donny and I were still hanging tough in A block aka the jungle. I was starting to get into my little groove of doing time, but wanted to be moved to C cellblock to have a single cell and hangout with Bobby in the evenings. I knew most of the prison tricks so I went to the doctor and told him that I would sleepwalk at night periodically; this is an automatic single cell change. After all, walking around unconscious in an eight-man cell at night could just end badly. I was moved to C block on the fifth tier in cell number 532. The advantage of being in a maximum security prison is most little requests are granted to keep the peace, and now I lived on the same tier and eight cells down from Bobby. I passed the information on to Donny on how to get a cell change, but Donny being the character that he was got it all fucked up. Donny went to the psychiatrist instead of the medical doctor. Doctor Karkas, the prison psychiatris, was this wack-job shrink who would wear his wristwatch on his ankle and talked with a thick German accent. Anyway Donny told the shrink that he heard voices and needed to change cells. Karkas put him in what is called the greenroom in the infirmary and heavily medicated him for two weeks. When Donny got out he was a little ringy from the medication, but he did get the cell change and ended up in 534 right next door to me. Naturally Bobby and I steadily razzed Donny about his bone-head doctor mix up.

C block was a good move for me, with the single cell I could sleep peacefully after the doors were racked shut and having my two road dogs in the block with me, things were as good as they could be given the situation. The prison violence never stopped but with

284

C block having less people it was simple math that it had less killings. Narcotics were everywhere and Donny, Bobby and I never went without. Bobby with his silver tongue always had his hooks into somebody who received visits with Bobby laying out the blueprints of what needed to be done to bring in the drugs. Donny was just a straight wild man always getting narcotics on credit, selling some and paying off his last drug debt, and because Donny had two life sentences, he was always running at full throttle. Though however little or much narcotics the three of us would have we made sure each other always got some, always. The snow had melted on the yard and although the air was still crisp I could smell spring coming, which meant summer was next and I hadn't had the sun on my face in a very long time.

With the weather nicer I found myself spending more time on the yard, walking after my run and work out with very few other prisoners around me. It was a nice break from the cellblock and in my heart I still appreciated the sky, the grass and just being outside in general. Bobby was like a reptile and didn't go outside unless the weather was warm; he never ran for long distances, smoked Camel non-filter cigarettes, drank the jailhouse pruno (homemade wine) and got high on heroin and weed as much as possible. Yet with all these bad habits he was a natural athlete that never liked to lose at anything, he was just an exceptional all-around athlete at everything he did.

Donny was gifted also and even with having all the habits as Bobby did sometimes he would show up and run keeping alongside of me for miles on the yard, and I was amazed how everything came easy for him. Being only five foot nine and a hundred and sixty-five pounds he was still a force. He had received double life sentences for two kidnap murders and everyone in the joint knew Donny was wound too tight, so most everyone stayed their distance, but with Donny and I everything was always relaxed and cool between us. He liked me and I liked him. But as for my routine I was constantly pushing my body to the limit, but still never to ever get ahead of Bobby physically on the iron, I may have weighed thirty pounds more and a half foot taller but Bobby was an animal when it came to the weight pile. Donny at times would get a new workout routine started but he always drifted after a short time, those two life sentences haunted him taking all the wind out of his sails and why wouldn't they? With any life sentence for the feds, and Donny had two, you only go to the parole board every ten years and that was usually for bad news.

This was no doubt the biggest penitentiary I had ever been in. There were two exercise yards simply called the big yard and the little yard. The weight pit was located next to building sixty-three on the big yard and at one time it was the area used as the prison hanging gallows for executions. The wall I would say was forty-five feet high and made out of brick, wide enough for a man to walk on the top and then it pyramided down going nine feet underground. There was a big concrete patch on a section of the wall located by the handball courts in the big yard from a small group of prisoners commandeering a supply train and hitting the wall with hopes of escaping years prior to me arriving in Leavenworth. There was a short section of train tracks coming in the back gate stopping at the furniture and shoe factory to bring in industrial supplies. Five desperate prisoners hijacked the train running it off its tracks for approximately three hundred yards while being shot at before hitting the wall. Between the battle of the train and the brick wall, the wall easily won.

A and B cellblocks connect the wall to a large rotunda in the front of the prison, with C and D cellblocks running off the round rotunda area like spokes on a wheel and having gun towers on every corner of the prison perimeter. This place was massive and with the double razor wire fence wrapping around the wall on the outside, it truly earned its title as the securest penitentiary in the nation. Another spoke that extended off the rotunda wheel area was center hall, leading to the chow hall, administrative offices and the movie house. With the infirmary and various outside construction maintenance buildings scattered throughout the prison this place had the feel of a city.

With an empty cell next to 532, I had stashed a knife in the cell door slot, but during a routine shakedown one of the bulls had found it, so it was time to get another knife made. My single cell was legally different than my ten-man 3i4 cell, in a community cell when they find weapons in a common area they (the feds) don't attempt to charge anyone. That's why we had the locker full of weapons in McNeil Island without any concern. But if any weapons are found in a one-man cell then that one man housed in that cell is charged with possession and the feds like to push a five year sentence on a weapon charge, but having a knife for me was mandatory since it seemed most everyone else did. Besides I had learned quick one of the most important prison phrases to be true, "It's better to be caught with a knife then to be caught without a knife."

I had already seen many examples of that prison slogan become a self-fulfilling prophecy and I wasn't going to go out like that. I relayed to Donny and Bobby about needing a new knife with Bobby telling me he was good with his, but Donny being the maniac that he was naturally wanted to get a bigger and better one. So Donny and I put our heads together and designed three sixteen inch heavy gauge steel weapons, we figured we could wrap the handle with four inches of tape and still have a bone-crusher, also I suggested we get a hole drilled in them to attach a strap to our wrist since I've seen a couple of prisoners killed with their own knife. After receiving the wire that the knives were made and with now my job smuggling them over to the laundry area, I then wrapped them in bed sheets that would be delivered to C block where Donny would be waiting. That night up on the fifth tier Donny and I took turns carving out the bricks around the corner by the mop sink from our cells, placing the knives in the wall hidden by the exterior bricks it meshed beautifully. The next morning we took the third knife out to the small yard and found a strategic spot and as I stood lookout on the gun tower Donny put it deep in the ground by stepping on it.

In the blink of an eye the weather in Kansas can change and on one late spring afternoon on the yard the temperature dropped and the wind was whipping through the brick buildings creating this miserable chilly afternoon. Two prisoners were playing handball at the far end of the courts, and I was working out on the pull-up bar located in the weight pit, other than us three the yard was empty. I noticed this prisoner starting to walk out onto the yard from the opening that connected the big and little yard, he looked like a nomad, a gypsy, with a T-shirt wrapped around the top of his head securing his long black hair and the way his clothes hung on him he looked like a character from *Lawrence of Arabia* walking out of the desert. It seemed to me he was walking a beeline in my direction and staring. Ever since my murder involvement in McNeil I became very cautious of people I didn't know and would think to myself that the victim of the killing had to have Homeboys as well as relatives. Slowly I grabbed a smaller curl bar from the weight area and laid it on the bench close to where I was doing my chin-ups, I would alternate from the pull-up bar to grabbing the curl bar and doing twists with the bar behind my neck. The closer he got the more I became sure he was looking my way, so I started to time his arrival making sure I had the curl bar in my hands in a nonchalant manner to make it look like it was part of my

288

callisthenic routine as he approached me. When he got close enough for me to see who it was I only somewhat recognized him as arriving in Leavenworth a few days prior, but had noticed all the California crew, especially the "powers that be" went out of their way to give him their respects. Now as he stood in front of me with the curl bar in my hands and with my heart beating fast I kept my eyes on his hands as he started to speak, "Whisper I'm Jay Tee from East Los Angeles and we have a close mutual friend, Sugar Bear."

I didn't say anything but only stood there watching his hands and listening, thinking he was trying to get me to drop my guard, and since I never carried my knife unless the situation really called for it, I felt like the curl bar could keep him away if something were to kickoff. Jay Tee continued, "Sugar Bear got out of McNeil last week and while he was sitting in his car in front of his house in the San Fernando Valley someone came up from the back driver side and shot him in the head using a shotgun."

A little more relaxed now, but still not saying anything Jay Tee continued with, "He talked highly of you Whisper, and I was a good friend to him as well, I just wanted you to know."

I slowly reached out my hand as a formal introduction to Jay Tee and as we shook hands Jay Tee added, "If you ever need anything let me know."

I relayed to him that I would, and as *Whatcha Gonna Do* by Pablo Cruise was finishing playing on my little radio, a lame-ass disco song started playing. Jay Tee asked me if I liked disco? I told him no, not at all, I'm a rhythm and blues man and went on to say how I thought disco sucked and please don't misunderstand me, I didn't like being locked up, but if I had to be locked up I was glad it was during the disco era. With the platform shoes and tight-ass shirts I told Jay Tee that we weren't missing anything. He agreed chuckling and started to walk off then turned around, "You are welcome to join me in the chow hall at our table if you want."

I nodded and after he took a couple of more steps, he turned around again saying with a smirk, "Whisper."

"Yeah?"

"You looked a little tense when I walked up, relax youngster."

I heard him laughing as he walked off and I knew that he knew what I was thinking when he rolled up on me, funny now but not funny then. After Jay Tee left I thought about Sugar Bear and how he lived by the sword and died by the sword. Later I heard that Sugar Bear was mixed up with some explosives involving the wrong people in Las Vegas, but I don't know for sure. But after that day meeting Jay Tee and getting that news, I would run my laps sometimes looking down at the shoes Sugar Bear had given me and kick that extra lap for him. I missed my friend Sugar Bear.

That evening as Donny and I were starting to sit down in the white neutral area of the chow hall, I looked over to see Jay Tee motioning me to join him and some of the fellas at his table in the elite California section. I pointed to the table Donny and I was standing at and as Jay Tee nodded his head, and made a gesture of tipping an invisible hat to let me know he understood one of the fellas at Jay Tee's table turned to look. It was the convict that had gutted the inmate in A block and we locked eyes for an awkward second and then I sat down to eat.

The menu for the federal prison system is the same in every federal joint with five weeks of a variety of meals, and on the six-week the menu starts over again. The exception of once a month they would serve soul food, Mexican food or corned beef and cabbage for the whites, so it becomes the same o same o when it came to food. But I will admit in the maximum-security penitentiaries they fed us good. The convicts prepared all the meals served, so pride was taken in everyone's prison kitchen job, and with the prison farm on the outside of the wall producing vegetables, as well as a slaughterhouse, the food was always of a fresh quality. Keep in mind there were prisoners doing life sentences, forty years, eighty years so the prison staff didn't want these hopeless convicts to be upset over the standard of chow being served. For a lot of these prisoners Leavenworth was home and it was where they would die, so some effort went into keeping the joint running as peacefully as the guards could make it, and except for all the killings they were successful in their peaceful efforts in other areas. That night was steak night, and after finishing eating when dropping off your tray and silverware in the dishwashing area a guard would stand by the trashcan making sure you got rid of the bone from the steak since everything was a weapon.

During that particular chow the prisoner that had opened up that inmate's stomach with a knife turned around once again glancing at me as Jay Tee said something, I pretended not to notice as I ate and held a superficial conversation with Donny. Leavenworth was like a chess game having to think three or four moves ahead and not letting your opponent know what you were thinking. And trust and believe when I tell you, you did not want to have somebody out think you, checkmating your ass with a knife then have game over.

The joint loosened up when summer came and I welcomed the sun but had to keep my T-shirt on for the first few warm days since I had gotten some new tattoos. I had "California" put on my back in four inch Old English style lettering along with "Whisper" tattooed over my heart in one inch lettering of the same style. On my back the letters were filled solid and on my chest, Buzz the tattoo artist used what is called ribbon shading. They looked good and I was more than pleased with the work and after my skin healed enough to get sun, I got sunburned for the first time in my life. I hadn't been in the sun for a couple of years but for as much as it hurt the sun felt good all the same.

I spent every minute I could in the yard with the weather warm and Bobby would join me playing handball and hitting the iron pile. Donny would show up also at times but he was very sporadic due to his two life sentence mindset. Jay Tee would regularly play handball with me and I started enjoying his company more and more, he was a very funny muthafucker and would make me laugh continuously. I had figured out he was very high up on the food chain of the "powers that be" but the more I got to know him the more I would see how personable and intelligent he was. Jay Tee would often throw me a package containing heroin that he received as extorted gifts and since he didn't smoke weed he would suggest to me that I should quit, saying it made the human mind weak. He also gave me the book *The Godfather* by Mario Puzo instructing me that I should read it carefully and pay attention to the finesse used to obtain things rather than from violence. Make no mistake about it, Jay Tee was a killer and relayed to me that murder was only as a last resort, but our brains are our true weapons. Jay Tee was a very deep individual seeming to have this spiritual connecting characteristic about him.

Summer was full on, and for as cold as it got in the winter the Leavenworth summer was the polar opposite, being very hot and very sticky with extremely high humidity. But it was summer which always had been my favorite time of year. I would see people on the yard that I had never seen before, who I imagined must've been just laid up in their cells during the cold months and stayed off the radar. With the time change and the nice weather the yards would be crowed and kept open until dusk. I would play handball, do my calisthenics or sit around with the fellas yuckin' it up and getting high.

Organized softball was one of the biggest events during the summer months, the softball field was always immaculate with the fresh cut grass and the white chalk lines. It was our version of Fenway Park. I joined a team called High Times named after the marijuana magazine of the late seventies. Donny joined the same team as I did but Bobby played for California Soul which was the premier team hand-picked for athletic ability and they would usually win the championship. California Soul was a mixed race team, which never was a problem, with sports in the penitentiary the racial divide is lessened and Bobby played shortstop because of his quickness and agility not because of his color. He would be warming up on the softball field with a Camel cigarette in his mouth catching grounders by putting his glove hand behind him between his legs or catch flies by putting his glove behind his back, he was so entertaining to watch. High Times was a combination of fuck ups and during practice sessions we would sit in the dugout and smoke weed rather than organize ourselves as a team. I wanted to win by practicing more but never said anything since most things in prison are just what they are. The comical part of the organized softball league was on game day we had prison inmate umpires complete with striped shirts and whistles. They could earn thirty days extra good time for being an umpire during the softball season, but not too many prisoners wanted the job. More than once did I see an umpire walk off the field during a game after his official ruling was disputed by some other prisoner guilty of the infraction and end up in his face screaming, "I WAS SAFE, I WAS SAFE MUTHAFUCKA."

You could hear the umpire mumbling as he left the field, "I'm not going to get killed over a fuckin' softball game, fuck this."

This didn't happen all that often, but when it did, it was comical as we would watch it unfold from the coliseum bleachers located behind the backstop. What can I say, not everyone was raised to be a good sport and some people are just extremely antisocial and are extremely fucked human beings. In the joint or not, it's still only a game. Donny played third base on our team of misfits and I played short center field or rover, in softball there are four outfield positions and I would position myself between the outfield and the infield roving and catching short fly balls hit in the gap or hot grounders missed by the infield. I was good and could throw someone out at home with my strong arm but a lot of the prisoners were exceptional athletes, exceptional, and I know for a fact some could've played in professional sports but lacked the skill of functioning in society.

Tumbleweed was a California boy who worked in the kitchen getting his name from his hair, he was a white boy with an afro and his hustle was sandwiches. For a pack of smokes you could have a sandwich delivered to your cell daily, homemade sandwiches at that, and I would get one under my pillow every afternoon for no charge out of respect. Tumbleweed would bring ace bandages to work with him in the morning and make upwards to seventy sandwiches to smuggle out, then wrapping the bandage around his legs and torso area to hold the sandwiches he would exit the kitchen. Although there was always a guard doing shakedowns looking for knives and other items being stolen from the kitchen standing at the chow hall door searching prisoners, Tumbleweed would throw the hack a couple of sandwiches to overlook the seventy wrapped around his body. Tumbleweed knew what was up, guards like free stuff and fat guards like free food. Everyone had some hustle even the guards, more than once did I see a kitchen freeman rolling out an entire side of beef through the rotunda area and out the front door presuming to take to his car and then home for his family. I had seen guards getting tattoos from prisoners, smuggling drugs as well as hearing about other bulls receiving sexual favors from homosexuals, we didn't look at them any different than us they just had the keys.

Living on the fifth tier had its advantages as well as its disadvantages; the po-lice wouldn't like to make the trip five flights up for a couple of reasons, the main reason was the fear of being thrown off. I'd seen a couple of people lose their lives that way and so far nobody the best I could tell could fly, the other reason was they were out of shape and overweight. But as for me, I might not have been able to fly but I could run up those stairs in a matter of seconds from being in such good shape. I would consider it part of my workout and the only drawback was if you forgot something in your cell on the way to the movies, yard or chow you would have to get back up all those stairs and back down. Still that would be just another workout for my young legs. Since the guards went out of their way to avoid walking the upper tiers it would be open season for tattooing, shooting dope and smoking weed. Even the old-timer guards would make sure they rattled their keys to give a heads up that they were on the tier to avoid confrontations completely. Four cells away from my cell on the corner of the cellblock was a shower that had been converted from a cell, which made it comfortable to use since it was a single shower and the door would slide closed. With the late hours of summer everyone would hit the cellblock from the yard at the same time hurrying to get cleaned up with lockup only being an hour and a half away at ten o'clock.

Coming in from the yard one late afternoon to avoid the summer shower rush I grabbed my towel, soap and only wearing my boxers and shower shoes noticed Tumbleweed was using the single shower, so I started the long walk to the opposite end of the tier. When I arrived at the three-man community shower and as I stepped in I noticed a black guy on the shower floor bleeding a one-inch solid trail of blood going into the drain, he was still alive and our eyes locked. Looking as if he were asking for me to help him I still couldn't and had to get out of the area quickly, so back at my cell getting dressed, I quietly yelled to Tumbleweed to go back out to the yard. As I was leaving my cell to get out of the block I heard the single shower being turned off. I thought about how I was probably the last face on earth that man would ever see. Back on the yard I found Bobby and Donny walking towards the center hall entrance and told them to stay on the yard with me and from my look they understood as the siren started to sound.

Understand me when I tell you it wasn't a matter of me wanting or not wanting to help a dying man, it was simply the discipline of survival and if it wasn't my business I wasn't going to make it my business. Even the responsibility of telling the staff that somebody was hurt on the fifth tier is no other prisoners business either, and with my track record from McNeil sitting on the shower floor holding a dying man's hand with his blood on me would end me up in federal court quick and in a hurry.

But there's one man that could help you in Leavenworth if you were stabbed and dying and that was Doctor Jarvis. Jarvis was a military medic in the

Vietnam War and he was one cool cat under pressure, which I personally witnessed the next day in the movie house. In retaliation for the dead guy in the shower another convict knowing who the assailant was in the shower killing crept behind the assailant in the movie house reaching around and stabbing him once in the chest right after the lights went off. The victim of the movie house stabbing, Eli I think his name was, jumped up and started chasing the dead guy in the showers Homeboy who had stabbed him. Some rookie guard who didn't know what was up then grabbed Eli as he ran by bleeding. As the guard held Eli, the guy with the knife came back stabbing Eli in the neck. Blood was pumping everywhere because Eli's jugular vein was severed and as we were all ordered down on the floor here comes Doctor Jarvis on the scene, cool as the other side of your pillow. What happened next I would definitely not believe unless I had seen it with my own eyes. Doctor Jarvis pulled out a ballpoint pen from his pocket, twisted it apart taking out the plastic filler and after breaking it in half he connected Eli's jugular vein back together. Fuck I thought as I was lying next to Jay Tee in the prone position right outside the movie house. Jay Tee looked over my way and all he said was, "We need to get Jarvis's home phone number."

We both snickered under our breath and it was just another day in The Big Top and although it was summer, violence didn't take a vacation in Leavenworth.

For all the natural athleticism that Donny had he was clumsy in other areas. Once coming into my cell opening up a balloon of weed he spilled the entire contents all over everything, another time dropping a weed pipe five stories we were sharing and smoking off the tier as he passed it to me. Then there was the one time he kicked my glass jar drinking tumbler off the fifth tier down the five stories shattering everywhere as it hit the flats below. That fumble caused a little heat from the guards thinking someone was targeting another individual which inevitably could lead to a riot. So one day as I was picking something up off my cell floor Donny had knocked over I looked at Donny, "Holmes, you're all thumbs."

He only shrugged his shoulders as I blurted out, "Thumbs! That's who you are, Thumbs."

And another nickname was born, so Donny was now known by me as well as everyone else as Thumbs and it fit him like a tailored suit.

The days started getting shorter with California Soul winning another championship, and another summer had gone and how quick it did go. I was still in the yard daily as the weather cooled while the yard crowd thinned out and Jay Tee would join me religiously after work in the afternoon walking the track, working out and listening to my little radio. Jay Tee had a love for music as I did and the hours would fly by as we laughed, talked and knocked down laps walking on the track. Jay Tee was a deep thinking individual teaching me many things, telling me how the birds that we would see fly over were God's creatures and we should respect them, and that we should do right in life with others. This was coming from a guy that had murdered people, even once killing the wrong person he was instructed to kill because of a name mix up. He didn't say so in words but he didn't like the life he'd chosen and always told me he wanted better for me, and that I was going to get another shot at life and to take advantage of it. And Jay Tee's golden rule was "Always think before you talk" stating that the tongue is where all our trouble starts, and if we can harness the tongue we can master life. Jay Tee was very deep, intelligent and extremely charismatic yet deeply involved with the game surrounding the "powers that be", but Jay Tee was also my friend and we had become very close in this war like atmosphere, and I knew in my heart of hearts that he always had my best interest in his heart.

Somebody had passed a girl's name and address on to Thumbs so he started corresponding through the mail and then later gave her a call on one of the cellblock telephones. When I first came in the federal prison system you were only allowed one phone call per month for ten minutes with the guard sitting across the table as you talked, now there were telephones mounted to the walls of every cellblock. I never used the phones even once, since I had no one to call and didn't need to know what was going on outside in the free world. I already knew the answer to that question of what was going on out there, and the answer was everything. During the transition of having phones readily available for prisoners the administration first came up with the bright idea of individual phone booths, which turned out to be a bad idea for some people. I had witnessed one of these unfortunate people earlier when I lived in the jungle. Since phone booths don't have a backdoor and are very confining, one day as I was walking by the phone area in A block I noticed a guy leaning against the glass wall of the booth with the phone hanging by his side. Instinctually his enemy realized this was a prime time to make his move stabbing to death the guy in the phone booth. I always wondered what the person on the other end of that phone conversation was thinking and hearing while all this was happening.

Things in my life kept running smoothly and I was knocking down the time and also picking up a new hustle being a runner for C block collecting the revenue on illegal parlay tickets for professional football as well as college football. My commission was twenty-five percent of the entire take of the gambling money which I would pass on to another prisoner in A block named William Williams who worked for another convict who in turn was the money man. Lots of people liked to gamble on football and the money and cigarettes were flowing. Even though gambling was a dangerous and tricky situation in the penitentiary, but with me I was well known and respected and everyone knew I was on the up and up and connected with the right people. It was cash or cigarettes only, except for Bobby and Thumbs of course, and Jay Tee didn't gamble, but I would never let Bobby and Thumbs or I get in any kind of jackpot by overextending. Bobby would come to my cell on Sunday morning handing me his NFL picks of the week, as I would say to him, "Who do you like this week, Maverick?"

Cracking that Paul Newman smile of his and handing me or not handing me the money his response would always be, "You're the one whose gonna have to be giving me money later Whisper, the Rams are a lock this week."

The Rams in the late seventies were pitiful, but football season was very lucrative for me and as Thumbs started to get visits from the woman who he had been corresponding with and had hopes of the visits becoming profitable also. After coming back from his first visit I put it right out there, "How fat is she?"

He proceeded to tell me she's wasn't fat at all, actually that she's kind of cute, I reminded Thumbs that he had been locked up for some years now and his definition of cute might have changed. But he insisted that she was okay looking and I pushed the issue with, "There is gotta be something wrong with her Thumbs, there always is with these love sick prison broads so tell me what is it?"

He danced around the question for a bit then he finally said, "Whisper she ain't got no teeth."

"What the fuck Thumbs," is all I could think to say as I was bent over laughing and as I became a little more composed I added, "You two probably make a cute couple, Thumbs and Gums, it has a certain ring to it. Don't you think Thumbs?"

"Fuck you Whisper," is all he could muster up to say.

The holidays were upon us once again and for Thanksgiving this year the kitchen staff decided to put tablecloths on the tables and fully dressed out cooked turkeys on display in the chow hall to add to the lacking ambience of prison Thanksgiving. It may have been Thanksgiving to the staff but it was Thursday to us, and with all the dressed cooked turkeys disappearing, back in the cellblocks prisoners were walking around chewing on a turkey leg as the guards shook their heads. That's the one thing that most of the guards didn't get, any kindness to us was perceived as weakness and it was our queue to do what we do, and in this case it was to steal the turkeys from the chow hall on Thursday.

I would be seen all over the cellblock listening to the football games in the fall and winter being announced on my radio, often standing by one of the four televisions that were provided for each cellblock while watching that same game on the screen. The first three televisions were for the main channels and the fourth one was for sports, but on game day all four televisions would be tuned into the games. Any sports, live or televised in prison seemed to loosen the tension creating a more common ground of interaction between prisoners which obviously was better for all of us. But in Leavenworth when watching television, you wear a set of oversized earphones to hear the audio portion of the television with the earphones plugging into a jack on the wall and anybody could do the math on this one; sitting with your ears shut off from everything around you this made you an easier target if you had enemies. So I would just lean against the heaters on the wall and watch the same game being announced on my radio. I got hooked on this method since the color commentators on the radio had the ability of making a dull NFL game more interesting, plus I always had to know what was going on around me, always.

Circus peanuts, cigarettes and an orange, these things marked another Christmas with more visits equaling more drugs entering the penitentiary and with the New Year flipping another calendar year off my ten years. I was in a deep groove of doing time and would still run daily no matter what the weather, but because of the yard closing fifteen minutes before four o'clock standing count in the winter months, this left a lot more time to be confined to the cellblock or the indoor gym.

With the New Year, not much had really changed other than the cabin fever felt by me and I can only imagine some others. My motor was still running on high with Thumbs always wound very tight, often we would be sitting in my cell after smoking weed or snacking and he would look past me with this odd stare, "I fucked up Whisper. I really fucked myself this time," was all he would say.

I knew he was referring to his two life sentences but I lacked any words so I never said anything, and that would be the extent of Thumbs expressing the reality of his life, or lack of one. Bobby was so much more relaxed about everything; he had always been, so conversation about doing time was nonexistent from him. But for Thumbs and I we were always on the move with some kind of prison mischief, smoking weed then trying to find something to eat or anything to do, even running up to the barbershop weekly located in the pool hall area. Cutting each other's hair by completely buzzing it all off with the clippers, which to me was the most comfortable in the joint. We just seem to have to be doing something at all times.

The barbershop was complete with authentic barber chairs, scissors and clippers, but no straight razors for obvious reasons. There was always a guard on duty in the barbershop, not for the weapon angle so much but to make sure all the hair was swept up and disposed of properly. This was in case somebody got the notion to make a dummy look close to real with human hair fooling the prison guards during one of the fourteen counts that were done daily. Counts done at night while we were sleeping had to let the guard see skin, so when a guard went by doing the overnight counts, he had to see human flesh and if he didn't he would tap his flashlight on the bars to wake you and loudly state, "SHOW ME SKIN".

Very irritating and with fourteen fucking prison counts every twenty-four hours, seven days a week with the four o'clock count being a mandatory standing count, which meant having to stand by your bunk, and that count eventually being called in to Washington DC to have the prison cleared so we could be unlocked once again, very fuckin' irritating. And as I would always say to the fellas, "They count us like diamonds and treat us like dogs."

Laying on my bunk after one of these standing counts I was flipping through the latest issue of Playboy magazine waiting for the doors to be unlocked and there she was, Janis Schmidt playmate of the month for February nineteen seventy-eight. I instantly had a major crush on this woman, not because of her naked foldout or other naked pictures in her pictorial, but a picture of Miss Schmidt standing while straddling a bicycle looking over her right shoulder wearing short white shorts, tube socks and staring right at me. Fuck she was beautiful and because of my lack of poon-tang going on years now I needed a girlfriend and she was her. I took a double-edged razor blade cutting her picture out and with toothpaste attached the photo to the wall across from my bunk. When the count was cleared and we were unlocked Thumbs came in my cell to get me to go to chow and while looking at my new picture on the wall at the same time as speaking, "Whisper you never have pictures up, who is she?"

"Thumbs, my boy, I would like to introduce you to Miss Janis Schmidt my new girl, and after this day I would appreciate it if you would never look at her again."

Thumbs while smirking and squinting said, "Whisper you are a crazy fool."

"You may be right, and I may be a zip damn crazy fool Thumbs, but I'm serious. Don't be looking at her, or me and you are going to have a problem."

We were both laughing as we walked down the tier on our way to evening chow.

24

Thumbs had started getting drugs brought in during his visits; marijuana mostly in small amounts since finding someone to send you a large quantity involved a lot of trust and plotting. It wasn't like you could post it on a bulletin board asking someone if they needed heroin or a pound of weed smuggled for a percentage. The reason that I had been so successful in the past on getting over with contraband and my personal involvement with violence was for one reason and one reason only, I kept my mouth shut. And Thumbs, Bobby, Jay Tee along with a couple other of the fellas shared this same simple philosophy, never say anything to people not involved.

Thumbs made me a wood frame complete with a Plexiglas front to put my paper girlfriend in, he didn't have the craftsmanship that Richie Rich had in McNeil, but it was much appreciated and enhanced Janis Schmidt's already enhanced attributes. Every morning part of my new routine while drinking my Taster's Choice coffee was to place two fingers on my lips and with a kiss I would put the same two fingers on Janet Schmidt's ass. I had also taken Jay Tee's suggestion and quit smoking weed, and now my new thing was fucking with administration even more than I had in the past. Besides, even without the weed high I still had my first love, heroin, and I wasn't going to be giving that up anytime soon.

When I would see Doctor Karkas, the psychiatrist with a screw loose, walking from the infirmary, I would always ask him what time it was, and like the nut he was, he would stop lift up his pants on his left leg and check his wristwatch on his ankle. Also the good prison shrink doctor came up with his own personal method of dealing with all the violence and killings in Leavenworth, he prescribed Valium to anyone that asked. Thumbs went to Karkas telling him he couldn't deal with doing all his time and the doctor gave him three five milligram Valium a day, trust me this was not the solution to calming Leavenworth Penitentiary. Prisoners would save up their Valium over a few days and then take all of them at once chasing the pills down with the prison pruno. Needless to say the Valiums and alcohol were a deadly combination. And any dealing with the prison psychiatrist the feds gave you what is called a P number which gave them permission to do anything they wanted with you, and I personally have seen this more than once when a maniac killer would disappear and on his return after a long length of time, he would be a completely changed person, but never for the better in my eyes. The feds would give the medication Prolixin to any habitual problem violent convict, it was shock therapy in a pill form and we called it Edison Medicine and it reduced men into vegetables, but with me I wasn't mental, I just didn't give a fuck and as far as I know there ain't no pill for that.

My little crew was always in and out of building sixty-three, but I was receiving more shots than usual, most of my shots had been for insubordination, that's running my mouth when the guards ask me a simple question such as how I was doing. After years in Leavenworth I was still flying low on the radar with my activities but high profile with the staff from the company I kept, and the guards targeted me for more searches than some. This was the cat and mouse part of prison. While stopping and searching me I would completely go off sometimes, mostly acting but the guard wouldn't know that, so when some screw tried to break the ice and asked me how I was doing, I became animated as my reply spilled out of my mouth, "How the fuck am I doing? Locked up in this shit-hole with you, no women for years and stuck here in bum-fuck Kansas what kind of question is that? Now you tell me, boss. How the fuck do you think I'm doing?"

Usually the guard would try calming me down by saying, "Take it easy I didn't mean anything by it."

Then I would go off again, "So you really don't care how I'm doing, then why the fuck did you ask me? You're confusing me boss, you act like you care then you act like you don't care, what the fuck, stop confusing me."

By now one of two things would be happening, nine out of ten times the guard would be trying to get far away from me, but that one other time the hack would call other guards to escort me to building sixty-three along with a shot for insubordination. So after getting tired of this routine I started not answering the guards when they asked me anything, now I would receive a shot for silent insubordination. They would take a minimal amount of good time away as punishment, then I would have to file an appeal to get it back. They always gave me my good time back, even the sixty days on my conviction of 001 in McNeil Island they eventuality reinstated. What a system, but this was only cat and mouse games to pass the time and it does seem stupid now that I think about it, but at the time it was about passing time plain and simple. And now it was summer again and Thumbs and I joined the softball team called High Times II with Bobby being asked to be on last season's champions California Soul again. A lot of the players would change over the year, but more surprisingly a lot of the players would be the same, it was amazing to me how many people were stuck in Leavenworth and I was definitely one of the ones that was stuck.

When playing handball with Jay Tee and Thumbs the one out of the three of us that was waiting for next game had the job of making sure the radio had a good song playing. We unanimously agreed fuck disco, so when Thumbs started to change the station one afternoon, I intervened by telling him to wait this song is a remake of an Eric Burton and the Animals jam and even though it's disco, turn it up and check it out, it's about us.

Santa Esmerelda started singing, "I'm just a soul that's intentions are good— please O Lord don't let me be misunderstood."

I was semi joking but we just stood there with all three of us silent while listening.

Softball season was over for another year, and the softball field had seen a lot of action that summer, but the biggest event on the infield wasn't during a playoff game or the turning of a double play, it was involving three prisoners from the Washington DC area. As Jay Tee and I played another game of handball the ball traveled over my head, and as I went to retrieve it I noticed something out of place on the yard, specifically the pitcher's mound of the baseball diamond. I gave Jay Tee an instant heads up for him to check this shit out. It was one prisoner on the ground stabbing another in the leg as he was being hit in the head with punches from the one being stabbed standing over him trying to get loose from the knife wielding prisoner's deadly grip on his shirt. While all of this was happening one of the DC Homeboys of the one being stabbed was walking onto the yard, his name was Fly and everyone knew him as being from DC as well as a serious threat if ever in a confrontation.

Once Fly caught focus of what was going down on the pitcher's mound he casually grabbed an aluminum bat from the equipment box and fast walked behind the one on the ground with the knife. Without hesitation he started to beat that man to death right out in the open on the yard and once the corner gun tower guard became aware of the situation he announced for Fly to put down the bat and step away. But Fly continued swinging on the already dead man's head as shots rang out from the gun tower into the yard. I immediately jumped behind a pile of concrete rubble in the weight pit area and Jay Tee jumped right next to me.

And after the usual lockdown and cleanup that evening Bobby whispered to me as we walked the yard, "What went down earlier?"

"It looked like a bottom of the ninth, two outs, bases loaded—Grand Slam."

Bobby moved his head side-to-side smiling and shortly the recall whistle blew and Bobby and I walked back to the cellblock and called it a night.

California Soul won yet another championship that year giving Bobby bragging rights throughout the winter. The recreation department also furnished a little cheesy trophy for first place and now Bobby had two. As I prepared for the cabin fever that would be setting in again, Thumbs started bringing more weed in from his visits, and since I had stopped smoking weed not only was my mind clearer but also I had more cash or things equivalent to cash. But the bigger thing I noticed was how cynical my view of murder was now. Thumbs had hooked up with this prisoner from B block named Ernest Hoyle, who back in the day was a marijuana smuggler, flying bales of weed from Mexico. Ernest would send Thumb's girl, Gums, a pound of weed at a time giving Thumbs half for bringing it into the penitentiary. I never learned Thumbs toothless

309

fake girlfriends name so I always referred to her as Gums. The pay off of half was for full discretion also but that was always understood by anyone we dealt with. Balloons of weed were equal to a heaping plastic picnic spoon, that's how they were measured and you could get anywhere from two hundred and seventy to three hundred and thirty balloons from a pound. Before his visit in the morning he would drink large amounts of water, and while on the visit he would swallow from seventy to eighty balloons. After getting back to his cell, as I would stand point (lookout) for the bulls, Thumbs would throw up the balloons in his sink. He could throw up almost all of them except for a couple, and after he rinsed and dried them he handed off the balloons to me. We would immediately separate, me going to the yard as he lay in his cell waiting to see if the guards rushed him. Thumbs was a machine when it came to swallowing and bringing back up the balloons.

The California crew or the fellas or whatever you wanted to call us, we were at the pinnacle of the narcotics, violence and it was like we had an invisible shield of protection around us. What separated us from the others is that we would kill our own without hesitation. If someone fucked up in any area which warranted being eliminated, then one of the California crew had no problem with killing another Californian. I have never seen any other region of people in these federal penitentiaries do this ever. This sends a definite message to others, and with fewer than twenty-five California boys at any one time in Leavenworth, we still were considered the untouchables. I was regularly eating with Jay Tee now at the California exclusive tables in the chow hall, Thumbs would join us sometimes but Bobby would rarely eat at these tables from personal choice. And if the fellas weren't in the chow hall those tables would remain empty and the same applied for the movie house with our three rows of theater seating down in the front of the auditorium.

Naturally the guards thought more was going on then there was most times at these tables, but truth be told it was usually just laughs and planning to meet in the yard for handball and shit like that. But there were a few times when plotting was being discussed in an extortion scheme or murder blueprint. One evening as I sat there at dinner chow two of the fellas were asking Jay Tee questions on where and when on a certain individual from Texas that owed drug money. I started to get up with my tray as Jay Tee looked at me saying, "You're okay Whisper to hear this."

I didn't want to hear anything, I didn't want to know anything, but I knew that Jay Tee trusted me completely and it would've been disrespectful for me to leave, so I sat back down and as I ate pretended not to hear the murder plot unfolding. And once I realized who they were plotting against, I glanced towards the Texas section of tables spotting the potential victim as he ate fried chicken and thought to myself, although he doesn't know it, this is his last meal. That evening I relayed to Bobby and Thumbs not to go to the gym that night, neither of them asked any questions they both just knew from my look. Later as Thumbs and I were playing cribbage in my cell with Bobby looking on a little before lockup, we could hear the siren sound and the commotion of jangling keys as guards ran towards the gym area.

That Thanksgiving there were no turkeys displayed in the chow hall for us to steal, fuck 'um if they can't take a joke. As far as I was concerned the administration had no sense of humor when it came to playing cat and mouse. But it was the holidays, more visits, and more narcotics but not soon enough for me the weather would finally break once again in Kansas. I was bored one evening in my cell after lockup so I decided to write a letter, the first letter I had written besides to Bobby years ago. I was writing through Playboy magazine to Janis Schmidt my paper girlfriend, and what I wrote was simple and to the point. I stated that I was a young healthy man, I used Dove soap, Mennen deodorant and could show her what a real gentleman was like, adding if she ever tired of that jet set lifestyle to write me and I signed the letter with my name and prison number. Thumbs thought I was completely fucking crazy but it was something I felt like I had to do. For a short time Thumbs would ask me on a daily basis, "Did you get a letter back from Janis?"

"Not yet. She's probably not tired of that lifestyle yet, I just have to give her a little more time but she will write. I fuckin' guarantee it Thumbs."

After the circus peanuts, cigarettes and orange, we were flipping another page on the calendar, and for me summer couldn't come quick enough as I could see the snow starting to melt earlier than in the past years on the yard.

I would still run for miles daily and I knew every crack in every brick in the wall. I would just run circles and circles in the big yard and it was the one thing that would let me think of things other than this penitentiary filled with craziness where I was living. I was scheduled to go to the parole board at the end of this year and didn't have much hope what the parole board would decide, so I just stayed in my routine of running, handball, reading and getting high on heroin every chance I got, which was starting to get more often since Bobby had once in a while lined up a package for Thumbs to bring in during his visit with Gums. Thumbs didn't have the luxury of swallowing the heroin balloons as he did the weed balloons, instead he had to keister them in the vault (inserting the balloons into his anus).

312

Spring came early that year and I was more than relieved so I shook off my cabin fever and got into my yard routine of being outdoors as much as possible, and as Jay Tee and I sat in the shaded corner next to the wall under the gun tower one unseasonably warm spring day we noticed Cinnamon on the yard. Cinnamon was this very flamboyant homosexual, who would dye his hair with black shoe polish, use the blue chalk from the pool hall as eye shadow and was always dressed with tailored blouses made from prison shirts and wear tight penitentiary issue pants. But for Jay Tee and I it wasn't his obscure dress sense that caught our eye, we both knew Cinnamon was never ever seen on the yard. We watched from our front row seats what happened next as Cinnamon ran up behind her current boyfriend hitting him once in the head and burying a claw hammer in his skull. The boyfriend stumbled but never went down as Cinnamon ran in the opposite direction crying and screaming while flailing his arms as he ran off the yard. Jay Tee and I were both laughing from Cinnamon's dramatic exit off the yard. As we continued to watch, the boyfriend with the hammer still half lodged in his skull was screaming Cinnamon's name and not to ever leave him as the boyfriend walked in a zig-zag pattern towards the infirmary.

But the real kicker was a few days later as Jay Tee and I were doing pull-ups in the weight pit next to building sixty-three the boyfriend, with a big ol' bandage wrapped around his head was serenading Cinnamon with his guitar as we could hear kisses being thrown out the window of segregation through the bars. Jay Tee looked at me, "Ahhh, springtime you can definitely feel the love in the air."

Within a week another crime of passion went down on the yard with the boyfriend this time stabbing his homosexual girlfriend. When the gun tower announced for the boyfriend to put down the knife and assume the position on the ground, the boyfriend then ran hiding behind the coliseum seating. As we laid in prone position on the yard two guards put the still breathing girlfriend in a gurney and started to transport him to the infirmary, then the boyfriend came running back out pushing both guards out of the way causing them to drop the gurney and started stabbing his girlfriend again while screaming, "IF I CAN'T HAVE YOU NOBODY CAN."

That was a bad spring for homosexuals but it didn't put a damper on the availability of generic *tang* available in Leavenworth. What always puzzled me though was how they never plotted their murders and were usually always busted and prosecuted all in the name of love, it just never made any sense to me.

Softball sign-ups came around again and I joined High Times III along with Thumbs as Bobby remained the starting shortstop on California Soul. What happened next was so out of the norm from what I had gotten used too. Now I definitely knew that Leavenworth was a fucked up place to be on any given day, and I also realized that I may never get out of here alive or otherwise. I had come to grips with this and that was my norm and mindset. I also had acceptance of whom I'd become and the things I'd done and still slept fine every night. But what really shocked me next was Thumbs with his request of wanting me to maybe be his best man at his wedding. Gums had been pushing the issue of if Thumbs really loved her or not, or was he just using her, and Gums literally had our lives in her hands with all the narcotics being mailed to her house and the felony risk involved in every visit. This was a very tricky situation since Thumbs had come to despise Gums because of her ignorance and hillbilly thinking, so after Thumbs apprehensively asked if he should really go through with it. I encouraged the wedding simply

314

stating, "Thumbs, she is the goose that lays the golden egg and always keep her happy, at all costs."

So the date was set with the ceremony arranged to take place in the visiting room during non-visiting hours. I wore my best military green pants, crisp white T-shirt and a pair of green suede Puma tennis shoes. The entire situation seemed surreal as I stood next to Thumbs as the prison minister pronounced them man and wife. I was looking at the bride and thinking to myself, what a good catch Gums, your new husband may be out in thirty years with good behavior and he doesn't like you, not even a little, yes Gums good fuckin' catch. Though that was my thoughts, what I said to the both of them was good luck as the minister asked us to bow our heads in prayer to bless these two individuals in their journey of marriage. And as he was praying, Gums put some balloons in my hand which I swallowed, and as the last balloon went down my throat I heard, "Amen."

And my job of best man was done and you know without me having to say how much I fucked with Thumbs about having to marry that crazy broad. The next day we were all sitting by the handball courts, Bobby, Jay Tee, Thumbs and I as Jay Tee asked, "Whisper how did Thumbs' wedding go?"

What an opportunity, so I slowly stood up and faced the three of them, "Bobby, Jay Tee, it was magnificent! It put Richard Burton's and Elizabeth Taylor's wedding to complete shame and there wasn't a dry eye in the house, truly fucking magnificent!"

"Fuck you Whisper. No fuck all you," Thumbs spit out while laughing, as we all lost it with the same laughter.

25

The score was tied at two apiece and the game had gone into extra innings in an ironic twist of events as High Times III was hosting California Soul for the softball championship of Leavenworth Penitentiary. With nobody on base Thumbs was up to bat with me warming up in the batter circle, I called time out and motioned Thumbs over and as I grabbed him by the shoulders I whispered, "Get on base Holmes and I'll bring you in."

The game thus far had been a seesaw battle of defensive plays and a large amount of shit talking between Bobby and Thumbs, this was our version of the World Series and with prisoners in the coliseum seating behind us watching, the focus of the yard was on this final softball game of the summer. With the crack of the bat Thumbs had himself a standing double. I slow walked up to home base locking eyes with Thumbs then sheepishly cutting my eyes towards right-center field. Thumbs received my signal clear as crystal and I tapped the first pitch over the first baseman's head, and with Thumbs' big lead off second base he never slowed down for third and scored the winning run. Fuck yes was my thought as the High Times III dugout erupted. Then the two teams lined up in the finishing gesture of good sportsmanship to shake hands and I puckered up throwing Bobby a little air kiss when we were face-to-face.

Thumbs and I would have all winter to talk shit about this championship playoff game to Bobby and without a doubt we would, but after that last game the summer becomes bittersweet knowing the frigid cold will arrive soon and the grass on the playing field will turn brown again until spring.

With the parole board only in session in the prison every six months, I missed my window of opportunity to be seen at this particular parole board hearing, representing the Kansas City region. But the holidays were here and my true motivation was to get high on heroin more, I wasn't going anywhere and waiting for the regional parole board to arrive was like everything else in the feds; It's always on their time, end of story, period.

After the Christmas formality of peanuts, smokes and a piece of fruit, I was more than ready to turn the page of the calendar once again, but this year coming up was unique. I would also be closing the chapter of another decade and the eighties would be born.

The two Puerto Rican nationalists that attempted to assassinate President Truman were given a presidential pardon that year by President Carter and extradited back to Puerto Rico. Since I read anything I could get my hands on I remember reading about them in *Time* magazine, and how they were hailed heroes after returning to their homeland. And the chaos of murder was getting closer to me as my neighbor on the fifth tier had his throat cut by a lawnmower blade as he laid on a weight bench doing bench presses in the gym that winter. Fatman was his nickname, Fatman Wilkins. Thumbs lived in 534 and Fatman lived in 528 on the other side of my cell with an empty cell between us the three plus years that Fatman was my neighbor. Fatman's nickname didn't derive from being overweight, quite the contrary.

317

Fatman was this extremely in shape individual and at only five foot seven he could dunk a basketball, along with being able to do an endless amount of pull-ups and chin-ups. Fatman's nickname came from him being *fat* with drugs and money. Often he would see me working the pull-up bar while doing my calisthenics and claim that any day I might take his premier position as pull-up king away from him. But even though in superb shape, Fatman couldn't stop the sharpened lawnmower blade from slicing his throat by the hand of some young buck that Fatman was trying to pressure for sex.

I was still C block runner for illegal football parlay tickets in the winters which gave me extra greenbacks to buy more heroin for me as well as Thumbs, Jay Tee and Bobby. We were always generous with each other so nobody kept track of who and how much, and we would all four be loaded on a weekly basis or biweekly at worst. I was robbing the federal government out of a lot more time by being high in the beginning of nineteen hundred and eighty. One evening as I was high, leaning in the doorway of Thumbs' cell waiting for him to finish doing his portion so I could stash the homemade syringe back in the shower wall, I started to smell smoke. Then the smell of smoke was mixed with a definite scent of flesh burning, fuck I thought as I realized someone had set a prisoner on fire on the fourth tier and the entire cellblock was engulfed now with this stench. I knew people were sometimes burned to death by their enemies, but I had personally never experienced until then being in the same cellblock while a prisoner was on fire and screaming. Someone had slammed the convict's cell door shut and wrapped a coat hanger around the bars and door to secure the victim in his cell. Then that same someone took a Taster's Choice jar of gas obtained from the landscape department, lit a piece of towel throwing it in the cell and walked off.

In a six foot by eight foot concrete and steel cell there is just nowhere to go for the person who's on fire. So I stood on the fifth tier loaded on heroin watching the flames arc from the fourth tier while hearing animal sounds coming from this human being that was trapped and on fire. Naturally they couldn't lock down the cellblock instead having to evacuate the entire block, minus one, taking us all down to the chow hall to wait for the C block situation to be cleaned up. This took quite some time since the steel becomes hot and twisted. So as I sat in the chow hall with Thumbs and Bobby, I appreciated the supreme quality of the heroin since I might have been upset if this murder had interfered with my high.

After the entire population of C block was escorted back, minus one, and as I sat in my cell locked in for the night, the smell of smoke lingered and I mentally felt the walls of Leavenworth closing in around me.

When I was nine years old and in trouble in school, I sat in my bedroom and prayed to not let this school trouble catch up with me and also for my father not to find out and punish me. And that night alone in my cell would be the second time that I said some kind of words in a prayer form to something or somebody that I really didn't know what was. With my makeshift prayer only asking one thing, and that was I would be stabbed to death in Leavenworth and not set on fire.

I knew exactly what I needed to do the next day and that was something that I would do periodically to feel a certain level of personal sanity. After my morning run, before work, I snuck up into the fourth floor stairwell of the shoe factory where there was a window that looked out on to this one small hill next to the penitentiary. Previous times I had seen buffalo grazing on that sacred hill and watching them would

319

some way comfort me, but this one morning as I looked out, there were no buffalo. Instead my eyes focused on white crosses stuck in the ground, crooked, staggered and appearing very lonely and cold. White crosses that I never noticed before while looking for buffalo out the shoe factory window.

Boot Hill was what it was called, and the white crosses represented prisoners who had died in Leavenworth for various reasons without anyone claiming their body. I could see the blurry prison numbers painted on the crosses and my mind let me know that within a matter of time I would maybe become one of those lonely crosses. There was actually a form that you fill out and sign asking who will pick up your body in case of death, and every time that I had to fill out this paperwork in the orientation process of receiving and discharge I put "no one". That is how I was sure I would end up on Boot Hill plain and simple. Now my only concerning thought left was how I had already planned my destiny and now was just waiting for fate.

With my shirt buttoned completely up to the collar of my pressed green prison issue clothing I sat in the federal parole board hearing, rigid with hawk like eyes and attentive to everything being said. The three members on the parole board listened as an officer read to them my progress report. It started with inmate 89759-132 being found guilty of 001, murder of another inmate in McNeil Island. The report continued to state said inmate was under federal indictment and no trial date had been set. The officer further read from my thick prison jacket listing numerous insubordination and silent insubordination write-ups along with suspected involvement of various offences and then concluded with, inmate 89759-132 has adjusted to Leavenworth Penitentiary with no major violent or weapon rule infractions in the last six months.

Thousands of thoughts ran through my brain, mostly how the progress report painted a negative picture of me. Hearing that shit I wouldn't let me out either. Why couldn't they have listed some flattering positive attributes that I possessed? In my mind the progress report should mention how I was a member of the championship softball team last year, was an excellent handball player who was very rarely beaten and could run like the wind for hours. But with my longevity of anger towards the feds I just sat quietly across the table from the parole board members concentrating on my posture.

After a short recess the chairman of the parole board gave me a release date of a little over two more years.

Seeing Bobby in the cellblock that afternoon, who had also gone to the parole board, he asked me if I got a release date and after telling him he said his release date was three months more than mine. He was livid telling me that in his hearing they only brought up one infraction of when he got caught stealing two cookies out of the chow hall. I just shook my head waiting for Bobby to release his steam since I knew he wasn't upset with me, it was the no rhyme no reason no method to their madness parole board Bobby was upset with. After Bobby cooled downed a little I did tell him, "You should've got some seriously violent write-ups, it worked for me." Adding, "Fuck 'um Bobby we are downhill now."

His smile looked like a smile of agreement as he said, "Yeah fuck 'um. I can use some more time to work on my handball game anyway."

We both agreed to downplay our release dates to Thumbs since he had almost five years more before he would even be considered for parole, and our two years and change would sound like a weekend to him. The start of this particular year seemed to be a little crazier than the usual with the increasing prison killings but I thought maybe it was just me, until I read an article in *Time* magazine. The article reflected how Leavenworth Penitentiary was declared the most violent and dangerous prison in the United States. It went on to say how the guards in Leavenworth had lost control of the prison and what should or could be done about it. This article reassured me that this place was really a fucking madhouse, and although I wasn't emotionally invested in most of the murders around me, I did definitely feel the pressure cooker affect that Leavenworth Penitentiary was taking on. But there's nothing at the time anyone, even administration could do about it. Leavenworth was labeled the worst of the worst living up to its reputation now more often than ever with violence in these explosive cellblocks.

So what happened next was equivalent to throwing gasoline on to an already out of control roaring fire. President Carter had made a deal with Fidel Castro agreeing to take some of Cuba's finest fuck ups. The Mariel boat lift portrayed in *Scarface* starring Al Pacino was based on a true exchange by the United States and Cuba in nineteen eighty and the first few hundred undesirables were brought to Leavenworth prison. They isolated the Cubans from general population and housed them under A block in cells that I didn't even know existed until then. The Cubans lived like animals, they would stab and beat each other with weapons in the chow hall, hallway or below in their subterranean cells, and when the guards intervened, the Cubans would point out the perpetrator in fear of being executed by the prison staff as Castro did in his communist country prisons. The Cubans rubbed feces below in A block on their cell walls and would defecate in the shower rather than use their toilets. But to the general population their animalistic behavior only took the staff heat off of us, increasing the existing penitentiary murderous problems at a rapidly increasing rate.

Thumbs was now used more as a mule to bring in narcotics by some of the heavy hitters from other parts of the country who had access to large quantities of raw heroin. Some of the outsiders who weren't connected with California would refer to Thumbs and I as *Dirty and Lowdown* from a song of the same title by Boz Skaggs in the late seventies. And given those apropos handles was just another way those outsiders were expressing how they viewed us as two muthafuckers who didn't give a fuck by always having our big toe in the dope game, with no regard about any and all consequences.

Summer came early that year and the heat only added to the overcrowded, over violent, over drug saturated Leavenworth, Kansas. Thumbs was picking up his own heat from administration and he was heavily suspected of drug trafficking, and once in a while after one of his visits he would be placed in what is called a dry cell, without a toilet and only a bunk, no sheets and only a blanket, with a guard constantly posted outside the cell. Thumbs would have to poop two poops in a tin pan then the guard would add water to the pan and check it for balloons, and if Thumbs gave two clean poops he would be released back into general population. We called this process the guards did looking for drugs *panning for gold*, but of course, Thumbs naturally figured out a method to get over on the po-lice by eating a large quantity of food before each visit. The guards would scratch their heads after panning for gold and having to release Thumbs without a clue on how he was getting over.

Another death that I witnessed while in Leavenworth was the death of disco. Punk rock was at the forefront of music, and although not being a punk rock fan, I would have rather listened to a screaming

323

prisoner on fire than have to listen to another year of disco. I couldn't relate to the punk rock genre of music and felt at times that one of these psycho prisoners could have wrote the lyrics to the new Sex Pistols song, "I'm an antichrist. I'm an anarchist. Don't know what I want but I know how to get it."

But I could always find some rhythm and blues to tune into on my radio as I would walk the yard with Jay Tee talking about anything and everything. Late spring started to feel like the middle of most summers in Kansas with the fifth tier extremely humid and my cell walls starting to sweat earlier than usual.

After reading a copy of *Runner's World* magazine, I felt I had what it took to run a marathon so one Saturday morning early I started doing my usual laps on the outside of the track and my body felt ready. So with a mental dedication to Sugar Bear, I set out to run twenty-six miles three hundred and eighty-five yards. I passed my usual five miles then seven and by now I was starting to float, I kept track of my miles with a book of matches, peeling one match down for every mile. Some of the fellas on the yard started noticing I was running extra-distance than my usual, and they would shout encouragement as I would pass them in the yard after another lap. The fog was starting to roll in as I dripped with sweat continuing to run at a faster than usual pace, I would peel another match down and I was close to twelve miles by now.

Without warning the prison whistle blew signaling to evacuate the yard and for all prisoners back to their proper cellblocks and we were locked in our cells. The dense fog had created a security risk and we remained locked down until the freak fog lifted. In my mind I knew that I could have run the other fourteen miles, but that was only in my mind. I never attempted another marathon distance after that muggy foggy spring day.

I joined High Times again along with Thumbs, and the team went to calling ourselves just High Times like we originally had, dropping the roman numerals for no apparent reason. Bobby was on California Soul once again and like in the previous years California Soul was highly controversial because everyone on the team wasn't from California, but truth be told it was because they were hard to beat. High Times that year wasn't the same either, two of our players were shipped out of Leavenworth on a prerelease program, our starting shortstop was in segregation on suspicion of extortion and didn't look like he would be getting out anytime soon and as for our cleanup hitter who played left field, he was killed that past winter in a stabbing. High Times didn't look or feel the same that year. But it was summer and summers in Leavenworth we played softball.

The heat wasn't letting up and every day started to feel like two Augusts wrapped in a July. Saddle Head, the prison laundry freeman, changed our hours of operation from eight to eleven instead of normal hours of eight to one in the afternoon because of the extreme heat. Every morning when I would get to work I would strip down to my boxers and tennis shoes to cool down while some of the other laundry workers would fill up the oversized plastic rolling laundry baskets with water and just sit in them trying to cool off. Since Thumbs who had to be dressed sharp every day of his two life sentences, I would press his clothes using the industrial clothes press and the steam gave me an irritating rash on my arms that wouldn't go away. It was a fucking hot fucking start of summer to say the least. And with every day it got worse. I had read in the newspaper fish were dying in the lakes from the heat, and this was documented so far the hottest summer in Kansas on record since nineteen thirty-seven.

Leavenworth was the wrong place to be during a heat wave, the already non-adjusted attitudes fed off this heat and extreme agitated irritability was around every corner with the margin of hate widened and only held together by a thin hair trigger thread of sanity.

Working in the laundry gave me access to clean dry sheets and towels every day for myself and my road dogs. And every night with the heat rising up to the fifth tier, ten minutes before lockdown I would stand in a cold shower and soak my towel with cold water so as I tried to sleep when lying on my bunk I could place the cold towel on my body. I cannot describe in words how miserably hot it was that summer, at one point the temperature didn't drop below a hundred degrees Fahrenheit even at night for thirteen days, even at night mind you. And with all this heat rising, the fifth tier was an oven and I would lie on my concrete floor some nights in my cell in an attempt to bring my body temperature down.

But the physical shape I was in was phenomenal and I would still run for miles on the yard often with Jay Tee no matter the heat. We would take an empty five gallon mayonnaise bucket filled with cold water placing it in the corner of the yard and on every lap we would dip a small towel into the bucket then placing it on our heads as we would knock down another lap. The institution had decided to close the shoe factory, as well as the furniture factory because of the sweltering climate. Something that I had never seen done before. I personally watched as this one wannabe fat Mafioso literally stagger and die as he was walking on the yard one mid-morning. And when we wanted to hit the iron pile or do our pull-ups, we had to cool the bars and weight plates with cold water to be able to touch them. And never to forget the killings continued even maybe increasing because of this hot humid summer.

California Soul nor High Times, neither won the softball championship that year, some obscure team out of the great lake region named the Detroit Mob took first place. Thumbs had missed a lot of our games from being in the dry cell, but even with him on the team it wouldn't have made a difference, we sucked that year. The losing teams blamed the heat for their losses but the fact was Detroit Mob had the big bat homerun hitters on their team. Michael their first baseman could hit the softball over the penitentiary wall, and in all my years in Leavenworth I only had seen two other prisoners be able to do that. It was amazing to watch as the ball would leave home plate sail over the homerun fence and keep going over the forty-five foot prison wall.

Doctor Jarvis had his hands full that summer also, sewing prisoners back together and mending the survivors of the attempted murders. With so many regular killings it creates more quantity of seriously wounded prisoners from stab wounds and pipings. Even one burn victim from D block survived after being lit on fire in his cell, but after a couple of days when he looked in the mirror he died of self-pity or so the infirmary prisoner orderly said. But with the summer heat finally becoming just a memory at the annual weightlifting competition in fall Bobby won first place for his weight division in the bench-press contest. Bobby benched three hundred and forty-seven pounds, keep in mind Bobby only weighed one fifty-five and he was just one cock strong individual. And in true Bobby fashion during his warm-up while lying on the bench he crossed his legs smoking a Camel cigarette and benched two hundred and seventy-five pounds ten times. I won the pull-up championship that fall by doing twenty-eight proper all the way down all the way up pull-ups. My closest pull-up competition in the past had been Fatman, but he wasn't in any condition to be competing this year.

After doing twenty-eight pull-ups I set a personal goal in my mind of breaking the Guinness world record, even though I didn't know what it was at that time. So after finding a Guinness world record book and after looking up the pull-up record I scratched that personal goal off my list. At the time the world record was one hundred and seventy proper pull-ups done by a sixty-three-year-old Chinese man, but I still remained the pull-up King in Leavenworth Penitentiary in the fall of nineteen eighty.

Thumbs was doing thirty days in building sixty-three after he shot out most of the windows in the furniture factory with an industrial staple gun while at work one afternoon. He would be out by the holidays so all was good since I liked to have my friends close during the holidays to get high, laugh and bring in the New Year. The cool late autumn weather was more than welcomed that year after the hellish summer that Kansas and I just had, and Bobby and I would play cribbage in his cell late afternoon or at night patiently waiting for the next calendar page to fall. Whenever Bobby and I were together the conversation would be at a minimum, for almost the last decade we had lived similar lives while being together and already knew each other's stories, so this left us little to talk about. One of those nights that we were deep into a game of cribbage I let Bobby know what a good friend I considered him and this adventurous ride that we were on would definitely not be the same without him. He only smiled.

The next thing, Thumbs was standing at the cell door with some of his personal property grinning. I immediately asked Thumbs, "Fool, why did you shoot all the fuckin' windows out in the furniture factory?"

"I don't know Whisper, I don't know."

Bobby jumped in, "Good answer, is that what you told the disciplinary board?"

While smirking I interrupted, "Maybe you should have told them that you were hearing voices and the voices told you to pull the trigger on the staple gun."

Bobby broke out the homemade pipe and Thumbs took a hit. Bobby and Thumbs smoked weed and soon after it was time for lockup.

The traditional Christmas gifts were being passed out and as I sat in my cell eating peanuts, I reached my arm through the bars to the next cell, trading my Camel no-filters to Thumbs for his orange, and in exactly one week we would flip the calendar page once again.

26

With only trace amounts of snow on the big yard, I would no longer need my gloves and knit hat while running my laps on the outer track. Thumbs was in the dry cell again which was becoming fairly routine, and after two poops he would be back out. Bobby would periodically show up in the yard coming out of his winter cellblock hibernation to walk or hit the iron. Another summer was coming to Leavenworth and the administration seemed to be tiring of the high murder rate, and I could feel changes coming. Guards were stopping the usual suspects more often and with their hand held metal detector wands. The guards showed no shyness when it came to putting us against the wall and waving their magic wand all over our bodies. A lot of the fellas went to knifes made out of Plexiglas to beat the detectors, but I was old-school, always with access to my steel knife around the fifth tier corner. I started to think that more time than usual had elapsed on Thumbs' two poop hiatus and also had a thought that something may be wrong. But it was Thumbs who never gave up anything to the staff, and a drug case wouldn't make or break his life, or should I say life sentences. For Thumbs it was about getting over to make his as well as his friends lives better and higher in the penitentiary. The dry cell was no more than an inconvenience of the cat and mouse game, and with Thumbs it was never personal.

I was given my first paid vacation ever in life, and my age now in my early thirties, I was a real overachiever. The vacation was for working in the laundry over the last few years, and with my pay at five dollars a month I was given two weeks off work with two dollars and fifty cents to vacation on. Where would I go? Big yard, the little yard or would I just be a wild man and go to both yards on my time off from folding sheets. With the late spring weather the humidity was low and the sun was shining so there I would be playing handball during the day in a yard of my choosing while on vacation. On certain warmer days there were a couple of homosexuals who were starting early on their tan, wearing their tailored two-piece bikinis and when I would walk by, without fail I would always give them a polite, "Good afternoon ladies."

"Heeeeey Whisper." I would hear, as I would stroll past laughing on my way to the handball courts.

The violence and the other shit that I would see on a daily basis became more comical since I was well-established in the pecking order of the penitentiary in Leavenworth. I relayed to Bobby my concern about Thumbs being in the dry cell longer than the usual and Bobby would just shrug his shoulders while saying, "Something gotta be up."

After six days in building sixty-three, specifically the dry cell I caught a glimpse of Thumbs coming out of segregation. I put my pull-ups on hold and ran over to catch up with him as we walked back to C block together. I asked if everything was okay and he said he would tell me when we got to his cell. While watching him unpack his personal property and put it back in its proper order on the shelf and sink area, he started to tell me the story. Sitting on his bunk I listened as Thumbs started explaining how after he gave two poops, a lieutenant showed up telling the officer posted outside his cell that he wanted five clean poops this time, that he was sure this inmate was smuggling drugs. Thumbs proceeded letting me know that he had in fact swallowed some balloons during his visit, along with two one hundred dollar bills, one torn width ways and the other torn length ways to easier swallow. Thumbs was getting very animated and started to say what happened next. How one night he felt after giving his previous four small poops the fifth would have the mother lode for sure and how he then got under his blanket pretending to be asleep and pooped in his own hand. After wiping the balloons and the currency off with a corner part of the blanket he then re-swallowed them. Thumbs was grinning at this point and told me to stand at the door of his cell and be lookout while he used the commode. After he was finished sitting on the toilet while standing at his sink he held up his hand with four pieces of two one hundred dollar bills along with several balloons in the other hand.

I had a hard time believing the story, yet I was looking right at the evidence in front of me knowing it was true and finally I had to say something, "Thumbs you are more of a man than I am or will ever be. Fuck Thumbs, that's so fucking crazy."

What Thumbs said next I will never forget till I die, "Whisper I'm being very serious now, whatever anyone ever tells you, whatever you may think, SHIT has no taste."

"Thumbs I'll take your word for that," I commented shaking my head slowly side to side.

Not too long after hearing Thumbs' *shit story,* I was walking the yard with Jay Tee and heard my name called over the loudspeaker to report to the lieutenant's office. I realized it couldn't be serious since they sent four guards anytime a lieutenant wanted to talk to you involving serious incidents. Walking in the office I could see it was Lieutenant Smith, and he was leaning back in his chair with his cowboy boots up on the desk. I sat and listened as he told me how we (administration) are tired of all you California boys running around Leavenworth thinking you own the place. My file was in front of him and as he flipped through it talking, all I could think was how thick it had gotten. It looked like a Los Angeles County phone book. He went on telling me how the prison population was going to be lowered so the murder rate would decline, and he personally was going to see the California boys split up the best he could and this would become his new mission in life. He added how I was considered part of the problem in Leavenworth, and even was bold enough to bring up I was under suspicion for selling narcotics, my affiliation with Jay Tee and also was suspected along with my cohorts of an unsolved murder in Leavenworth in nineteen seventy-nine. I just looked him right in the eye knowing he was only fishing with all these bullshit accusations, believe me if the feds have any concrete evidence you end up in segregation and with a new federal charge. He finished by saying that since I had state time to serve concurrently with my ten years federal time he was going to see that I would be transferred to the state penitentiary in which I owed them for a supermarket robbery. Then he asked, "Any questions?"

"No, no questions boss. Am I free to leave?"

Lieutenant Smith nodded excusing me and as I started to walk out the door I turned around and had to fuck with him in some sort of way, "Nice fuckin' cowboy boots boss."

Jay Tee was lingering in the hallway waiting for me to come out of the office and I updated Jay Tee on the information I had just been given as we walked back out to the yard. I would only further pass this transfer information on to Bobby and Thumbs. People are real fucked up in prison and some of the nut-jobs suffer from this weird envy and seeing anyone leave creates this odd paranoia of jealousy, just too weird to explain. I didn't owe money to anyone and I hadn't done anyone wrong without justification, but in some of these psychotic prisoners' minds they feel they should be the one leaving not you, even though I was going to another penitentiary.

I knew how it worked, that one day I would hear my name to report to receiving and discharge and I would be gone, so I needed to take care of everything I needed to take care of immediately. First business at hand was I had to break up with my paper girlfriend, Miss Janis Schmidt, and this was going to be a difficult separation for me since she had an ass that could make a priest kick out a stained-glass window. So after the clearing of the standing four o'clock count, and with the doors un-racked I snatched her picture off my cell wall and went next door handing her to Thumbs as I sang the lyrics of a J. Geils song, "My blood runs cold—my memory has just been sold—my Angel is a centerfold."

We both were laughing, but there was still that uncomfortable knowing that I would be leaving and make no mistake about it I would miss Thumbs, Jay Tee and my main man Bobby the exact same as I would be missed. The closeness that comes from adversity is unmatched by any other bond that I have ever experienced, ever. After that it was hard to engage fully in any kind of handball game or my constant calisthenics and running, my mind was taking some of my strength as all I could think about was what's next.

Hearing my name to report to R and D, I gathered my one box of property as Bobby and Thumbs walked with me down the tier to the stairs and doorway of C block. Outside in the rotunda area Jay Tee waited, joining the three of us as we all now slowly walked to receiving and discharge. I stood a moment looking at the three of them, after an awkward pause my three comrades shook hands with me and said things I can't remember, but I definitely know one of the encouraging comments was, "See you on the other side, or Broadway."

My property was taken from me; I was strip-searched and given a set of wrinkled prison issue clothing complete with Peter Pan shoes, and then wrapped in chains and handcuffed. The guard slid the black box over the chain connecting my handcuffs and an extra set of shackles were placed on my ankles. I was then escorted by two prison guards brandishing weapons down the stairs of the front of Leavenworth Penitentiary and onto a waiting bus. The guards treated me different as I entered the bus, and I noticed some of the other prisoners on the bus would look at me and look away quickly, like I was a rare to be seen survivor of Leavenworth Penitentiary. I was given a pack of Camel no-filters for the ride, and since I didn't smoke I would make sure someone besides a lop or a lame would get them to maybe smuggle into the next overnight stop. As I slowly walked down the aisle of the bus with double shackles on my legs and the black box on my cuffs, some of the prisoners seem to scooch over in their seats to give me more room that I didn't really need. I found a seat close to the back of the bus and sat there staring at the big dome in the front of Leavenworth. I was so much more relaxed than my first bus ride many years before when leaving Leavenworth to go to McNeil Island and as we pulled out I could see the buffalo grazing, but in a matter of moments as the bus traveled down the road away from The Big Top the buffalo were not to be seen.

27

I noticed the route the bus was traveling was north, and I'd never been on the federal bus in this direction before, even on my diesel therapy excursion. But I did start to see things that were familiar and soon realized it was the same road when the marshals had driven me and Bobby to Leavenworth after our convictions, what seemed now like light years ago. Late afternoon the bus pulled to the side of the road and sat idling, then shortly an unmarked state vehicle pulled up in front of the bus with two state prison guards getting out of the vehicle. The federal and state officers conversed for a moment while looking at my paper work with one of the federal guards getting back on the bus and calling my name to exit. Now as I stood on the side of the road as the two jurisdictions started trading chains on me, I stood there looking out at the endless prairie and thought that the air tasted different outside the walls of Leavenworth. After this process of wrapping the state chains around my body and removing the federal chains, I was escorted to the back of the unmarked vehicle and we drove farther north. The state guard riding shotgun turned around asking me some superficial questions, but I never uttered any form of conversation back, I just looked out the window as if the two men upfront were invisible to me. My ability to size up people and situations had reached a new level and noticing the young age of the shotgun guard and his demeanor I came to the conclusion that he had never had a prisoner of my caliber in his custody before, and I played off that fact by keeping him guessing by not talking. My years in the penitentiary had changed me into this predatory animal like some great white shark constantly circling and ready to seize any opportunity for my advantage, and I would try to take full control of any situation in a power struggle of minds. *Animal Factory* was a book written by Eddie Bunker that I had read previously. Eddie was on McNeil Island also and now I realized the full concept of Eddie's writings. I was definitely a product of the factory that produces animals. Pulling off the main road I could see the brick building in the close distance and surmised this was the state penitentiary in which I was headed, it looked small compared to Leavenworth and the wall didn't seem higher than thirty feet. As we got closer I became thankful for the wall instead of a double fence, I still didn't ever want to see outside when I was doing time inside.

Inside R and R, receiving and release, front and side photos were taken and I had to show the rookie guard how to roll my fingers when fingerprinting me because of his obvious nervousness. After the state's version of orientation I was assigned a cell on the second tier in the larger of the two cellblocks. This place didn't feel right from day one, and I decided then and there just to do the little bit of time I had left and not engage with the other prisoners who already didn't live up to my expectations of true convicts. I missed my friends in Leavenworth, with Bobby, Thumbs and Jay Tee every morning when I woke up I knew what I got as far as the solid characteristics that each one of them possessed. This prison in the Midwest state of where I was convicted of supermarket robbery had a country-fried atmosphere and I wasn't down for any sort of interaction with the others in this hillbilly heaven of a prison. The *wire* was received long before I got there of my arrival and a couple of transplanted

California prisoners approached me, Red and Eugene, to welcome me and offer me anything I needed. Although I was courteous, I let them know immediately that I was very resourceful and self-sufficient with only around a little more than a year left of my sentence. I was fine with just riding out alone the small portion of time I had left. There were three other transplanted prisoners from California doing time there but in my opinion were straight up lames, and my mindset was to be released not waste my time schooling others how to act. I made it known to Red, who worked in the auto body vocational training school, that I would need a knife made *pronto,* and naturally I was willing to pay. He stutter-stepped with his answer saying I probably wouldn't really need one, and I responded firmly, "I definitely do need a knife."

I could see in his eyes after my strong will was forced upon him that he fully agreed to satisfy my request, and when supplying me with the exact knife I had blueprinted, he took payment for making the weapon, and I was a little taken aback. I hadn't paid for anything in years but had put a little money and some balloons of weed in the *vault* before leaving Leavenworth for situations such as this. Next I got into a poker game with Red's road dog Eugene, in charge of the gambling as well as dealing the cards. I jumped in with both feet to this Disneyland structured prison since opportunity had opened the door by showing me obvious weakness existing in this Midwest so called maximum security prison. With my reputation preceding me, and with Leavenworth as my alma mater, I felt like Moses parting the Red Sea when walking to the chow hall, on the tier, or going to the recreation yard, which was extremely small, smaller than the small yard in Leavenworth. My first week on the main line of general population I won a television and radio along with cigarettes from the poker game in which Eugene was the house dealer. I noticed right away how Eugene was dealing dirty with me as the beneficiary. Usually my values don't tolerate cheating, since poker is an honest gentleman's game, but Eugene's eyes let me know that he fully agreed how weak these hillbilly prisoners were as he would deal me the cards I would need to rake in another pot. Both Eugene and Red were alright, so I gave them the cigarettes I won.

Red walked up to my cell door one afternoon and handed me a folded twenty-dollar bill wrapped in cellophane, it was the same twenty that I had given for the knife and he wanted to give it back. I told him to keep it and thanks for his offer. Red was one of those guys that would do shit and think about it later and then have to undo it in a final attempt to make everything copacetic. He had realized, through Eugene I imagine, that he should have never expected or accepted payment for the knife. "Golden rule, Red, think before you talk," I said.

Passing on to Red what I had learned from Jay Tee.

But Eugene on the other hand, now he was one sharp muthafucka and I knew that he understood my convict thinking and I liked him. He was also intuitive enough to realize I was the guy that was just trying to kill a little time and leave, so he never crowded me. Eugene also offered to hook me up with forged paperwork from a prisoner that worked in the clerk's office on my radio and television, so I gave him back the television as his cheating payment from the card game and said I would only need paperwork on the radio since I was strictly a music guy. Eugene relayed to me also that this extremely fucked up state penitentiary locked all the prisoners down every couple of months for a two-week period to check paperwork on entertainment appliances, not search so much for weapons, but only televisions and radios to keep extortion to a minimum. I thought this was so crazy when he was telling me this. But Eugene turned out to be the guy that could get things done and I appreciated that. So now I was set to run the yard, do my calisthenics, read and kill time waiting to turn another calendar page of this ten year fiasco that had become my life. All of the seasons had done their changing and I had gotten high a few times, but never could engage fully with the other prisoners on a trust level. But one prisoner kept me entertained over this last short year and that was Wong.

Wong was a very unusual person. I have known a cast of characters, excluding Bobby, Jay Tee and Thumbs through my travels and in my ventures into the penitentiaries around the nation. Wong stands outs because he never spoke. He could speak, but for some reason he never uttered one word to anybody, very unusual. I knew his name was Wong and that is all I knew about his name, first or last name nobody or I knew. I was in this Midwest penitentiary with him for the past last year where the weather would change to extreme winters of snow and cold to even more extreme summers of sweltering heat equaling or worse than Kansas. But Wong looked the same every day, penitentiary boots, denim issue pants, and a denim issue prison jacket always buttoned at the top, finishing it all off with an old school prison hat with the bill cut off. Wong dressed like this every day of that year, no matter how cold, no matter how hot.

I was housed in the same cellblock and would often hear the swatting sound of a newspaper hitting the inner cellblock prison wall, and I would automatically know that Wong was killing flies. The sound would bring me out of my cell and I would lean on the rail of the upper tier and watch because I knew what was coming next. When Wong got tired of killing flies with the rolled up newspaper he would start kicking flies out of the air while still wearing his penitentiary boots, and keep in mind these boots were heavy. Now kicking flies out of the air is a masterful feat in itself but with boots on, unheard of, and I definitely would not repeat this story if I had not seen it with my own eyes.

During basketball season Wong would shoot baskets for hours alone and silent. During the fall when everyone was playing football, he would again for hours throw a football to an invisible receiver, walk, pick it up and throw it again and again. And baseball season, you could see Wong on the yard with a bat hitting a ball in no particular direction, throwing the ball up into the air swing the bat then walking in the direction of the ball, pick it up off the grass and do it again. Through that year Wong never changed, dressing the same, participating alone in seasonal sports the same and kicking flies out of the air. Never, let me repeat never saying one word.

Then one sunny summer day high noon on the tiny big yard I watched as Wong had walked from the cellblock to the yard carrying a homemade rope and a homemade hook, and ending up at the prison wall, which separated society from us. Wong swung the rope over his head a few times trying to get the homemade hook to catch the top of the wall, the same twenty-four inch wide wall that kept us all from freedom and eventually the hook grabbed on the row of top concrete bricks. This was all done in plain view of all the gun towers whose only job was to secure the wall perimeter. Simultaneously a group of prison guards started running in the direction of Wong and surrounding him. They grabbed him and after cuffing Wong escorted him off the yard. I never saw Wong after that day, but I have never forgotten about him either, Wong was my entertainment that year.

Doing push-ups in my cell one afternoon while the prison was on lockdown status again for the bullshit television and radio shakedown, a guard appeared at my cell door telling me to pack my property I was being transported.

With a little more of another year passed and gone, I was being driven in an unmarked vehicle by two guards to intercept a federal prison bus. After standing on the side of the road having my chains switched from the states jurisdiction to federal jurisdiction and another bus ride going somewhere new, I ended up in a federal prison directly west of the state of which I had just completed doing time for the supermarket robbery. Fuck I thought, how time had certainly picked up speed and it was becoming reality that I would be released in a little over a month.

Excitement wasn't the right word to describe my thoughts of being let back out into the free world, I can only best define my thoughts as every day something seemed different than the days of the past few years. After once again going through the receiving and discharge process, and all my paperwork in order, my parole date was now weeks away and entering my cell one day I noticed I had institution mail lying on my bunk.

Naturally I thought this was some form of prerelease information, but it was a notice declaring I was given a retardation of parole date for a hundred and twenty days. My thoughts instantly went to how these fuckin' feds are past being just muthafuckers. Retardation of parole date is a federal institutional term used when the region on which you were assigned, in my case the Kansas City region, feels fit to take your original parole date and retard it for a maximum time of four months. Here's the crazy part, the region doesn't have to show any cause or disciplinary infraction, they simply can because they're the federal government. I wasn't upset, I wasn't mad, these are two emotions that no longer existed in my human makeup and I didn't depend on for survival anymore. Once again this wasn't any more than the cat and mouse game being played by the feds and I for the past several years. And I knew in my heart of hearts why they did what they did, I still hadn't gone to trial for the murder in McNeil, which only told me they must have a very weak case and that probably upset them tremendously, and I was not a model inmate while in Leavenworth or McNeil, but quite the contrary. So I fully understood as my mind went right to fuck 'um, I guar-an-fuckin-tee I can do a hundred and twenty more days.

Later I was called to a prerelease hearing and showed up wearing a T-shirt and shorts, showing no respect to the *suits* in my prerelease hearing to discuss my parole plan. I had done some reading in the law library and discovered I could be paroled to the state I was born, which was California, or the state that I had been federally convicted. I stated to the prerelease board that I had chosen the Midwest state of which I was convicted of bank robbery to parole to, convincing them that I wanted to start fresh, a clean slate so to speak. But the real truth of the matter is I had a personal hidden agenda that no one, not even Bobby knew of. So in a matter of a couple of months more, I would be released to a federal halfway house in this fucking awful backwards Midwest state in which I only knew one person who only maybe now lived there and that I needed to pay a visit.

So I continued my running, reading and calisthenics routine just waiting with under forty days to pass. My prison job on this short stay was to keep this small series of walkways snow free by shoveling and any debris off them by sweeping, with these walkways connecting the barbershop and chow hall to the cellblocks. And administration was completely leaving me alone at this point. The year prior to my arrival at this federal penitentiary a guard was killed by two convicts from California, and now these country guards stayed completely clear of anyone associated with California, which was more than fine with me. Not much attention was given when we were killing each other, but when a prison guard lost their life the rest of the guards would get a loud wake-up call on how everyone is vulnerable to the violence produced through the prison environment.

With only days left now and as I walked in the chow hall I noticed Richie Rich from McNeil Island days eating alone at one of the chow hall tables and wearing wrinkled prison clothing. I assumed Richie must have just arrived that morning off the bus. I would approach Richie apprehensively since I hadn't seen him for years and people change, plus with one foot out the prison door I had to let him know I didn't want to get sucked in to doing any more time by some *bull-shit* foolishness. I grabbed my lunch tray and slowly walked in his direction and as soon as we shook hands and started talking I could see that Richie was a changed man. He started telling me how he had been stabbed in the face in a murder attempt over narcotics in Lewisburg prison and now he just wanted out of this crazy nightmare. He added that he was very tired of this fucked up lack of life and didn't even use heroin anymore, he sincerely just wanted the fuck out. I immediately relayed back to Richie that was good news and I was almost on the exact same page except I still loved my heroin.

Also I said to Richie I could almost smell my freedom and within days I would be walking out in the free world. It was so good to see the new and improved Richie, and as he eyeballed my left arm to inspect how my peacock tattoo was holding up, we both reflected in conversation of how much time had gone by and that life was definitely a fucking mystery. Richie also commented how he heard I had ended up in Leavenworth and said how he often thought of me and wondered if I would be all right given Leavenworth's reputation, and as Richie smiled he said, "Whisper, I heard crazy things about you, and I started hearing more and more so I really didn't think you would be one of the few to make it out. No disrespect meant by me saying that."

"I'm the long shot horse Richie. You should know that by now."

Within a couple of days I was in receiving and discharge getting pictures taken front and side, but this time it was to have a current picture of me for the government's file upon my release. The feds furnished a mandatory suit to leave wearing and I was bringing with me three sets of green prison clothing crisply pressed, new T-shirts, socks, and boxers, a couple of pairs of tennis shoes along with a manila envelope containing all my paperwork. I signed for and received the hundred-dollar kick out money and having to wear that clown suit that was provided I walked through the front prison gate a free man. Then walked directly into the visitor's bathroom and immediately took off the outdated suit throwing it in the trash and putting on my prison greens.

With no conversation, none whatsoever, the prison guard whose job was making the daily prison mail run transported me to a small café located on the outskirts of the animal sanctuary in which this federal penitentiary was located, dropping me off out front. With my prison bus voucher in hand I went to a small window located inside the café to trade my voucher for a Greyhound bus ticket to the federal halfway house that was over six hundred miles away. I ordered a cup of coffee in the café while I waited for the Greyhound and noticed how the customers were all staring. I knew they knew what was up and where I was coming from, so I asked for the coffee to be made to go and after exiting the café, I waited outside in the cold with nothing else for miles around me. This place was located in the middle of nowhere, but I was free, although nothing seemed to make sense I just stood there drinking my coffee on a two-lane highway wondering which direction the bus would be coming from.

The bus driver stared at me as I stood outside the open bus door not getting on, as if I was waiting for his permission to enter the bus. Finally my brain caught up with my body and I boarded. As I sat in the far back of the bus staring out the window on my way to the federal halfway house I thought of absolutely nothing...

28

With the sand under my feet as I stand on Silverstrand beach again, I wonder if some of the grains are the exact same grains of sand that I stood on as a kid. Looking out towards the ocean, the rocks that make up the rock island in the distance are in exactly the same place and the jetties on both sides of me haven't moved. But when I turn around where the bungalow beach houses that we would rent for under a hundred dollars are now multimillion-dollar homes and they call it beachfront property. Things have changed at Silverstrand. Everything changes, everything including me. I am older now and on some days I am wiser, but when I look at the full circle of life that is my life I can't help but remember days gone past and the people that I have shared time with on this earth.

The three small, medium and large Lupien brothers ended up all successful on their own levels, but that's no surprise since they always did everything together. Steve "Deer" Deerington ended up buying a house on Silverstrand and lives there today with his high school sweetheart who he married and has always shared his life with. My good friend from past days Melby, David Melborn, stayed connected to the ocean, buying a sailboat and chartering trips to far places throughout the Pacific Ocean and eventually became a boat salesman. Bennie Tee retired from his City of Oxnard job that he had obtained in the late sixties while we were still little crazy surfers with no direction. Not every story ended like a fairy tale, Jimmy Pierdon as well as Dudey Wares and not to forget Eddie Kane my first mentor on being low-profile all died of natural causes before they were sixty years old. Tough generation, what can I say. Gary Shanklin, the wild do anything on a dare one of our crew attempted to rob someone with a knife and had the knife taken away from him and was stabbed to death.

And as far as what happened to me? I wish I could tell you that after sitting on that Greyhound bus that cold winter morning, while leaving the penitentiary on my way to the federal halfway house in the Midwest, that I had learned my lesson, seen the error of my ways and was a changed man. But things didn't go exactly like that.

As soon as I was in the halfway house, I was scheming, leaving the local bus route laid out on my bed every morning next to the want ads while circling potential jobs and writing fake footnotes of potential job interviews. It was all bullshit to keep the halfway house counselors off my back. I would leave the halfway house early every morning under the guise of looking for work, but instead I would be running the streets like a crazy man. Within days I met a woman who became enthralled with the image of an ex-con gangster and whose father owned a restaurant where illegal sports betting took place. Her dad was also a fence (someone who buys stolen items), so naturally I hit the ground running in this criminal environment with about three years to do on parole. And trust and believe my federal parole officer and I had a tumultuous relationship, which is the most civilized way I can put it. My girlfriend of convenience had money and willing to share but I was still acting a fool by always carrying a pistol, sometimes two, and looking for that quick buck. I had this enormous three fifty-seven chrome long barrel and also a twenty-two-magnum pearl handled derringer, which became my sidekicks on a daily basis. I was never without one of these guns unless I was in my parole officer's office, which with my high risk parole category was three times a week and I hated every Monday, Wednesday, Friday visits. Fuck him, my parole officer. Catch me if you can muthafucker, I had been playing cat and mouse with the best in Leavenworth for years. I had paroled to the Midwest for one reason and one reason only and I had a constant thought that I needed to take care of something, and until I did I could never be at peace.

So borrowing my unsuspecting girlfriend's Chevy Camaro Berlinetta, and since she never asked questions, which is why I think I was really with her, I started driving the two hundred or so miles to Tony Lofton's house after finding his address in the phone book. I was on a mission. It was to make sure that the rat that had sold me for reward money to the feds would not breathe the same air as me. It was a simple plan; if Tony was still driving truck I would follow him and wait for one of his stops then jump up in the cab of the truck and empty my pistol into him. If for some reason he wasn't driving truck, I would just wait for opportunity and that would be that. So I parked across and down the street from his house that night waiting for morning. Finally I could see his front door open and out came Tony, but with him were his wife and two children who looked exactly like him, so my mind processed the situation quickly. As if it was another crossroad in my life I made a conscious decision in a matter of a second to not make his kids orphans, and I turned the Camaro around and started driving back to where I lived. I've never regretted or thought about that decision since and I never mentioned it to Bobby ever.

I was living the high life but soon was back in federal prison on a maximum nine-month parole violation, for giving my parole officer a dirty urinalysis for heroin. I was using heroin every day for quite some time while on parole and getting over by giving my parole officer clean fake urines, and the one time I showed up dirty he violated me. Fuck him, I liked getting high, so I was sent to a federal penitentiary to give them nine months more time off my ten years. It was mentally like I had never left prison and doing time there I did my usual routine of handball, running for what seemed like only minutes as that three quarters of a year flew by.

This entire time whenever I was free, I made sure I sent packages to Jay Tee and Thumbs when I would hit a score. As for Bobby, he was in a halfway house in Santa Barbara and driving a linen truck when he first got out, but while still in the halfway house he picked up new gun charges. Being the solid helpful ex-con that Bobby was, he was approached by another ex-con and asked to store some weapons. Bobby refused at first, explaining how he was on parole and was just trying to stay out of prison. The party with the guns kept pushing the issue, and finally Bobby agreed to store the weapons in the trunk of his car, stating firmly that he would only hold the guns overnight. Long story short, right after Bobby locked the trunk and turned around the FBI grabbed him, charging him with 'felon in possession of firearms' then Bobby was sent back to federal prison on a new mandatory five-year sentence. It is what is called an ambiguous statute, and your actual time is only two years instead of five and you're out in eighteen months, but it was still a fucked up situation since it was a sting operation and they were using this rat ex-con as a pawn to put federal felons back in prison. Bobby was now doing his time in Terminal Island California and I was still in the Midwest not giving a fuck, and we still

350

hadn't seen each other in person since we had both gotten out of Leavenworth.

Thumbs in a letter asked me to pick up one of the new disposable cameras and send him pictures of women, lots of pictures of women or any activity that I was involved with so he could vicariously live through me somewhat. So naturally I sent Thumbs and Jay Tee hundreds of pictures of me at the lake or random places or pictures of women that I would stop on the streets, just pretty much anything that would take them out mentally of where they were. I never forgot how it was in there, never.

While out of prison I had no regard for laws, much less my stipulations of parole. I was on a terror, and my next move I hooked up with a burglar with lock picking talent. We would drive all night out of state and burglarize pharmacies, taking everything on all the shelves and sorting it out at home. I was rich in a week on the first of many big scores this way and immediately I bought an almost new dark green Sedan Deville Cadillac. My parole officer stayed eternally upset with me but I was giving him clean urines and producing pay stubs from the restaurant my girlfriend's father owned. I was beating the urine tests and the pay stubs were forgeries, and my whole life was one big parole violation. But it's not what you know, it's what you can prove. And adding to my parole officer's constant attitude was me driving a Cadillac while my monthly reports stated I washed dishes on the weekends to satisfy my job commitment of parole. I hit another pharmacy soon after, and along with all my other little hustles I had a nice supply of money, and Thumbs, Bobby and Jay Tee would benefit every time I would profit.

I had everybody mad at me by now, including the federal parole officer, along with my state parole officer from the supermarket robbery, who always just wanted money so I could start paying on that fine that the judge had given me along with the ten years. Even my playing-house girlfriend was constantly complaining about my lack of coming home at nights, she knew exactly what I was up to. The crime didn't bother her, the money didn't bother her, but other women for some reason bothered the shit out of her. Naturally, I always denied anything and everything, but the truth of the matter was I was hitting everything but the lottery sexually when it came to women. I was in my late-thirties and all I was trying to do was catch up on the years that I had lost, nobody in my life had any understanding during these times, none whatsoever.

I was so busy all the time and after one time being two weeks late on my monthly report to my federal parole officer, he violated me once again. Really? Only two weeks late on a monthly report and I was back in federal prison with the parole board telling me now to CTE, continue to expiration, and I was given the maximum second time parole violation time of one year with no good time. This was all becoming a blur and the parole board that had ruled on my one-year violation time added four months to my ten-year sentence for absconding, saying I was on the run during the four months the Marshals were searching for me to arrest me. I wasn't on the run, I just wasn't anywhere I said I was and stopped reporting to my state and federal parole officers completely. Along with me driving a better car than my federal parole officer and my attitude, that's the real reason I went back on my second violation, not the petty two weeks late reason he filed the warrant for. After all, he wasn't stupid, and I wasn't doing anything to help myself or even look like I was attempting to succeed on parole.

On this violation in yet another federal prison I formed my own softball team calling them the Dirty

UA's, standing for dirty urinalysis. We won the first place championship that year and I had a mixed bag of players. My pitcher had a glass eye, my right fielder was a homosexual who could bench-press almost five hundred pounds and my first baseman was a crazy country boy I nicknamed Big Boy. The other players fit the definition of characters also and we had a good time that summer. I worked in the recreation department and would crosscut mow the softball field and chalk the lines around the bases and would also always write Dirty UA's in chalk in front of our bullpen. Some of the other teams would complain about my favoritism with the chalk, but fuck 'um, its prison, stop whining. Big Boy was my cellmate that entire year and I was pleased about that because of the trust factor. He was a good man and made that one-year violation tolerable. I still owe him a little money from a deal we did, and Big Boy I got your money, just circumstances beyond my control I wasn't able to give it to you then. During this particular violation I received a letter from Thumbs, his letter only had one purpose and that was to inform me that Jay Tee had been released from Leavenworth back to East Los Angeles, and shortly thereafter was killed in a shootout. This news broke my fuckin' heart.

The guards went out of their way to fuck with me that year only because they didn't understand what was really going on. It looked like I was doing nothing because I was doing nothing, nothing major anyway. Because of my Leavenworth history, my Leavenworth prison number and my oversized prison file those hacks that year tried to make my life miserable. I would always tell the guards who would fuck with me the most, "I will be getting out soon and close to being done with my ten year sentence, but you hacks are doing a life sentence eight hours at a time."

Released again, now with only twenty-six days left on my original ten-year and four month federal bank robbery sentence, I could not wait to call my parole officer. As soon as you are released from the penitentiary, you only have twenty-four hours to report to your parole officer, and I wouldn't wait that long this time to call.

As soon as I was back home I picked up the phone and dialed my parole officer's number and the secretary connected me, and after I told him who it was, all I said was, "Fuck you."

He relayed to me that he understood how I felt and wouldn't put in for a warrant for violation (not reporting) on my last twenty-six days of my ten year four month sentence. He also wished me good luck, which I thought was odd.

Within days of being off federal parole, state parole and my five to life and one to life sentences completely extinguished, I packed a bag for the West Coast. I left instructions for my now constantly nagging girlfriend not to drive my Cadillac, leave my guns alone and don't let Sancho wear my clothes. California was calling me. I planned on a one or two week vacation, from not working, and also to look up my old friend Bobby who was now out prison.

As the commercial airliner started to descend over the Sierra Nevada Mountains, I got that feeling for the first time of being free from everything. After landing, I took a shuttle north to Ventura and walked down to The Point where California Street meets the ocean. It had been over a decade and a half since I had this feeling of being young again, I felt exactly like I did when I would stand on Silverstrand as a young boy. I stood at the edge of the asphalt parking lot that had replaced the dirt where we had parked our cars in the late sixties and early seventies when surfing. As the sun was shining making the ocean sparkle dance I thought my ears were deceiving me when I heard a familiar voice across the parking lot. I knew that voice well, and as I looked at the silhouette caused by the sun behind him, without a doubt I knew it was Slurp Dog. He damn near broke my ribs hugging me when I walked up on him after realizing who I was. He hadn't seen or heard from me since that one visit in McNeil Island many years before. Slurp insisted on me staying with him at his house on Ventura Avenue and Slurp had also recently divorced. His pain from the breakup was very obvious to me and through his bewilderment, he was a wild man again, like I remembered him when he was younger. Slurp always wrestled with good and evil his entire life, but no matter what was going on with him his heart for others would always remain gold.

Staying with Slurp, on mornings when he would go to his construction job as a crane operator, I would make my way down to the beach or look for other mischief to get into. With my money getting low again, Slurp let we know in a direct manner that I was headed right back to the penitentiary from the way I was acting and the things I was doing, adding he didn't want to see that happen to me again. So my good friend Slurp Dog got me a job in the union as a laborer for the same construction company that he was employed by. The money was good and since I was in excellent physical shape the hard work didn't bother me. But with my first paycheck I bought an ounce of cocaine and was back in the dope selling game again. I think in the late eighties I was the only one in Ventura who didn't use cocaine and the money was rolling in hand over fist.

Easter Sunday I was working in Slurp's yard trimming the bushes and mowing the grass. I never liked yard work as a kid but now after my experiences of not being able to garden, for some inner satisfying reason, I liked working in the yard. So this particular Easter with the music going and my shirt off doing

355

yard work, I caught the eye of this young little strumpet driving by. After stopping and chatting for a moment she realized I had nowhere to go on Easter, so she invited me to spend Easter with her at her house in the hills behind Ventura, a town called Ojai (pronounced O-hi). Soon after, I let Slurp know I was making more money selling cocaine than working, but appreciated the break that he had offered me. Naturally Slurp understood as a friend and I transplanted to Ojai living with this new little filly that I had met. Ojai became too much of a hassle because of location for my cocaine business and soon I rented a split townhouse in a nice section of Ventura off Aurora Street. Things fast forwarded quickly and people would buy cocaine all day and all night, I still had my old rules of not letting people know where I lived so I had employed some runners to deliver the twenty dollar packages of cocaine. Those twenty dollar packages added up quickly and I bought myself a black Oldsmobile Delta ninety-eight, completely furnished the townhouse and became criminally established in California again in a relatively short time.

Shortly thereafter, I left a phone message with Bobby's mother to have her son get a hold of me. I could tell by Bobby's mother's tone she wasn't none too happy about the probability of Bobby and I being together again. But within a few days Bobby called me at my home on Aurora Street, saying he was in Oxnard and would drive up to Ventura. It was so fucking good to see Bobby again, and after doing some heroin we took off in my Olds ninety-eight. Cruising around with Bobby again along with the laughs it was definitely like old times. In an ironic twist of fate Bobby let me know that he was now living with Gene, the minister who was busted with us by the FBI in Scotts Valley over ten years prior. Bobby further informed me that Gene had raised his two kids, Baby Bobby and Vanessa, sending them to private school, getting them

356

music lessons and they were pretty much grown and turned out okay. Nice I thought, Bobby always cared about his kids although he never wore his heart on his sleeve about anything or anybody. Bobby also let me know that he had caught a state felony case in northern California but was completely tired of doing time, so he had obtained false identification, complete with drivers' license, credit cards and a new Social Security number. Gene had bought a house in Phoenix, Arizona so that's where Bobby had settled and asked me to visit anytime. Bobby would visit his mother often, but didn't like being in the state of California with false identification or not. I filled him in on my cocaine dealing and let Bobby know my life was good also. We had both made it to the other side, and I cannot tell you how truly good it felt to see Bobby besides on the fifth tier of Leavenworth.

Within a year things were getting bad on the home front. I seemed to always pick women in my life that lacked any kind of understanding. When I would disappear for days or weeks at a time, as soon as I would walk back in the door after one of my disappearing stunts, they would want to know immediately where I had been. They lacked understanding what can I say.

So with my suitcases in the trunk containing my clothes I drove my Oldsmobile to Phoenix, Arizona, and stayed with Bobby and Gene for a short time until I got my own place in the Cinnabar Apartments in Phoenix, completely furnished, twenty-four hour pool and Jacuzzi, I fuckin' loved it. I was financing everything now by cashing forged payroll checks and life continued to be better than good. Bobby and I would play handball in the parks, get high, gamble and go to a lot of movies. Though I did start to notice how Bobby would tire easy and looked extremely skinny, but figured it was from his forty years of age, smoking

Camel non-filters his entire adult life and the constant use of heroin over the last twenty plus years.

One day while waiting for Bobby at the methadone clinic in Phoenix, I ran into Jerry Roward from my old Oxnard neighborhood. I had been friends with his younger brother Richard in school, and Jerry informed me that his mother and my mother kept in touch over the years. Jerry let me know also that my father was very sick and dying. Nineteen years had gone by since I had talked to my folks, so it was awkward to say the least when I picked up the phone and called my mother after Jerry got her number for me from his mom.

I let Bobby know my plans to visit my dad who now lived in Florida, and he completely understood since his own father had died without him being there. I wanted to thank Jerry Roward for the heads-up information about my father, but Bobby let me know that Jerry had died from a heroin overdose the day before. Selling the Oldsmobile, along with my fraudulent check money, I asked Bobby to drive me to the airport, and on the way he let me know that he wanted me to know something that he found difficult to tell me before that day. Bobby informed me that he had contracted the AIDS virus from a dirty syringe a little over a year before in San Jose, California, and had been waiting for the right time to tell me.

I said nothing, just continued to stare out of the window of Bobby's car as he dropped me off at the departing flights section of Phoenix's Sky Harbor Airport. On the plane headed to the east coast, I had no tangible thoughts and just sat there quietly among the other passengers on my nonstop flight to Florida.

When departing the plane and walking into the airport I could see my parents from a distance, they both looked so old and frail. Instantly I could see my mother's look as a look of long-suffering and apprehension seeing her son after so many years. I know my own look had hardened, like life had continuously tested me and the jury was still out on who would win, life or me. My father looked disheveled from the dementia he was experiencing and the reunion lacked compassion, empathy or any bond that should exist within a family. I knew I was the center of this uncomfortable, chaotic, after two decade rejoining.

I found a pristine Eldorado Cadillac, white with white leather and purchased it after a couple of days of my arrival, and without words my mother's look screamed disgust because she knew. She knew everything, my bank robbery conviction, my other robbery convictions as well as my murder indictment. Somehow through the Federal Bureau of Prisons and reports from around the neighborhood she had followed my life of crime, and now the only glue that was holding us together was my sick father. And she also knew her son never worked yet had money, with my mom one and one is always two.

I spent time with my father but his mental level was too far past for any comprehension and he died shortly thereafter. My dad's wishes were to be cremated and that his ashes be put in the ocean so he could travel everywhere, and that's what we did. I settled into a beach house not far from my mother's house, but after only staying in touch a couple of times with her we drifted apart again. We just never got along.

I would keep in touch with Bobby, and he would send me tar heroin, but I never felt comfortable selling drugs in Florida. The people there had a way about them, a way of distrust. Or as some people say, "Florida is a sunny place for shady people."

Bobby even hand-delivered one package and we spent a week driving around in my Cadillac, high and going to the movies and dog track. But Bobby's physical condition was weakening right before my eyes and I still couldn't come to grips on what was really happening. After Bobby went back to Phoenix, I would fly out and see him once in a while since we just always had that relationship of picking up where we left off.

Back in Florida one day while driving down Beachfront Avenue, I noticed something that looked out of place on one of the many liquor stores in this college spring break town. Buildings right on the beach are elevated because of the tides and changing water levels and this one particular liquor store was missing a wooden board nailed around the bottom of the building which was for cosmetic appearance. I could see the corner of the floor safe as I further inspected under this raised liquor store. So with very little planning on one moonless night, I crawled under and removed the safe and it turned out to be a very nice score. The next day I got on the telephone and called Bobby asking if he needed any free cash?

He abruptly said he didn't, but within an hour he was calling me back now questioning me, how much money you talking? I told Bobby I would send him a chunk, and fuck it I was gonna get on a plane the next day and fly out to Phoenix and everything would be on my tab for at least a couple of weeks. We had such a good time going to the fights, gambling, just the usual shit that Bobby and I would do whenever together.

Within less than two months of me arriving back from Phoenix after another visit, my beach house phone rang and I didn't hear Bobby's voice on the other end, but because of caller identification I knew it was him. A wave of understanding came over me and I knew this would be the last time that I would speak with Bobby. Spontaneously the words came out of my mouth, "Bobby I have already said everything to you, I have left no stone unturned in our friendship."

My good friend Bobby died two days later.

While still in Florida I tried my hand at a couple of semi-legit jobs. I collected money for a psychiatrist in the Palm Beach area and was successful, but he said he had to let me go because my tactics were overzealous. I worked in nightclubs during spring break and was paid excellent money, but tired of the drunken stupid atmosphere that went along with the job. I even body guarded for some opening B list music acts, my favorite being Otis Day and the Knights from the movie *Animal House* fame. Otis was one cool cat but I still wasn't cut out for legitimate employment. So back in the crime game again, I started doing a credit card scam in Florida and worked my way all the way up the eastern seaboard making quick and easy money.

So many more years had passed and somehow I ended up in Massachusetts, not knowing a soul there but doing the same o shit. One day and I don't remember the exact day, but I took a look at my life for what it really was and not what I thought it was. I felt alone in the universe with most of my good friends gone. I had lost track of Thumbs in the federal prison system, I'd been using heroin for over thirty-four years and doing crime even longer. And financially, I felt like I was still chasing the same dollar, over and fuckin' over. I realized at that point I needed to make some drastic changes if I ever wanted to be at true peace, whatever my definition of peace was at this stage of life. It felt at that moment like I had the devil on one shoulder, and a more fucked up demon on the other shoulder, with one definite question surfacing in my mind. How could or would I start to change?

The answer for my personal change came in a very subtle form of simplistic logic. The one constant in my life since being a child were relationships with people who I called my friends. Now, alone with heroin and crime, my only two friends, I needed to cut them loose and move on to relationships which had substance and wouldn't put me in harm's way. So I made a definite conscious decision to stop doing the things I was doing and see what would happen.

And today I'm here to tell you things worked out, not always the way I wanted, and sometimes not as easy as I wanted, but they all worked out. Saying goodbye to crime and narcotics was not an easy task because this lifestyle had become part of my DNA, but saying goodbye is what I did.

I live back in Oxnard now, and like everything Oxnard has changed dramatically. Most of the farm fields have all been replaced with homes and apartments; even where the city dump was located is now a gated community. Under the expensive homes and golf courses are buckets of oil, lead paint, tires and years of unknowing biological hazards. A lot of the beautiful eucalyptus trees have been cut down and the pace of Oxnard has increased tremendously. Even one of the former farm fields is now a man-made harbor complete with expensive boats and exclusive waterfront property, but I realize everything changes and I am no exception.

I live a peaceful existence now, and the proud overseer of many potted plants and succulents, and with my nutty brain I'm always on snail patrol by *securing the perimeter* of any outside threats who might damage my plants. Often I walk the shores of Silverstrand again and the territorial reputation that we once established is only that, a repetition from days long ago. I rarely talk of my prison life to anyone, but often still tell humorous stories about Bobby, Jay Tee,

Thumbs and me, mostly to keep their memories alive in my mind and to remind me of our deep undying friendships. I sometimes see some of the "powers that be" on the television that I was with in McNeil Island and Leavenworth, and while watching those hour long informative documentaries, my heart goes out to those California boys, they have never since or will never be able to walk the beach like I am able. Also I read a book a while back about Leavenworth called *The Hot House* and the entire book is as inaccurate as the title, Leavenworth was never called *The Hot House*. Most of the violent incidents mentioned in the book happened while I was serving my time in Leavenworth and the writer for whatever reason got the facts all twisted, but in my opinion the day of the true convict is gone, like the cowboys eventually disappeared from the plains. I even read recently a group of prisoners filed a class-action lawsuit stating there wasn't enough cheese on the macaroni and cheese at chow. I can't fathom the mentality inside the walls now and I don't need to, these things only add to the list of the already many reasons I have for not doing the past things that would end me back in prison.

With a new life I also have a new cast of characters in which I call my friends; although few, I've always been someone that was about quality not quantity. East Coast Rich probably is the first person that gave me a cornerstone to build on by telling me, "Stop doing narcotics, stop doing crime and a lot of things will fix themselves."

And then there is my man Che-Cho, who not only became my good friend but also employed me and bought my Cadillac SLS to help finance my trip from Massachusetts back out West. Che-Cho is unique because of his old school flavor and values, although he is still a very young man who's already ahead of the game. Incidentally my calypso green Cadillac SLS was the first car I obtained legitimately in my life at fifty-five years of age.

There's also Stevie Ree, who is ten years my junior and has a memory of Oxnard like I do, and we often cruise around reminiscing about how our hometown used to be while laughing at the things we see and hear. Stevie Ree periodically employs me and is the only boss I've ever known to overpay and under work me, always to make sure I have pocket money. His vigilance on helping others in need is unmatched.

Another Stevie, is Stevie Dee with his cynical humor, logic, intelligence and helpfulness in my life is on my short list of friends also. His nickname is Clark Kent because he looks like Clark Kent, and I haven't seen him go into a phone booth and change into a cape yet, but with all the projects he takes on and his constant success at various endeavors, it would not surprise me all that much.

My friend L. Max always lets me know that I'm still on the right path in life. L. Max is definitely cut from the same cloth as I am, and when spending time together we never talk about penitentiary life, instead we focus on the here and now and let the past remain in the history books.

Although I can't run as fast as I used to as a young man and I miss my youth almost daily, and whenever I dream it's always the same reoccurring dream that people are trying to kill me, I count myself very fortunate to be one of the few still standing and having the solid friendships that I've accumulated over my lifetime thus far.

And my extra special gift from the sky is my Baby Turtle Egg, as I call her sometimes, because of her fragileness and unconditional kindness. The first time I saw my Angie I knew, trust me on this one, I just knew. Angie and I are as contrasting as night and day on paper, but in everyday life we go together like toast and jam. She shares the same simple hearts desires as I, and we often go camping, walking the hills or end up at a five-star resort, just doing everything together while enjoying each other's dedicated friendship. Coffee on the beach is one of our favorite make-the-world-go-away activities. As we walk the different coastlines of California, Angie picks up shells and rocks and I search for sea glass; truly we are a match made in heaven. Can you imagine how happy it makes me to have a woman placed in my life who likes shells and rocks, and not gold and diamonds? Also another first, I listen when she speaks with her intelligent perspective of life and me always knowing and aware she has my best interest at heart. After jumping into my first time sincere relationship with a woman, with both of my feet, I also inherited a bonus of being stepfather to two cats. You read correctly, I said two cats, named Diesel and Girlie-Girl. Now I'm a pit-bull kind of guy, but I said that I had changed. With Angie, I feel like I hit the jackpot, so I stopped putting quarters in the slot machines since I've already won the sought after brass ring by being able to share my life with her.

I still love my music and pretty much stayed up on whatever was current since I was never one for getting stuck in the past. I liked the New Jack genre of music in the late eighties and followed the Rap Movement with Tupac and the Notorious B.I.G. talking of social issues in which I could fully relate. But in the late nineties I became disappointed with the overall music game. So I went back mostly to what I know, and I'm still a rhythm and blues man, what can I say? And one of my overall favorites in this lifetime so far is by William De Vaughn, "Though you may not drive a great big Cadillac—and you may not have a car at all—just be thankful for what you got."

Another person in my life, which adds to the irony, and unexplained coincidences that life provides is Slurp Dog's nephew Mikey. Slurp's body just stopped one day and he died a few years ago at a young fifty-six, another product of the generation of hard living. But I'm sure he would be smirking from wherever he is to know that his nephew Mikey and I are in each other's lives. I often tell Mikey stories about his uncle Slurp and how he was definitely the real deal; naturally my favorite story is how Slurp would use Wesson cooking oil to tan with. Slurp had a simple logic, "If it makes chicken brown on the stove it will make me brown in the sun."

Shortly after meeting nephew Mikey, he guided me back to school, and now I go to college and am considered a student in good standing along with a high GPA, and in a little less than a year I will have a degree and that's another first. Now I ain't the biggest kid in school, but I'm definitely one of the oldest and my teachers seem to like the life experiences that I bring to the classroom. Recently in my English composition course I was asked to write about my future and where I would like my life to be in ten years, and this is the essay that I wrote...

My Future

A lot of my future is already here; a lot of it has passed and a little is yet to come. Being older now, the word future doesn't have the meaning that it once had. Ten years from now I picture myself on the deck of a beach house having a really good cup of coffee and watching the ocean change moods with every wave.

Now rewind a little bit. I've had coffee on the beach in the morning many times and I have stared at the ocean over many years, but what I am finding out about my future which is partly here now, is the sunrises and the waves haven't changed all that much but I have. My perspective of so many things to put in words is rather hard; it's one of those many things in life that the experience of it is the only true way you could know what I am really saying.

I've lived by the ocean most of my life, walking the shoreline maybe to the count of thousands of miles. When I was younger I would notice sea glass in the sand, the jagged edges smoothed by constant rolling in the sand from the waves and the changing of tides, but I never stopped to pick it up or look at it closer. With youth comes hurry. But now, I not only stop and pick it up I bring it home and put it in a little glass jar, for what reason I don't know but it satisfies me. I am not in a hurry anymore and every day of life seems more like the scenic route instead of the freeway.

In ten years I can only hope that I am a better man from learning through life and others, realizing that my legacy could be what others think of me instead of what I think of myself. My insides have never matched my outside, but they are closer than they've ever been, and in more time there is a chance that they could connect.

For me personally, I was given a second chance, a life do over. So even though I don't know what is waiting for me in the years to come, I know it won't be like my past because I am not that past person. So I can only now hope that there will be a good cup of coffee in my future, an original sunrise and people in my life that understand me and let me be me. Maybe even having somebody similar to myself when I was younger put in my life having questions like I had at their age, and giving me the opportunity to answer or having my questions answered by them. This is not any earth-shaking plan that I have for my future. But you asked me about my future, not yours, and walking the beach for a lifetime picking up, or not picking up sea glass has made me come full circle. It worked for me when I was young, it works for me now, and in ten years I am highly confident that it will continue to work.

59058484R00210

Made in the USA
Lexington, KY
21 December 2016